CW01668584

a30118 009219324b

Income Tax

Made Simple

The Made Simple series
has been created
especially for self-education
but can equally well
be used as
an aid to group study.
However complex the subject,
the reader is taken
step by step,
clearly and methodically,
through the course. Each volume
has been prepared by experts,
taking account of
modern educational requirements,
to ensure the most
effective way of
acquiring knowledge.

In the same series

Accounting
Acting and Stagecraft
Additional Mathematics
Administration in Business
Advertising
Anthropology
Applied Economics
Applied Mathematics
Applied Mechanics
Art Appreciation
Art of Speaking
Art of Writing
Biology
Book-keeping
Britain and the European Community
British Constitution
Business and Administrative Organisation
Business Calculations
Business Economics
Business Law
Business Statistics and Accounting
Calculus
Chemistry
Childcare
Child Development
Commerce
Company Law
Company Practice
Computer Programming
Computers and Microprocessors
Cookery
Cost and Management Accounting
Data Processing
Economic History
Economic and Social Geography
Economics
Effective Communication
Electricity
Electronic Computers
Electronics
English
English Literature
Financial Management
First Aid
French
Geology
German
Graphic Communication
Housing, Tenancy and Planning Law
Human Anatomy
Human Biology
Italian
Journalism
Latin
Law
Management
Marketing
Mathematics
Metalwork
Modelling and Beauty Care
Modern Biology
Modern Electronics
Modern European History
Modern Mathematics
Modern World Affairs
Money and Banking
Music
New Mathematics
Office Administration
Office Practice
Organic Chemistry
Personnel Management
Philosophy
Photography
Physical Geography
Physics
Practical Typewriting
Psychiatry
Psychology
Public Relations
Public Sector Economics
Rapid Reading
Religious Studies
Russian
Salesmanship
Secretarial Practice
Social Services
Sociology
Spanish
Statistics
Technology
Teeline Shorthand
Twentieth-Century British History
Typing
Woodwork

Income Tax

Made Simple

Henry Toch BCom

MADE SIMPLE
BOOKS

HEINEMANN : London

Copyright © 1985 Henry Toch
All rights reserved, including the right
of reproduction in whole or in part
in any form whatsoever

Printed and bound in Great Britain
by Richard Clay (The Chaucer Press) Ltd, Bungay, Suffolk
for the publishers, William Heinemann Ltd,
10 Upper Grosvenor Street, London W1X 9PA

This book is sold subject to the
condition that it shall not, by
way of trade of otherwise, be lent,
re-sold, hired out, or otherwise
circulated without the publisher's
prior consent in any form of binding
or cover other than that in which it is
published and without a similar condition
including this condition being imposed
on the subsequent purchaser

British Library Cataloguing in Publication Data

Toch, Henry
Income tax: made simple,—(Made simple books)
1. Income tax—Great Britain
I. Title II. Series
336.24′0941 HJ4707

ISBN 0-434-98606-2

00921932

68599033

LANCASHIRE LIBRARY
ROSSENDALE

DR	DB	DC	DE	DH	DS	DX	DW	WB	MR
✓									

Preface

This book is addressed to the growing number of people, who need to have a better understanding of the effects of taxation on the financial side of life. According to Inland Revenue evidence in 1980 one in three tax assessments were incorrect and more recently over half the firms examined did not operate PAY AS YOU EARN correctly. I estimate that some ten million people overpaid tax in 1984/85.

The book will be helpful to students of business law and accountancy preparing for examinations of all the major professional bodies; e.g. Institutes of Chartered Accountants, for England and Wales and Scotland, Institute of Bankers, Institute of Scottish Bankers, Association of Certified Accountants, Chartered Institute of Secretaries and Administrators, Institute of Cost and Management Accountants, and the Law Society. It is also suitable for students on Degree Courses at Universities and Polytechnics and BTEC students in accountancy, business studies and law.

It is a comprehensive book including tax reform proposals in relation to the 'poverty trap' and the Government Green Paper on the 'Taxation of husband and wife'. The last chapter on 'Tax Planning' sets out how the individual can reduce his or her tax bill at various stages during one's life-time.

At a time when the number of Citizens' Advice Bureaux and public welfare services have been substantially reduced, this book will prove invaluable for people who wish to plan a sound financial future for themselves. I would like to thank Robert Postema, publisher of the Made Simple Series, for painstakingly reading the text and suggesting improvements.

Henry Toch

Contents

1
Introduction

1.1 Why Pay Taxes?

Mr Justice Wendell Holmes, the famous American judge, is reputed to have said that 'taxation is the price we pay for living in a civilised society'. Historically, the growth of administration and taxation went hand in hand. When the first census was carried out in ancient Rome, its purpose was to record the property of each citizen for the levy of taxes. Similarly, the English Domesday Book, which is the basis of so much historical research, had as its purpose the collection of taxes.

Another aspect of Mr Justice Wendell Holmes' dictum is the fact that taxes are compulsory payments for which no value or service has to be rendered in return. Thus a nuclear scientist who objected to paying for nuclear defence on the ground that it was inadequate was made to pay for it. Another way of illustrating the point is the story of an elderly lady who was faced with tax under PAYE (Pay As You Earn) when it was introduced in 1943. She wrote to the Inspector: 'Dear Sir, I appreciate the number of letters you have sent me, and have considered the matter carefully. I have decided that on balance, I do not wish to join your club.' In spite of this letter she was duly enrolled.

1.2 Basic Definitions

Taxation is based on an arbitrary system of laws passed by Pariament and interpreted by the judiciary, giving effect to what one must assume to be the democratic will of the citizens. Since the terms used contain political and economic assumptions, those most frequently encountered have to be defined. The following definitions, moreover, are in the words of a famous judge: 'Clear in outline, but blurred on the borderline.'

(*a*) **Direct and indirect taxes.** Direct taxes are taxes where the incidence cannot be shifted. The person who pays the tax also suffers it. The most common example is, of course, **income tax**, even if paid under PAYE where the employer deducts the tax on behalf of the employee. One normally includes under direct taxes **capital gains tax**, **capital transfer tax**, **development land tax**, and **corporation tax**. The borderline case is corporation tax, which is a direct tax as far as companies are concerned, but an indirect tax for shareholders. In the United Kingdom, direct taxes are collected by the Inland Revenue and indirect taxes by Customs and Excise.

(*b*) **Progressive taxes.** When considering the term 'progressive', a value judgement is included and political prejudice is involved. Although this book is of an educational nature, the fact that taxation is a highly political matter cannot be denied, as any general election leaflet makes clear. A progressive tax is one which is levied according to the person's ability to pay. Income tax is assumed to be a progressive tax, since an individual with a high income does not only pay more tax, but pays tax at a higher rate. However, since the higher rates of tax do not operate until a single person in 1984/85 has reached an income of some £17,400 and some £18,550 in the case of a married couple, most people pay **proportional** or **neutral tax** (see below). Income tax, therefore is progressive at the lower end, because in 1984/85 a single person receives the first £2,005 tax free and a married person £3,155. Similarly, for people with incomes in excess of £17,400, if single, higher income tax rates begin to operate, which makes income tax progressive at the upper end. Most people's income in 1984/5 is between £2,005 and £17,400.

(*c*) **Regressive taxes.** A regressive tax, being the reverse of a progressive tax, is one which bears more heavily on those least able to pay it. Probably the most regressive tax is the excise duty on tobacco and cigarettes. An individual smoking 30 cigarettes a day pays the same tax on them irrespective of his income and therefore it is paid by poor people who are below the threshold for income tax.

(*d*) **Proportional and neutral taxes.** A proportional or neutral tax is one which is neither progressive nor regressive. Income tax and VAT satisfy this test for most people. The rate of tax is the same as a proportion of income. Additional earnings are taxed at 30%, the same rate as existing earnings, the recipient paying more tax but not at a higher rate.

The political nature of these terms has already been referred to. Normally, **progressive** taxes means higher taxes on income and lower VAT, whilst **regressive** taxes will involve a higher flat-rate VAT and import duties and lower income tax. At election time, the political parties normally propose conflicting measures in the field of taxation.

1.3 Taxation and incentives

Two views often vigorously expressed are that a high rate of tax on additional income acts as a disincentive to people in doing more work, e.g. overtime or to take on more responsibility and that the British pay the highest income tax in the world. Both views are broadly untrue. How people decide what kind of work to undertake and whether to take risks or do overtime etc., is a complex economic decision and the level of pay is only one factor out of many to be considered. Economists when analysing price movements distinguish between two principal considerations individuals take into account;—the **income and substitution effect**. They claim that each change in price affects people's income. In terms of income tax, this means that an increase in the tax will make the taxpayer worse off than he would have been without the increase. Normally one would expect an increase in income tax to make the taxpayer work harder, the reason being that the increased tax has made him poorer and he can afford less of all things including leisure. The extent to which the **income effect** will influence the taxpayer will depend on the proportion of the individual's gross income which goes into tax, or his *average* rate of tax. The effect of the **substitution effect** is the opposite. It measures the extent to which an individual substitutes goods or services for each other as their relative prices change. In terms of *income tax*, it measures the extent to which an individual will substitute work and leisure as a result of a change in his taxes. For example if the tax rate is increased, he will have to work harder to earn an additional £ in take-home pay. The **opportunity cost**, to use another economist's term, of leisure in terms of work has increased and the individual will be inclined to substitute leisure for work and work less. In other words, an increase in tax, which reduces the **marginal** or additional benefit from work will discourage further work effort. The reader will notice that the **income effect** depends on a person's **average** rate of tax; e.g. a married man with an income of £12,000 in 1984/85 pays £2,653.50 tax, giving an average rate of 22.11 per cent $\left(\frac{£2,653.5 \times 100}{£12,000}\right)$ although the **marginal rate** is 30 per cent (the rate at which each additional £ gross earnings is subject to income tax).

Theoretically then, it is impossible to predict what the actual effect of a change in the tax rates will be on work incentives, since the income and substitution effects tend to have the opposite effect. Empirical evidence suggests that most people do not realise what their marginal tax rate is, although many believe that it has a disincentive effect. Evidence has also shown that at different income levels the value of leisure as an alternative to paid employment varies. Moreover, some work is more interesting than other work, and some people may not mind doing overtime when the work is interesting. It is also true that the disincentive effect of rising taxes is greater for married women than for single women or men, because their income is often not the main source of income, which is provided by the husband, and in such circumstances the substitution effect will outweigh the income effect.

To answer the question whether or not the British are the most highly taxed people on income is equally difficult. It has already been shown that the average tax rate is substantially lower than the marginal tax rate. For 1979/80 the highest marginal rate was 98 per cent on investment income and 83 per cent on earned income and these rates were probably the highest in the world. It was, however, possible to reduce the tax burden (as can be seen in Chapter 14) by various legitimate means, which reduced the average rate of tax to, say, 50 per cent. Since 1979/80 the marginal top rates of tax have been reduced.

Even these generalisations have to be qualified. In the USA social security payments are provided by the municipality and paid for separately, and state taxes are more important than local authority rates in the UK. Moreover, there is no National Health Service in the USA and each individual provides himself with health insurance, which in the UK is paid out of taxes. Comparisons with other countries are equally difficult.

1.4 The Poverty Trap

It has been demonstrated that a high marginal rate of tax will deter high income earners from working harder and taking more responsibility. This also applies at the other end of the scale when the income of a family is low. The cause of this is not only the low tax-free threshold for income tax, but also the interaction of a wide range of ad hoc means-tested benefits, including supplementary benefits, rent and rate rebates, free school meals, etc.

National Insurance Contributions (NIC) were introduced for all UK residents in 1948 and since then have had a chequered history. The rate has risen over the years and for 1984/85 the Class I contribution, standard rate, not contracted out, for an employee is 9.00 per cent and the employer's contribution 10.45 per cent, making a combined contribution of 19.45 per cent. It starts with an annual income of £1,768 (compared to the income tax threshold of £2,005), when NIC is £343.72, but has a cut-off at an annual income of £13,000 when NIC is £2,528.24. The reason for the upper limit is that since the contribution provides for sickness, unemployment pay and retirement pensions, which are not earnings related, a limit should be applied. The employer's share of the NIC has been included in these figures since it will affect and possibly reduce the amount he can offer to pay.

Radical changes take effect from 6 October, 1985:

(*a*) The upper limit of £265 per week is abolished for employers, but not for employees. The new contributions are as follows:

Employers' contributions		*Employee contributions*	
Earnings £pw	*% on earnings*	*Earnings £pw*	*% on earnings*
35–55	5	35–55	5
55–90	7	55–90	7
90–130	9	90–265	9
130 and over	10.45		

The rates are for contracted-in employees.

The **poverty trap** arises when a married man will pay 19.45 per cent NIC on income between £1,768 and £3,155 in 1984/85, when he would not be liable to income tax. A married man pays NIC £343.22 on an annual income of £1,768 in 1984/85 but is not liable to income tax of £345.28 until his earnings reached £4,306. In other words, if a married man worked part-time earning £1,767, he paid no NIC in 1984/85, but if it was increased to £1,768 he paid £159.12 NIC and was therefore £159.12 worse off. If one adds to this the Supplementary Benefit paid when the family income is below a certain figure, it becomes apparent that an increase in income due to more hours being worked will result in more NIC, less Supplementary Benefit and possibly more income tax, the marginal loss of take-home pay or spending money being reduced by more than 100 per cent. Moreover, since the threshold for Supplementary Benefit is higher than the income tax threshhold it is possible to pay income tax and at the same time receive Supplementary Benefit.

The poverty trap arises not so much from the fact that the income tax threshhold is too low, but from the fact that wages are low and well below the poverty level (fixed for Supplementary Benefit). What seems to be required to make it worthwhile for the very poor to find work when unemployed is to replace the present system with a combined tax and welfare system, as suggested in the Tax Credit System of 1972, which was not proceeded with.

The table shows that when working for 6 months, he is £221 worse off, or £8.50 per week, but this does not allow for fares or petrol to get to work and meals etc. at work, which clearly will normally cost more than £8.50 per week. So it is better from a financial point of view to work 6 months rather than a year. Not working for the whole year will reduce his income by a further £775 or £30 per week and compared with being employed for a year his income is reduced by £996 or £19 per week. It is clear that the incentive to take a post for six months when unemployed is very small, or negative.

Table 1.1 Annual Income Of A Married Man With Two Children 1984–1985

	In work throughout year	*In work for 6 months Supplementary Benefit afterwards*	*Supplementary Benefit for whole year*
	£	£	£
Earnings	5,000	2,500	Nil
Child benefit	689	689	689
Supplem. benefit, say		1,500	3,000
Income tax	−554		
NIC	−450	−225	
Disposable income	4,685	4,464	3,689

1.5 The Effect of Inflation

Inflation can be defined essentially as a fall in the value of money caused by rising prices—too much money chasing too few goods. It has a number of causes and can be measured in various ways. The most common measure used is the **Retail Price Index** (RPI), which is compiled by the Department of Trade. Taking 1975 as 100, the recent figures were as follows:

Year	1950	1960	1970	1975	1979	1980	1981				1982	
Quarters							1	2	3	4	1	2
	24	36	54	100	166	196	219 218	219	220	221	222	222

The figures show that prices have risen over 600 per cent in 22 years. The rate of increase has been very small in 1982, compared to 1980 and 1981. Income tax is not normally regarded as a factor causing inflation, but is subject to **fiscal drag**, a term which denotes the effect rising prices have on incomes and rising incomes which will affect the tax disproportionately at the progressive ends of the income tax structure.

Example 1.1 A married man born 1.10.1914 has the following income:

Tax year	1980/81	1981/82	% increase	1982/83	% increase
	£	£		£	
Occupational pension	1,400	1,491		1,563	
National retirement pension	2,004	2,437		2,561	
Investment income	2,100	2,020		2,250	
Total income	5,504	5,948	8	6,374	7
Age allowance	2,895 (Restricted)	2,863		3,295	
Taxable income	2,609	3,085		3,079	
Tax at 30 per cent	782.70	925.50	18	923.70	

Example 1.1 shows that when income rose by 8 per cent in 1981/82 the tax paid increased by 18 per cent, giving a fiscal drag of 10 per cent, but the increase in income of 7 per cent in 1982/83 was accompanied by an increase in tax free allowances, giving rise to no fiscal drag.

1.6 The Relative Importance of Individual Taxes

The following table is compiled from official figures.*

Table 1.2 Sources of tax revenue—1981/82 and 1982/83

Year	*1981/82*	%	*1982/83*	%
Taxes on personal income	£m		£m	
Income tax	28,504	30.6	30,775	30.9
National Insurance Contributions	20,500	22.1	20,477	20.6
	49,004	52.7	51,252	51.5
Taxes on company income				
Corporation tax	4,800	5.2	4,850	4.9
Petrol taxes	4,430	4.8	4,330	4.3
Special tax on bank deposits	355	0.4	—	
Development land tax	35		40	
	9,620	10.4	9,220	9.2
Taxes on transfers of capital				
Capital transfer tax and estate duty	486	0.5	475	0.5
Stamp duties	800	0.9	810	0.8
Capital gains tax	540	0.6	600	0.6
	1,826	2.0	1,885	1.9
Taxes on commodities, etc.				
Value added tax	12,300	13.2	14,750	14.8
Oil	4,550	4.9	5,100	5.1
Tobacco	3,325	3.6	3,525	3.6
Alcoholic drink	3,000	3.2	3,275	3.3
Others	9,309	10.0	10,601	10.6
	32,484	34.9	37,251	37.3

* Chancellor's Autumn Statement as per *Economic Progress Report, No. 151*

1.7 Taxation in Different Countries

Reference has already been made to the difficulty of making meaningful comparisons of the tax burden in different countries. Attempts are made from time to time, and the proportion the tax revenue bears to the gross domestic product at market prices can be used as the measure for comparisons. The figures published in the 10 August 1983 issue of *The Times* for 1982 are as follows:

Table 1.3 The tax burden, 1982.

Country	*Percentage of GDP*
Sweden	50.32
Norway	48.80
Netherlands	45.37
Denmark	44.49
France	43.73
Austria	41.01
Irish Republic	40.51
United Kingdom	40.00
West Germany	37.00
Finland	36.84
Canada	35.89
New Zealand	34.03
Luxembourg	33.33
Portugal	31.12
Switzerland	30.98

The table shows that the UK ranks eighth in a list of fifteen countries and confirms that the British do not bear as heavy a tax burden as they seem to believe.

1.8 Revision Test

In this book each chapter ends with a test-yourself section, which acts both as a chapter summary and a revision test. Cover the page with a sheet of plain paper and uncover the first question. Try to answer it from your knowledge of the chapter. Lower the paper and read the answer to question 1. Then read question 2 and try to answer it, and so on.

Answers	*Questions*
1. A compulsory annual payment from income imposed by Parliament.	**1.** Define income tax?
2. A direct tax is one, which the payer suffers, and an indirect	**2.** Distinguish between direct and indirect taxes.

one is one the payer can pass on.

3. A 'progressive' tax is based on the payer's ability to pay.	**3.** What is meant by a 'progressive' tax?
4. A 'neutral' tax is one which is fixed at the same rate irrespective of income.	**4.** What is meant by a 'neutral' tax?
5. According to economic research an increase in the tax will tend to make the taxpayer work harder to maintain his standard of living (income effect), but at the same time tend to make him substitute leisure for extra work (substitution effect). So it depends on the taxpayer's circumstances.	**5.** Does an increase in the income tax rate reduce the incentive to work harder?
6. This arises when the marginal rate of tax and National Insurance Contribution and loss of benefits exceeds the increase in income.	**6.** Explain the term 'poverty trap'.
7. Inflation will automatically increase the tax burden, unless the tax-free allowances are increased or are index linked.	**7.** Is income tax affected by inflation?
8. 'Fiscal drag' is the measure of the increase in tax paid as a result of inflation.	**8.** What is meant by the term 'fiscal drag'?
9. According to OECD comparisons for 1982 the UK ranked 8th in the league table of 15 countries.	**9.** How do UK taxes compare with other countries?
10. They must be treated with caution since national and local taxes are different in each country.	**10.** How useful are international comparisons?
11. This is largely a political question. All industrial countries have a mixture of both types of taxes.	**11.** Would you favour a shift from 'direct' to 'indirect' taxes?

2
The Present System and its Administration

2.1 The History of the Present System

Income tax was first introduced in the UK in 1799 as a temporary tax to pay for the Napoleonic wars. It was abolished in 1815 and reintroduced in 1842, still as a temporary tax which had to be reintroduced each year by means of an annual budget. The present law still provides that the income and other direct taxes lapse unless reintroduced by means of an annual budget. The only change has been that in order to run the economy, Chancellors of the Exchequer have found that more than one budget per year is often required.

The 1842 budget imposed a single rate of income tax of 7*d* or 3 per cent. During the Crimean War (1854–56) it rose to 7 per cent on income exceeding £100 annually, affecting some 500,000 people. Income tax replaced some customs duties on imported goods. The number of taxpayers did not exceed one million until Lloyd George introduced his 'People's Budget' in 1909, which increased the rate of income tax to 8 per cent and introduced **supertax** on incomes over £5,000 per year, equivalent to over £100,000 per year at 1982 prices. Supertax was changed into **surtax** in 1920 and abolished in 1973, when it was replaced by higher rates of income tax and incorporated into the income tax system, except that tax on higher rates and investment income surcharge was still separately assessed on taxed investment income until 1983/84.

During the First World War, income tax rates were increased and the highest marginal rates were over 50 per cent, but since the threshhold was £225 in 1939 for a married couple, most people still did not pay income tax. The majority of the working population started to pay income tax in 1943/44 when Pay As You Earn was introduced. The system was not changed until 1973/74, when the present 'Unified System' was introduced.

2.2 The Officials

The day-to-day administration of income tax, capital gains tax, development land tax, corporation tax, capital transfer tax, oil taxation and stamp duty is in the hands of the **Board of Inland Revenue** with a staff of over 70,000 people, who collected £39,950m tax at a collection cost of 2 per cent in 1981/82. The Board consists of a Chairman, two Deputy Chairmen, two Directors General and a number of other members. Board members are known individually as **Commissioners of Inland Revenue** and are responsible to a Minister, the Chancellor of the Exchequer, like other full-time civil servants. But apart from having to implement Government policy, the Board has a distinct constitutional existence of its own under the Revenue Regulation Act, 1890, which specifically entrusted it with the 'care and management' of the collections of these taxes and gave it powers, for example, to prescribe tax return forms, for the purpose.

2.3 Organisation

Under the general supervision of the Board, operational responsibility for the bulk of the work rests with the various Head Office Divisions—Policy, Technical, and Management (including Finance)—all situated at Somerset House, London, WC2, with networks of local offices dealing with the practical task of assessing and collecting income tax, capital gains tax and corporation tax and with a small number of specialised offices dealing with capital transfer tax (Capital Taxes Office) and others. In addition there is a Solicitor's Office and a Valuation Branch which carries out valuations for local rating purposes, with local offices throughout the country.

The Policy Division is itself divided into seven separate divisions:

P1 Personal taxation
P2 Collection and enforcement; stamp duty; pensions
P3 Capital taxes (capital transfer tax)
P4 Taxes on business profits
P5 International matters
P6 Taxes on capital gains and land
P7 Oil taxation

The technical Division is divided into three sections and the Management Division into five. These specialised offices deal with stamp duty, development land tax, superannuation funds and foreign taxed income, as well as capital transfer tax.

2.4 Regional and Local Offices

The fifteen regional offices, each covering a distinct geographical area, provide a management link between Head Office and local offices. Each is headed by a Regional Controller who is responsible for supervising the standard of work in the local offices in its area.

There are over 1,000 local offices, which fall into two categories. Nearly 800 are **tax offices** concerned with the determination of tax liability for both individuals and companies. The remainder are **collection offices** responsible for the payment of taxes. Although the **Collector of Taxes** sends out tax demands, he is not responsible for the tax demanded, which has been notified to him by the **Inspector of Taxes** to be found in a tax office. Any objection to the amount of tax demanded must be sent to the local Inspector of Taxes, since the Collector of Taxes is an expert in debt collection, not income tax.

Each tax office is in the charge of a District Inspector (one of a number of Inspectors of Taxes), whose name appears on the letter heading and who is personally responsible for the work carried out by some 60 staff, including three or four fully trained Inspectors. Each office handles on average the tax liabilities of about 40,000 people, but PAYE work, dealing with some 20 million taxpayers, has been centralised. In Scotland, Centre 1 in Glasgow has 2,000 staff and deals with PAYE for the whole of Scotland. There is a similar number of staff at the office at Cardiff, dealing with Public Departments divided into a number of PD offices, which deal with all the civil servants, etc., and public service pensioners. Most PAYE operations for London are dealt with by LP (London Provincial Offices) situated in Manchester, Salford, Leeds, Southampton and Edinburgh.

The degree of decentralisation has made it necessary to open some 80 local Enquiry Offices where general PAYE queries can be dealt with. In fact, the lack of a localised structure has made PAYE less convenient for the taxpayer and this was borne out by the evidence given by the Chairman of the Board of Inland Revenue in 1980 to the Public Accounts Committee of the House of Commons, when he admitted that a random check had shown that 27 per cent of all PAYE assessments were wrong.

A fundamental reorganisation of the structure of the Inland Revenue Department took place in 1975 and yet, as the evidence disclosed suggests, one in three of the 26 million taxpayers was wrongly assessed. This is not the fault of the organisation of the Inland Revenue, but due to antiquated tax laws dating sometimes as far back as 1842, which are not suited to present-day conditions.

2.5 The Procedure of Assessment

(*a*) **Commencing employment.** When a person first starts work in the UK as an employee the local tax office will become aware of him through the PAYE system. If the individual cannot produce a **Form P45** (see Chapter 10) the employer notifies the tax office on **Form P46** and follows instructions contained in the *Employer's Guide to PAYE.* The Inspector (i.e. the tax office) will then write to the new employee, enquiring where he or she has made the last tax return. If the employee can produce Form P45 this means that tax has been deducted by the previous employer and the new employer can continue to apply PAYE in the normal way. Only after he has discovered that no tax return has been completed will the Inspector issue one in order to ensure that only *one* tax return form has been completed for *one* tax year; otherwise two forms may result in two sets of tax free allowances being given when only one was due.
(*b*) **Self-employed and non-employed persons.** In case of a self-employed person, the Inspector will become aware of the person if he employs labour and has to operate PAYE. If the person's income is from letting property, the Inspector will usually obtain the name of the purchaser from the vendor of the property or be made aware that a new unknown owner has taken over. If the income received is untaxed interest or from untaxed National Retirement Pension, the Inspector will be notified by the bank or similar institution, which has to make a annual return of all interest paid in excess of £15 per year. If the income is in the form of taxed interest or dividends (including building society interest) tax has been deducted at source before payment was made. In such cases taxpayers have to write to the Inspector to claim their tax-free allowances and get a repayment of the tax overpaid.

Retired people with occupational pensions as well as National Retirement Pensions often find that the PAYE system works badly as tax is deducted on income before it is received. Tax overpaid has to be reclaimed at the end of the year and this applied particularly if the income for 1984/85 exceeded £8,100, as explained in Chapter 3.

2.6 The Black Economy

The term 'black economy' has come into popular use in recent years as a general description of economic activities which escape detection or measurement by the authorities. In its evidence to the Keith Committee (Report Cmnd 8822, March 1982) the Inland Revenue defined the black economy as covering 'activities which are concealed from the revenue-collecting authorities with the specific intention of evading tax'. They can be divided into two broad categories:

(*i*) Activities which are known but where the amount of income or turnover is understated, and

(*ii*) Activities which are not reported to the authorities at all.

A third category is the case where expenses are wrongly claimed or overstated.

The main component of the second category is commonly referred to as **moonlighting**, which is usually a secondary source of income that is undeclared. Opportunities for moonlighting are probably greatest among tradesmen and there can be few people who have not provided cash payments to such persons and have suspected that no tax was paid on it. To show that a person has income which has not been reported to the tax office, however, is no proof that tax was due to be paid on it. Legitimate expenses can be claimed against the income before it becomes taxable, and tax-free allowances often cover part-time earnings. The Inland Revenue has recently stepped up their investigation work, so it may well pay people to keep records of income and expenditure; it may result in the payment of a little more tax, but will have the beneficial effect of peace of mind.

It must be stressed that the black economy comprises the sum total of all the various methods of **tax evasion** (breaches in the law), but does not include **tax avoidance**, which consists in the exploitation, sometimes by artificial arrangements, of tax reliefs and loopholes in the tax laws.

The attitude of the Courts to tax avoidance schemes has changed in 1982, when it was decided in the case *W. T. Ramsay Ltd v. CIR (1982) Ac 300* that the Courts could look at the substance of the scheme, as well as the form, which was laid down in the famous dictum of Lord Clyde in *Ayreshire Pullman Motor Services v. Ritchie (1929) 14 TC 754*:

'No man in this country is under the smallest obligation, moral or other, so to arrange his legal relations to his finances or to his property as to enable the Inland Revenue to put the largest shovel into his stores. The Inland Revenue is not slow—and quite rightly—to take every advantage which is open to it under the taxing statute for the purpose of depleting the taxpayer's pocket, and the taxpayer is in like manner entitled to be astute to prevent, so far as he honestly can, the depletion of his means by the Inland Revenue.'

A number of attempts have been made in recent years to estimate the size of the black economy. In 1979 the Chairman of the Inland Revenue claimed that it was 7½ per cent of GDP, or £3,500m, but the Central Statistical Office revised this estimate to some 2 per cent. They are not necessarily incompatible figures, one being the maximum and the other the minimum of an intelligent guess.

2.7 Annual Tax Return

The Taxes Management Act, 1970, provides that each person with taxable income or capital gains should notify the **tax office**. Certainly, there are penalties for not notifying liability to tax and not completing a tax return issued by the Inspector of Taxes. Yet persons under PAYE are sent an **annual tax return** only once in three years and as a result sometimes overpay tax.

When the income is received untaxed, under Schedule A dealing with income from property (see Chapter 5) and Schedule D dealing with trading profits, interest, overseas income, etc., the Inspector will normally issue a tax return each year. The form divides into two sections: the 1985/86 tax return will contain particulars of income and chargeable gains for the year to 5th April, 1985, in Section One and the claim for tax free personal allowances for the tax year 1985/86 in Section Two.

If a taxpayer fails to complete the annual tax return, or the Inspector from information in his possession has reason to believe that the income disclosed is less than it should be, an estimated assessment to tax will be raised, against which the taxpayer can appeal in writing within 30 days of the date of issue, specifying the reasons for the appeal and agreeing to pay an amount of tax 'not in dispute'. On appeal, the burden of proof is on the taxpayer and the Appeal Commissioners will usually ask the trader to prove that the assessment is excessive, by submitting proper accounts. The annual tax return must also be completed within 30 days of issue, but Inspectors normally accept them after the time limit has expired.

2.8 Additional Assessments

Section 29 of the Taxes Management Act, 1970, provides that if the Inspector *discovers* additional liability, he can make an additional assessment within *six years* of the end of the year of assessment in which the additional liability occurs. Thus in 1985/86 the Inspector can raise assessments for any year after 5 April, 1979.

The term 'discovers' has been given a very wide meaning by the Courts. The cause of the under-assessment may be due to an understatement by the taxpayer, or simply that the Inspector comes to the honest conclusion that an under-assessment has occurred. It may be simply a change of mind by an Inspector. This was established by the decision in *Commercial Structures Ltd v Briggs (1948) 31 TC 477*, amongst others, but these wide powers of the Inland Revenue were reduced by the decision in *Cenlon Finance Co. Ltd v Elwood (1962) 40 TC 176*, when it was held that where an assessment has become final after an appeal, even if the appeal was settled by agreement, the Inland

Revenue cannot re-open the matter by making a further assessment. On the other hand, the Revenue is free to make additional assessments where the facts on which the previous assessment was based were incomplete or no appeal was made.

In addition, since 1971 where an underpayment of tax arises from *official error*, tax is remitted in certain circumstances. (See 2.10.) Moreover, the six years time limit is removed in cases of **fraud and wilful default**. In cases of **neglect** the time limit has not been removed entirely. In practice, since it is difficult to distinguish between neglect and wilful default, the Inspector has little difficulty in going back more than six years. In the case of deceased persons the time limit for **additional assessments** is three years from the end of the year of assessment in which the person died.

2.9 Error or Mistake Claims

Just as the Inspector can raise additional assessments if he discovers an under-assessment of tax, so the taxpayer may claim relief for tax overpaid under Schedules A, D and E (dealing with income from property trades, interest etc., and employment) if he discovers that some **error or mistake** has been made in a return of income or statement of account. This is provided for in Section 33, Taxes Management Act, 1970. The relief under Section 33, however, is much more restricted than the power of **discovery** of the Inspector. The Section provides that the Inland Revenue must enquire into the matter and give by way of repayment of tax such relief as is *reasonable and just* and there is no appeal to the High Court under this section (see page 27). Moreover, no relief is due if the return or statement was made in accordance *with some basis or practice generally prevailing at the time when the return or statement was made.*

In other words, if a taxpayer has overpaid tax in 1982/83, due to an error, the Inspector can deduct any tax underpaid in earlier years to arrive at a just and reasonable solution. Moreover, if the taxpayer wishes to change a previous claim on the ground that it would have been more advantageous to make a different claim, this would not be regarded as an *error* since the previous claim was in accordance with the *general practice prevailing*. Lastly, if assessments were estimated and too high, but not appealed against, no claim can be made that they were in *error*, because the taxpayer who has not made a return or statement cannot claim to have made an error in such a return.

Comparing the rights of the Inland Revenue to recover tax underpaid with the rights of the taxpayer to have tax overpaid refunded, it can be seen that the Revenue powers are much wider.

2.10 Tax Remission due to Official Error

There is an **extra-statutory concession** which enables taxpayers with relatively low incomes to avoid paying additional tax which was not collected earlier due to official error. The remission limits for 1984/85 are as follows:

Gross income limits		
General	*Aged 65 or over or on Government pension*	*Amount of tax remitted*
(£)	(£)	(%)
7,500	9,500	100
9,500	11,500	75
12,000	14,000	50
14,500	16,500	25
20,000	22,000	10

2.11 Penalties

The penalties for neglecting to deliver a tax return or for failing to make a correct return are heavy and are contained in a number of sections of the Taxes Management Act 1970. The most common provisions are those dealing with fraud, wilful default or neglect. The maximum penalties can and usually are mitigated by the Board of Inland Revenue. When mitigating the penalties, the Inland Revenue will compute the tax lost, charge interest on the amount in accordance with interest rates applicable at the time and add some penalty loading to take account of the circumstances of the case.

In practice, once the tax lost has been agreed between the Inspector and the taxpayer and interest has been calculated the taxpayer is asked to sign a **Certificate of Full Disclosure**, certifying that all relevant factors have been disclosed and to make an offer to settle the matter, which will involve a mitigation of penalties. If it is discovered later that the Certificate of Full Disclosure deliberately omitted taxable sources, the penalties will be severe and may involve criminal prosecution outside the Taxes Management Act, 1970.

Taxpayers faced with **back duty investigations** (the term used by the Inland Revenue for investigations involving penalties) are well advised to seek early professional advice and to cooperate fully with the Inspector, since the taxpayer's conduct will affect the extent of the penalties imposed. Indeed, it is in the taxpayer's interest to disclose any inadvertent omission from the tax return and thus confirm that the error was not deliberate and therefore did not involve fraud, wilful default or neglect.

Table 2.1 Maximum Penalties

Offence	*Penalty*
Failure to give notice of tax liability	Not exceeding £100
Failure to submit tax returns	£50 for each form plus tax unpaid or £10 per day after Court Declaration
Incorrect tax return	£50 plus twice the tax lost in case of fraud and wilful default. £50 plus tax lost in case of neglect
Assisting in preparing incorrect returns	£500
False statement made by sub-contractor to obtain exemption	£5,000

2.12 Interest on Unpaid Tax and Repayment Supplement

Section 86 of the Taxes Management Act, 1970, provides that interest is charged at 12 per cent for the period from the **due and payable date** until the tax is paid, except that if the interest on any one assessment is less than £30 the Collector of Taxes will not normally make a charge. For periods after 1 December, 1982, the rate charge is 8 per cent.

The due and payable dates, except if under appeal, are shown in Table 2.2.

Table 2.2 Due and payable dates for payment of tax, 1984/85

Type of income	*Due and payable date*
Schedule A (property, etc.)	1.1.1985
Schedule D, Cases I and II	Two instalments 1.1.1985 and 1.7.1985
Schedule D, Cases III–VI	1.1.1985
Schedule E (Employments)	If not paid under PAYE, within 30 days after demand is issued by Collector of Taxes
Corporation tax	Normally 1.1.1985
Higher rates and investment income supplement on taxed income	1.12.1985
Capital gains tax	1.12.1985

In case the assessment is under appeal and part or all the tax is postponed, the rule for interest on unpaid tax is modified as follows:

(*i*) If the notice of assessment for 1984/85 was issued before 2.6.1985 the due and payable date is either 30 days after the issue of the notice or 1.1.1985, whichever is the earlier, and interest runs from that date.

(*ii*) Under appeal, the interest on the postponed tax will run from

1.7.1985 but on not-postponed tax as under (i), or

(*iii*) 30 days after the appeal is settled, where this occurs between 3.12.1984 and 1.6.1985.

Repayment supplement is due when tax repayments are made late and are calculated on tax repayments of £25 or more at the current rate of 8 per cent, but for periods prior to 1 December, 1982 at 12 per cent. The repayment supplement under PAYE will not be paid in 1984/85 for a tax overpayment in 1983/84, but for earlier years.

Lastly, it must be remembered that interest on unpaid tax has to be paid out of taxed income since no tax allowance can be claimed for the payment of such interest. Similarly, a repayment supplement is tax exempt.

2.13 Taxation at Source

Whenever practicable, the Inland Revenue endeavours to collect income tax at source, from the person who makes the payment rather than from the recipient. Thus **PAYE** is operated by the employers, **tax credits** on dividends are paid by the companies and not the shareholders in the form of **advanced corporation tax**. The same applies to alimony and other **annual payments**. The Courts have defined the term 'annual payment' as follows:

(*i*) It must be made under a legal obligation (Court Order or covenant),

(*ii*) Extend for more than one year, and

(*iii*) Be income in the hands of the recipients.

Alimony payments and covenants are common methods used to reduce tax liability, since these payments are made after tax at the basic rate has been deducted, enabling the recipient to reclaim the whole or part of the tax paid if not liable to tax, without extra cost to the payer. Income tax law distinguishes between two types of payment:

(*a*) **Annual payment paid wholly out of profits.** Where these payments are paid wholly out of profits or income brought into charge to tax, the payer is entitled to deduct tax at the basic rate from the payment, but if he omits to deduct it, he cannot legally recover the tax from the recipient.

(*b*) **Annual payment not paid wholly out of profits.** In such cases the deduction of tax is mandatory and the Inspector will make an assessment on the payer to recover the tax.

Before the recipient can claim tax repayment in respect of tax deducted from an annual payment, he has to obtain a certificate from the payer on **Form R185** to show that the tax deducted has been paid to the Collector.

2.14 Appeals Procedure

If a person is aggrieved by an assessment made on him, he can appeal **within 30 days** from the date of the issue of the notice of assessment. The appeal must be in writing to the Inspector, stating the grounds for appeal. An appeal form is received with each assessment issued under Schedules A and D and on taxed income. The form requests the taxpayer to indicate what proportion of the tax charged is not in dispute. The Inspector will postpone the collection of the disputed amount, until the appeal is settled. If the Inspector regards the undisputed amount too small, he will reject the taxpayer's proposal and ask him to agree to a revised proportion.

Most appeals are settled by agreement with the Inspector after the outstanding information in the form of accounts or statements and tax returns have been submitted. Moreover, if the appeal is made late, after the 30 days' time limit has expired, the Inspector will accept it, provided some **reasonable excuse** such as absence or illness, etc., is given. In contentious cases where agreement cannot be reached with the Inspector, the appeal will be heard by **Tax Commissioners** of whom there are two kinds: General Commissioners and Special Commissioners.

(*a*) Normally, the appeal is heard by the **General Commissioners of Taxes** and questions of tax-free personal allowances must be heard by them. They are members of the public appointed by the Lord Chancellor. They are like Justices of the Peace and in many cases are in fact JPs as well. They are lay people and unpaid and are appointed for a geographical division, except in Northern Ireland, where the Special Commissioners hear all the appeals.

(*b*) If the taxpayer prefers, he can ask for his appeal to be heard by the **Special Commissioners of Taxes** and this choice should be made on the original appeal form. Technical questions such as claims of error or mistake (page 16) and **annual payments** (page 19) are always heard by the Special Commissioners, who are seven in number and are paid civil servants with legal qualifications. They can be compared with stipendiary magistrates.

The General Commissioners, like lay magistrates, are usually assisted by a legally qualified clerk (solicitor), whilst the Special Commissioners are assisted by a minute clerk.

2.15 Procedure at the Appeal Hearing

Before the hearing both the Inspector and taxpayer will normally make great efforts to settle the appeal by agreement and it is usually in the taxpayer's interest to reach a reasonable compromise with the Inspector. Where agreement cannot be reached with the Inspector, the appeal is settled by the Commissioners.

The FA, 1984, S.127 and *Schedule 22* introduced new provisions in respect of Commissioners to take effect from 1.1.1985.

Special Commissioners in future must be solicitors or barristers of not less than ten years standing and cases will normally be heard by a single Commissioner. The Lord Chancellor is also empowered to appoint *Deputy Special Commissioners*, who must be similarly qualified and have the same functions as *Special Commissioners*.

The taxpayer's right to elect that the case be heard before the *Special Commissioners* is qualified by the provision that upon receiving notice from the Inspector, the General Commissioners may direct that such an election be disregarded, where the appellant has not satisfied them that he has arguments or evidence to present in pursuit of his appeal. The *General Commissioners* were also given the power to refer complex cases to the *Special Commissioners*.

The effect of the new procedure will take some time to be felt. The Special Commissioners had a long waiting list of cases to hear and in the interest of speedy justice and fair play, frivolous claims should be excluded from their list. It may turn out, however, that genuine cases will now require two Commissioners' hearings, before the General Commissioners to determine whether the appellant can satisfy them that he has a case to be heard by the Special Commissioners and the hearing before the Special Commissioner. This may in practice reduce the right of appeal by making it more difficult to bring it to a hearing and thus reduce the taxpayer's right of appeal against the decision of a mighty Inland Revenue represented by an unreasonable Inspector.

The time and place of the hearing is notified to the taxpayer by the Clerk to the Commissioners. The procedure follows the rules of proceedings in a Court of Law, but in practice the procedure before the General Commissioners in particular is more informal. The appellant makes his case and calls witnesses, who are not normally sworn. Witnesses will be cross-examined by the respondent (the Inspector), who will then reply and produce his witnesses, if any, whom the taxpayer can cross-examine. The final word is with the appellant, after which the Commissioners will consider their decision in private. The decision of the Commissioners is final on a question of fact, but this does not prevent the loser expressing immediate dissatisfaction that the decision was erroneous in point of law, since the question of whether the evidence supported the Commissioners' decision is in itself a question of law.

Having expressed dissatisfaction, the party concerned has 30 days to pay £1 and ask the Commissioners to prepare a **case stated**. The case stated is usually prepared after consultation with both parties, and sent to the loser. He will send the Case Stated to the High Court for its opinion and a fee of £5. The other party is informed and sent a copy of the Case Stated.

In due course, the appeal will be heard by the High Court (Chancery Division), from which further appeal lies to the Court of Appeal and, provided leave is granted, to the House of Lords.

2.16 Costs Involved when Disagreeing with the Inspector

One reason for so few cases being taken to actual hearing is the actual cost involved. The normal rule applies that costs follow the event, i.e. the loser pays the costs for both parties. In most cases the tax forming the subject of the appeal is too small to justify the cost of engaging professional help with the appeal. There is the additional hazard that when the appellant conducts his own case before the Commissioners and wins, he may still incur heavy legal costs if the Inland Revenue appeals to the High Court and wins. Moreover, should the taxpayer win in the High Court and the decision is reversed either in the Court of Appeal or House or Lords, he will be faced with costs of many thousands of pounds.

In fairness it must be stated that the Inland Revenue in cases where an important principle is involved will not insist on recovering its costs, when winning, but the taxpayer does not know this when he attends the Commissioners' Hearing, after which the matter may well be out of his hands. Many people have campaigned that the question of costs substantially reduces the right of appeal and the taxpayer's chance to have his tax reduced.

2.17 Adequacy of Inland Revenue Powers

The claim made by the Chairman of the Board of Inland Revenue that more powers were needed to deal with the black economy has already been referred to; the question arises whether further powers are needed. The existing powers of the Inland Revenue are twofold:

(*a*) *Investigatory powers.* These were greatly increased in 1976 and enable the Inspector with the consent of the Board of Inland Revenue to require a taxpayer by notice in writing to supply him with documents which he considers may have a bearing on his tax liability. Moreover, the Inspector may require other people, including the taxpayer's family, to produce such documents, but before he can do this he must obtain the consent of the General or Special Commissioners, who will ensure that the request is justified.

Where fraud is suspected the Inspector can obtain a warrant from a circuit judge who is satisfied that on sworn evidence produced by an officer of the Board of Inland Revenue, to enter a taxpayer's premises to remove any documents and other evidence required for relevant proceedings. The warrant is valid for 14 days. These powers are hardly ever used and then only in cases where serious fraud is suspected involving substantial sums.

(*b*) **Normal powers under the Taxes Management Act, 1970.** It has already been stated (page 00) that the Inland Revenue can demand annual returns from the taxpayers themselves, their employers, banks, etc. If one adds landladies, businesses employing subcontractors, etc., it presents a comprehensive list. Moreover, the power of the Inspector to make estimated assessments is very effective. In order to have such an assessment reduced the taxpayer must appeal (page 15), and on appeal the burden of proof that the assessment is excessive is on the taxpayer. There are many cases of small traders and others who claim that they were overcharged because they could not produce evidence that certain sums of money received were not taxable receipts—e.g. betting wins, gifts from deceased relatives, etc.

(*c*) **Need for further safeguards for taxpayers.** The wide powers of the Inland Revenue have been described; they are not matched by safeguards against arbitrary acts of Inland Revenue officials. If an Inspector demands that the taxpayer produce extensive evidence to show that there were no omissions from the annual tax return, the taxpayer may incur extensive and irreversable costs to prove his innocence. There are no penalties for unreasonable behaviour of officials outside the normal complaints procedure through MPs and the Ombudsman. Indeed, since the cost of fighting an unreasonable official is great, most people would rather 'pay up and shut up'.

2.18 Revision Test

Answers	*Questions*
1. It was introduced in 1799 as a 'temporary' annual tax to pay for the Napoleonic wars. It still has to be reintroduced each year.	**1.** When was income tax introduced and why was it a 'temporary' tax?

2. The Board of Inland Revenue has a staff of some 70,000 and has its headquarters in London, 15 regional offices and some 1,000 local offices.	**2.** How is the Inland Revenue organised?
3. The Inspector issues the annual tax return, makes the assessments, receives appeals and represents the Revenue before the Commissioners. The Collector is a debt collector.	**3.** Distinguish the functions of HM Inspector of Taxes and the Collector of Taxes?
4. Each taxpayer is obliged to make a return. Moreover, traders and others make returns. When no return is received the Inspector makes an estimated assessment.	**4.** How are taxpayers outside PAYE discovered?
5. The 'Black economy' has been defined as covering 'activities' which are concealed from the revenue collecting authorities.	**5.** What do you understand by the term 'black economy'?
6. If the Inspector 'discovers' additional liability, he can raise 'additional assessments' within six years of the end of the year of assessment in which the additional liability occurred.	**6.** What do you understand by the term 'Additional Assessment'?
7. These provisions enable the taxpayer to rectify an incorrect statement or omission to claim allowances due. If no return was made no error can occur.	**7.** Explain the 'Error or Mistake' provisions?
8. There is a sliding scale for tax remission in these circumstances depending on whether the taxpayer is over 65 or receiving a Government pension or not and on his income.	**8.** In what circumstances would a 'Tax remission due to official error' arise?

9. There are extensive penalties for omitting to declare full tax liability due to 'fraud wilful default or neglect'.	**9.** How do penalties arise?
10. If a tax repayment is over a year late for whatever reason, tax free interest of 8 per cent is paid.	**10.** In what circumstances does the taxpayer qualify for a 'repayment supplement'?
11. 'General Commissioners' are like Justices of Peace, unpaid lay persons, who are assisted by a qualified clerk. 'Special Commissioners' are solicitors or barristers of at least 10 years standing and are paid.	**11.** Distinguish between 'General' and 'Special Commissioners'.
12. The taxpayer is rightly reluctant to press his dispute with the Inspector to a hearing. The costs are considerable and if he wins and the Inland Revenue takes the case to the High Court and wins, he will have to pay its costs as well, usually out of all proportion to the tax in dispute.	**12.** Why are so few cases taken to a personal hearing before the Commissioners.

3
General Principles of Income Tax

3.1 The Income Tax Year

The year of assessment for income tax purposes runs from 6 April to the following 5 April: this does not seem to be at all convenient. The financial year predates the introduction of income tax to 1753, when the calendar was changed and the new style calendar made the year end 31 December, instead of 25 March (Lady Day) as before. In the process eleven days were lost and the financial year ended eleven days after Lady Day, or on 5 April. As a judge once remarked, what one finds surprising is not how the date was arrived at, but that it was not changed by Parliament in over 200 years. In fact, for practical purposes 5 April is ignored, unless the difference is significant, and by general consent the year is taken to end on 31 March.

Although income tax has to be reimposed each year, the machinery for assessment and collection of the tax is kept alive from one year to another by the provisions of the Provisional Collection of Taxes Act, 1968.

3.2 The Nature of Tax Law

Income Tax law has some special features:

(*a*) **Statute law.** This applies to the whole of the UK, including Scotland, and is made up of Finance Acts (at least one a year) and other Acts of Parliament. The principal Acts consolidate the law from time to time. They are:

(i) *The Income and Corporation Taxes Act, 1970*, reputed to be the longest Statute.

(ii) *The Taxes Management Act, 1970*, dealing with administration, etc.

(iii) *The Capital Allowances Act, 1968* (see Chapter 6).

(iv) *The Development Land Tax Act, 1976.*

(v) *The Capital Gains Tax Act, 1979.*

(*b*) **Case law.** This has to be distinguished from common law in

England, the ancient customary law of the land as developed by the judges. In tax law, the judges do not evolve what is *just*, but confine themselves to interpreting statute law. No intention not expressly shown in the statute can be assumed, no logic and no fairness.

3.3 Basic Questions

All income tax questions can be reduced to four:

(*a*) What is income for tax purposes?
(*b*) How much is it (since mortgage interest, etc., can be deducted)?
(*c*) How is it taxed (some is tax-free and some liable at the higher rates)?
(*d*) How is the tax paid (monthly under PAYE and see Section 2.12 for others)?

3.4 What is Income for Tax Purposes?

The **Income and Corporation Taxes Act, 1970**, nowhere defines income, but enumerates sources of income, because a sum of money which would be treated in the hands of one person as a capital receipt may be income in the hands of another.

Table 3.1 The Schedules (Sources of Income).

Schedule A	Income from rents, etc. (Chapter 5).
Schedule B	Notional income from occupation of commercial woodlands.
Schedule C	Income from public revenue dividends from which tax is deducted at source.
Schedule D	Case I: Trading profits (Chapter 6).
	Case II: Professions and vocations (Chapter 6).
	Case III: Interest, annuities and other annual payments (Chapter 11).
	Case IV & V: Overseas securities and possessions (Chapter 12).
	Case VI: Miscellaneous income not covered elsewhere (Chapter 11).
Schedule E	Income from employments and pensions.

3.5 Who is Liable to Pay Tax?

Income tax in general is payable annually by all UK *residents* (see Chapter 12) not only on income arising in the UK but also on income arising abroad. If foreign income is subject to tax in the country of origin, **double taxation relief** is due (see Chapter 12). Moreover, income receivable in the UK is subject to UK income tax, whether the recipient is **resident** or not. Thus a person resident in the US pays UK income tax under Schedule A in respect of rents received in the UK, and a UK resident pays UK income tax on rents received in the US under Schedule D, Case V. The only person who escapes paying UK income tax is a *non-resident* (living in the US) on foreign (US) income and the reason, is of course, that the Inland Revenue has no means of collecting tax on such income.

3.6 Income Specifically Exempt from Tax

Certain income is specifically excluded from tax. The more common exempt income includes the following:

(*a*) The first £70 per annum of interest on deposit with the National Savings Bank (ordinary) account payable to an individual. This exemption does not extend to the National Savings Bank (investment) account, which pays 12½ per cent, compared to the 6 per cent on the ordinary account. It should be noted that husband and wife are entitled to £70 each, but the exemption cannot be transferred from one spouse to the other.

Example 3.1 Mr Jones' annual tax return for 1984/85 discloses that he received National Savings Bank interest from an *ordinary* account of £50 and his wife £90. The position is as follows:

Interest received self £50 covered by exemption.
Interest received wife £90—exemption £70=£20 taxable.

The unused £20 exemption cannot be transferred from the husband to the wife. In such circumstances one should not normally suggest to Mrs Jones that she should transfer £400 from her account to her husband's in order to save £6 of tax, since although it may be good tax advice, Mrs Jones would hardly regard it as good financial advice for her. Investing £1,200 but no more in a National Savings Ordinary Account may be good advice to a taxpayer with a high marginal rate of income tax.

Example 3.2 B has earned an investment income of £30,000 and £7,000 respectively in 1984/85. Investing £1,166 in a National Savings Bank (ordinary) account will result in 15 per cent interest return after tax has been taken into account. In other words, with a marginal rate of tax of 60 per cent, B has to receive taxable interest of £175 before he gets a net income after tax of £70.

Save As You Earn schemes are also tax free and restricted.

(*b*) Interest on National Saving Certificates, which also form a useful tax saving investment for people paying a high marginal rate of tax. For this reason the number of such certificates is restricted to so many per issue.

(*c*) Certain Social Security benefits, including:

(*i*) Earnings-related supplement to unemployment benefit, but statutory unemployment and sick pay became taxable from 1982/83 onwards.

(*ii*) Maternity benefit and grant.

(*iii*) Death grant.

(*iv*) Attendance allowances and mobility allowances.

(*v*) Child benefit payments and family income supplements.

(*d*) Certain pensions:

(*i*) Wound and disability pensions.

(*ii*) War widows' pensions.

(*iii*) Pensions paid to Victoria Cross holders and others holding gallantry awards.

It should be noted that the normal National Retirement and widow's pension are taxable.

(*e*) Income from scholarships, bursaries and similar educational endowments, though most graduate fellowships, etc., are taxable.

3.7 Receipts not Regarded as Income

Certain sums of money received are tax-free because judicial authority has established that they do not fall within the scope of income as defined by statute. Such sums are not specifically exempt, but are outside the statutory definition of income.

(*a*) Capital receipts (see Chapter 6).

(*b*) Gambling profits, including lottery wins and Premium Bond prizes.

(*c*) Gifts of a personal nature, e.g. wedding gifts. (They may attract capital transfer tax in certain circumstances.)

(*d*) Compensation for loss of office and redundancy payments unless in excess of £25,000 (see Section 10.14).

3.8 Persons Specifically Exempt from Tax

Just as certain income is free of tax, whoever receives it, so certain organisations or persons are exempt from income and certain other taxes, whatever their income:

(*a*) Certain literary and scientific institutions (Section 363, Income and Corporation Taxes Act, 1970).

(*b*) Certain friendly societies and trade unions (Section 334).

(*c*) Non-residents (see Section 3.4) on foreign income and not ordinarily resident persons on certain income, specified in Section 99. Persons not domiciled in the UK are liable only on income remitted except under Schedule E (Chapter 10).

(The terms **resident**, **ordinarily resident** and **domiciled** are explained in Chapter 12.)

(*d*) Certain saving banks and pension funds.

(*e*) Charities (Section 360). What is a charitable purpose has been questioned from time to time, since the definition dates from 1891. The definition of charitable purpose was in the case of *Special Commissioners v. Pemsel (1891) 3 TC 53* as dealing with one of the following objectives:

(*i*) The relief of poverty.
(*ii*) The advancement of education.
(*iii*) The advancement of religion.
(*iv*) Other purposes beneficial to the community.

Under (*ii*) some of the most expensive public schools have charity status, but under (*iv*) Amnesty International was refused charitable status on the ground that since it opposes the imprisonment of political opponents this objective is political, but not party political, and no political objective can be *for tax purposes beneficial to the community*. Amnesty's 'Prisoners of Conscience Fund', on the other hand, has been given charity status by the Charity Commission.

3.9 The Concept of Total Income

This concept deals with the question: 'How much is the income?' Since some payments can be deducted it would be possible for an individual to have income of, say, £1,500, but subject to mortgage interest of £1,600, so that the total income for tax purposes is nil. Annual payments (see Section 2.13), annuities and certain interest can be deducted as well as superannuation payments and pension provisions for the self employed.

(*a*) **Certain bank interest paid.** After 1982/83 bank interest can be claimed only in the following circumstances:

(*i*) Interest paid on a **mortgage** in respect of the only and main residence of the borrower, his divorced or separated spouse, or one dependent relative, up to a loan of £30,000 for 1983/84 (but £25,000 for earlier years). The mortgage, etc., need not be for the purchase of the property only, but the loan also qualifies if it is for improvements—for example, the cost of installing central heating, the cost of extensions including the erection of garages and garden sheds, cost of conversion into flats, double glazing, etc. It should be noted, however, that the relief does not extend to a **second mortgage**; many a hapless taxpayer who increased his existing mortgage on his home to pay for a new car or holiday abroad has discovered that such a loan is not for the *purchase and improvement of land and buildings* as required by the statutes and therefore the interest does not qualify for tax relief. (Banks and building societies issue certificates showing the purpose of the loan and these have to be produced before the relief is given.) There is also no relief on interest on an **option mortgage**.

(*ii*) Interest paid to a bank on a loan to enable the taxpayer to purchase another main residence before the existing one is sold (known as a **bridging loan**). Relief in such circumstances is allowed for 12 months or such further period as the Board of Inland Revenue (Inspector) consider reasonable in the particular circumstances. It is quite possible that in such circumstances the mortgage will exceed the £30,000 limit. From 6 April, 1983, mortgage interest is paid net, after the tax relief at 30% has been deducted provided the mortgage does not exceed £30,000 (**MIRAS**).

Example 3.3 A person with a mortgage on his main residence of £17,000 at 12 per cent purchases a new main residence on 6 October 1984, with a bridging loan of £17,000 at 12 per cent interest, his old residence remaining unsold on 5 April, 1985. The relief due would be calculated as follows:

6 months when only one residence owned: interest £1,023 allowable

6 months when two residences owned: interest paid £2,040. Relief

$$\frac{£30,000}{£34,000} \times £2,040 = £1,800$$

Total relief for 1984/85

$$£1,020 + £1,800 = £2,820$$

(*iii*) Interest on a loan which is wholly and exclusively for the business, known as **business interest relief**. There is no restriction on such a loan and it also applies where the loan is used to purchase plant, such as motorcars, which are used privately as well. It should be noted that a loan may qualify for relief under (*i*) and (*iii*), in which case the taxpayer must make a choice and the method chosen will be adhered to as long as it remains applicable.

(*iv*) Interest on loans to **purchase or improve land, houses or caravans**, etc., which are let at commercial rents for more than 26 weeks out of any period of 52 weeks falling wholly or partly within the year of assessment. For the rest of that 52 week period when not let it must be available for letting at a commercial rent, or prevented from being so available by repairs, etc. It should be noted that the property, etc., must be let commercially—not to a friend or relative at a nominal rent. It must be available for letting throughout the year, and excludes the holiday home, which is not let while required by the owner. There is no restriction on the amount of the loan, but interest can only be claimed against income from the property in question or against any other income from letting property. Lastly, any allowed interest can be carried forward and be allowed against future income from letting.

Example 3.4 Smith purchased a property for letting on 1 January, 1981, with a mortgage and has no other letting income. The recent history is a follows:

From 1.1.81 to 10.5.1981, the property is empty whilst being renovated. From 11.5.1981 to 31.12.1982 it is let commercially at a rent of £15 per week, the tenant paying all expenses including insurance, after which it is left vacant and offered for sale.

Interest payments were as follows: 1980/81 £100, 1981/82 £400, 1982/83 £350. The interest qualifying for relief will be calculated as follows:

1980/81: No income from letting—	£100 to be carried forward.
1981/82: Rent 48 weeks at £15	£720
Less interest £400 + £100	£500
Schedule A assessment	£220
1982/83: Rent 39 weeks	£585
Less interest ¾ of £350	£263
Schedule A assessment	£322.

It will be noted that the interest for the period when the property was vacant and not available for letting does not qualify.

(*v*) Interest on loans to **purchase an interest in a partnership**, irrespective whether or not the claimant is personally involved in the conduct of the business.

(*vi*) Interest on a loan to **contribute capital to an industrial cooperative.**

(*vii*) Interest in respect of a loan to **acquire ordinary shares in a close company** (family company controlled by the directors) and interest in respect of a loan to purchase plant (e.g. motorcars) for use by the employee in his employment and provided he can claim capital allowances (see Chapter 7).

(*viii*) Interest on certain loans raised by representatives after the death of the deceased to **pay capital transfer tax**.

(*ix*) Interest on loans to **purchase annuities** for people over 65.

(*b*) **Annuities.** These are payments made net after deduction of tax at the basic rate, which are made to a former owner of the business or retired partner.

(*c*) **Court Order (alimony) payments.**

(*d*) **Payments under a separation agreement.** These are treated the same way as Court Order payments.

(*e*) Payments under **deeds of covenant**. This is a very popular way of making payment after deducting the tax at 30 per cent; the recipient can recover the tax deducted without it affecting the tax bill of the payer (except in certain circumstances when the payment is not made wholly out of taxed sources—(see page 19).

For 1980/81 and subsequent years one has to distinguish between deeds to charities and deeds to individuals.

(*i*) Deeds of covenant in favour of charities must be for *four years* (unless they exceed three years they are not valid) and from 1981/82 onwards these payments are deductible from total income for higher rates of tax up to a total of £3,000 gross per year. This limit was increased to £5,000 for 1983/84 and 1984/85 and to £10,000 for 1985/86.

(*ii*) Deeds of covenant in favour of individuals must be for a period exceeding six years, and are therefore made for *seven years*. They are a useful way of giving an allowance to the daughter or other relative acting as housekeeper or paying an impecunious relative. Most commonly they are used to make allowances to students over 18 attending university or other full-time education or training. No allowance is made for such payments against higher rates of tax.

Example 3.5 Jones has a salary of £24,000 in 1984/85; he is married with a son 19 attending a polytechnic and a daughter of 21 attending university. He pays £140 per year to his favourite charity and £1,400 to each of his children, who have no other taxable income during 1984/85. These payments have been made under properly executed deeds of covenant, signed, sealed and witnessed for the purpose. The position would be as follows:

(1)	Mr. Jones' position—salary	£24,000	
	Less: Personal Allowance	3,155	
	Taxable Income	20,845	
		15,400 at 30% =	£4,620
		2,800 at 40% =	1,120
		2,645 at 45% =	1,190.25
			6,930.25
	Less higher rate of tax on payment of covenant to charity £200 at 15% (45%–30%)		30
			6,900.25
	Net cost of payment to charity £140–£30 = £110		

(2) Income received by charity—net payment (£140) + tax at 30% (£60) = £200. It will be noted that the Inland Revenue contributed £90 to Mr Jones' contribution or increased it by 82%.

(3)	Income of son £1,400 + tax £600 =	£2,000
	Less personal allowance	2,005
	Taxable income	Nil
	Tax paid	600
	Tax repaid	600

(4) The position of Mr Jones' daughter is the same as for the son. It can be seen that out of a tax bill of £6,930.25 the Inland Revenue paid back to Mr Jones £30, the charity £60 and the children £1,200—a total of £1,290 resulting from the *deeds of covenant*.

(*f*) **Superannuation payments to a pension fund approved by the Inland Revenue** under section 19 of the Finance Acts 1970.

3.10 Tax-Free Personal Allowances

Tax-free personal allowances are given to all *resident* individuals (the term is defined in Chapter 12) and to *non-resident* individuals in certain circumstances as provided by Section 27 of the Income and Corporation Taxes Act, 1970 (see Chapter 12), provided a claim for relief and a return of income has been made. The allowances are:

Table 3.2 Tax-free personal allowances—1985/86

	1985/86	1984/85
Age allowance—single person	2,690	2,490
Age allowance—married person	4,255	3,955
Single person	2,205	2,005
Married man	3,455	3,155
Wife's earned income allowance	2,205	2,005
Additional personal allowance	1,250	1,150
Widow's bereavement allowance	1,250	1,150
Dependent relative allowance—single woman claimant	145	145
Dependent relative allowance—others	100	100
Housekeeper	100	100
Relative taking charge of younger brother or sister	100	100
Son's or daughter's services	55	55
Single blind person	360	360
If both husband and wife are blind	720	720

(*a*) **Age allowance.** This allowance is available to any individual who has reached the age of 65 during the year of assessment. It is interesting to note that a woman is entitled to the National Retirement pension on reaching the age of 60, she has to wait for the tax allowance another five years. In the case of a married man living with his wife, the tax-free allowance is £3,955, provided either spouse reaches the age of 65 during the year. If the income exceeds £8,100 during 1984/85 the allowance is restricted by *two-thirds of the excess.* This restriction has important implications for retired people with money in a building society account. In 1985/86 banks also pay tax at source at the composite rate (CRT) and the income limit is £8,800.

Example 3.6 Brown, a single man, reaches the age of 65 on 10.11.1985 and has the following income:

Salary (to date of retirement)	£6,320	tax paid £1,250
National Retirement pension	1,600	
Dividends + tax credits	950	
Bank interest	50	
Building Society interest received	210	
Total	9,130	

Since the building society interest is received after deduction of tax, it has to be grossed at 30 per cent.

$$\frac{210 \times 100}{70} = £300$$ making total income £9,220

Less: Age allowances	£2,690		
Less: 2/3 (£9,220–8,800)	280		
	2,410		
Building society interest	300	2,710	
Taxable income		6,510 × 30% =	£1,953
Less: tax deducted under PAYE	1,250		
Tax credits	285		1,535
Tax due 1985/86			418

Example 3.7 Assume that the facts are the same as in Example 3.6, except that Brown is married. The figures would be the same, except that the National Retirement pension would be say £2,050. The computation would be:

Total income		£9,670	
Less: Age allowance	£4,255		
Less: 2/3 (£9,670–8,800)	580		
	3,675		
Building society interest	300	3,975	
Taxable		5,695 × 30% =	£1,708.50
Tax paid			1,535
Tax due			173.50

It should be noted that if a tax repayment is involved the tax deducted from building society interest cannot be reclaimed and for this reason retired people should review the position.

Example 3.8 Green, a married man of 64 with a wife of 65, has the following income in 1985/86.

Salary		£11,800	
Less age allowance	£4,255		
Less restriction 2/3 × £3,000	2,000		
Age allowance not claimed	2,255		
Personal allowance		3,455	
Taxable income		8,345 at 30% =	£2,503.50

It will be noted that the **marginal adjustment** (restriction of the age allowance) ensures that the age relief is not cut off abruptly. If this were not so, a small excess of income over £8,100 would suffer tax at more than 100 per cent. The marginal adjustment is found in other parts of the tax structure, e.g. corporation tax.

(*b*) **Personal allowance.** A married man is entitled to the *higher* personal allowance of £3,455 for 1985/86 provided his wife is living with him, or is wholly and voluntarily maintained by him. The wife is regarded as living with her husband if the spouses are living together in intention, although temporarily apart, e.g. if the husband has to go abroad for business or private reasons. The higher personal allowance is reduced by one twelfth of £1,250 for each month which passed before marriage in the year of marriage. If the spouses are living apart, the husband can still claim the higher personal allowance as long as he makes voluntary payments substantially maintaining his wife.

Any other person is entitled to the lower personal allowance of £2,205. Although the wife's income is normally aggregated with that of the husband (see Chapter 4) this does not apply in the year of marriage.

Example 3.9 Mr A married Miss B on 6 July, 1985. His income for 1985/86 is as follows: Salary £6,000, building society interest received £55, building society interest paid (on mortgage of family home) £850. Miss B continues to work after her marriage and her salary is £5,000 for the year.

Husband: Salary		£6,000	
Less personal allowance	£3,455		
Less restriction $\frac{1}{4} \times 1{,}250 =$	312	3,143	
Taxable income		2,857	at 30% = £857.10
Wife: Salary		£5,000	
Less personal allowance		2,205	
		2,795	at 30% = £838.50

The following principles have emerged from the above examples:

(*i*) Personal allowances, except the higher personal allowance during the year of marriage, are given for the whole year and are not apportioned.

(*ii*) Building society interest paid and received is normally excluded, since tax has been deducted before payment, unlike National Saving Bank interest which is paid gross. From 1985/86 all bank deposit interest is taxed at source at the *composite rate*, which hitherto only applied to building society interest received. Under this system the banks etc. pay less than the full basic rate of 30%, but the recipient if not liable to cannot reclaim the tax overpaid.

(*c*) **Wife's earned income allowance.** For tax purposes, the family is treated as a unit. As explained in Chapter 4 this means that the wife's income is treated as belonging to the husband. The **earned income** of the wife is given particularly favourable treatment and receives an additional allowance of up to £2,005 for 1984/85 and £2,205 in 1985/86 and one can claim to have it assessed separately (Chapter 4). Wife's earned income includes not only her earnings from another firm, but salaries paid by the husband—though not housekeeping money.

The **wife's earned income allowance** was first introduced in 1920—when most other tax-free allowances were introduced—and was increased to the present level of being equivalent to the single personal allowance in 1942 to encourage married women to go out to work. This resulted in some six million married women being employed and was particularly helpful during the Second World War. At a time of high unemployment it encourages married women to seek employment and creates a greater difference in living standards between families where both spouses are working and where they are both unemployed. It also pays to send the wife to work and let the husband stay at home to look after the children, rather than the other way round. *The allowance is £2,005 for 1984/85 or £2,205 in 1985/86 or the wife's earnings, whichever is the lower.*

(*d*) **Widow's bereavement allowance.** This allowance applies from 1980 onwards. The allowance for 1984/85 is £1,150 and for 1985/86 £1,250. It is due only in the year of the husband's death and the subsequent year, and cannot be claimed by separated wives who are widowed.

Example 3.10 Mr C died on 6 October, 1985 and the income was as follows: Mr C—salary to date of death £10,000, tax deducted £2,932.50; Mrs C—salary for the year £6,000, less tax deducted £1,330.50 and dividends received by Mrs C, June 1985, £1,400 and December 1985, £700. The 1985/86 position is:

(*i*)	Mr C to date of death—salary		£10,000	
	Mrs C to date of death—salary		3,000	
	Mrs C's investment income (gross)		2,000	
			15,000	
	Less: Higher personal allowance	£3,455		
	Wife's earned income allowance	2,205	5,660	
	Taxable income		9,340 at 30%	=£2,802
	Less tax paid £2,932.50 + ½ Mrs C's £665.25 + Divs. £600			=4,197.75
	Claim repayment of tax overpaid			1,395.75
(*ii*)	Mrs C (widow)—salary from date of death		3,000	
	Investment income (gross)		1,000	
			4,000	
	Less Lower personal allowance	2,205		
	Widow's bereavement allowance	1,250	3,455	
	Taxable income		545 at 30% =	163.50
	Less tax paid £665.25 + Divs. £300			965.25
	Claim repayment of tax overpaid			801.75

Widowhood is a sad and traumatic experience, but it usually results in substantial tax repayments which should not be overlooked.

(*e*) **Additional personal allowance for single persons with children.** This allowance of £1,150 for 1984/85 and £1,250 for 1985/86 is available to any single person who has a child, or maintains the child of another person. The child must be either under 16 on 6 April, attending full-time instruction at any university, college, school or other recognised educational establishment, or undergoing full-time training for a trade or profession, lasting for two years.

Example 3.11 Mr and Mrs Green were divorced on 6 July, 1985 and their daughter's custody was given to Mrs Green. She is five years of age. Mr Green pays £10 per week maintenance for the child under a Court Order. Mr Green's salary was £6,000 and Mrs Green's £4,000 for working throughout the year 1985/86.

(*i*) Tax liability of Mr Green: Salary		£6,000	
Wife's salary		1,000	
		£7,000	
Less: Court Order payment			
39 × £10		390	
		6,610	
Less: Higher personal allowance	£3,455		
Wife's earned income relief	1,000	4,455	
Taxable income		2,155	at 30% = £646.50
(*ii*) Tax liability of Mrs Green: Salary		3,000	
Court Order payments		390	
		3,390	
Less Lower personal allowance	£2,205		
Additional personal allowance	1,250	3,455	
Taxable income		Nil	

(*iii*) Moreover, if the Court Order payment is made in favour of the child Mrs Green's liability will be reduced by £520 at 30% in 1986/87 without it affecting Mr Green. Lastly, it should be noted that the restriction applying in the year of marriage (Example 3.9) does not apply in the year of divorce.

(*f*) **Dependent relative allowance.** If the claimant maintains a relative of his or his wife's (including a child over 16) who is incapacitated by old age (exceeding 65) or infirmity from maintaining himself, or his or his wife's widowed mother, whether incapacitated or not, he can claim an allowance of £100, but if the income of the dependent exceeds the normal national retirement pension, the allowance is restricted by the excess. If the allowance is claimed by a woman, it is £145.

In recent years a growing number of such claims are being made by people who support dependent relatives overseas. In such cases the Inland Revenue will ask to be satisfied not only in respect of the dependent's income, but also that he or she actually exists (through identification by a local dignatory or British consul) and that the money was actually sent abroad by bank transfers or money orders.

If the value of the claimant's contribution is less than the allowance, the allowance is reduced to the actual amount, and if two or more people jointly maintain the relative the allowance is apportioned.

(*g*) **Housekeeper allowance.** The allowance of £100 is available to any widow or widower who has resident a relative acting as housekeeper (who need not be a woman). If the housekeeper is not a relative, the allowance is available provided he or she is employed. In both cases, the housekeeper must reside with the claimant to qualify for the allowance, and the housekeeper must not be a married woman for whom her husband claims higher personal allowance.

This allowance is not claimed very much these days, since any individual, not necessarily widowed, can maintain a friend living with him or her by means of a *covenant* (see Section 3.9).

(*h*) **Son's or daughter's services allowances.** If the claimant, by reason of old age or infirmity, is compelled to depend on the services of a son or daughter resident with and maintained by him, he is entitled to claim an allowance of £55. It will be noted that the relief is less than the *housekeeper relief*, but in order to claim it the claimant does not need to be a widower. It is claimed even less often than the *housekeeper* allowance and for the same reasons.

(*j*) **Blind person's allowance.** An allowance of £360 can be claimed by a person who is (*i*) either a married man who for the year of assessment had his wife living with him, and one spouse was and the other was not a blind person throughout the year, or (*ii*) a registered blind person himself throughout the year. If both spouses are registered blind persons the allowance for 1984/85 is £720. A condition of the allowance is that the son's or daughter's services allowance claim of £55 has been relinquished.

(*k*) **Life assurance relief.** An allowance is given by the deduction of 15 per cent from the premiums paid to approved life assurance companies or friendly societies, provided the policy is a life policy which includes an endowment policy. It also applies to deferred annuity premiums. The relief is restricted as follows:

(i) £1,275 (£1,500 less 15 per cent) or **one sixth** of the claimant's total income, whichever is the greater. The payments for deferred annuities may not exceed £100 (gross) or £85 net in the year. The deduction of the 15 per cent at source is not available in the case of *non-residents* and in other special cases. The relief was withdrawn for policies taken out after 13 March, 1984.

Example 3.12 G, with a total income of £6,000 in 1983/84 and £10,500 in 1984/85, pays life assurance premiums to approved companies of £1,000 and £1,600 in 1983/84 and 1984/85 respectively.

The relief is calculated as follows:

1983/84: No restriction since £1,000 net is below the £1,275.

1984/85: Assuming that all policies were accepted before 14.3.1984, the premium is in excess of £1,275, therefore the 1/6th limit may apply.

Gross premium $\frac{£1{,}600 \times 100}{85}$ £1,882

Maximum relief available 1/6 of £10,500	1,750
Restriction of relief to be recovered by Inspector	132

Claw-back of relief in certain circumstances (see 11.13).

(*l*) **Retirement annuity relief.** Self-employed individuals and others in non-pensionable employments are entitled to an allowance of 17½ per cent of **relevant earnings** (excluding investment income) provided the date of birth was after 1933. For older people the relief is greater.

Born between	1916 and 1933	20%
	1914 and 1915	21%
	1912 and 1913	24%
	1910 and 1911	26½%
	1908 and 1909	29½%, but no one aged 75 or over

qualifies.

Since 1980/81 the premiums not being used in the year in which they were paid can be used and set against the *net relevant earnings* of the previous six years and if this does not exhaust the relief the balance can be carried forward for one year. If one takes out a premium of say £5,000 in 1984/85, it can be partly claimed for the years 1978/79 to 1985/86 (eight years). The contract has to be of a kind approved by the Inland Revenue, whose conditions include:

(*i*) It provides an annuity payable during the life of the individual.
(*ii*) It commences between the ages of 60 and 70, except in special cases.
(*iii*) Annuity to be payable to the individual, his widow or his personal representatives.
(*iv*) Up to 5 per cent of net relevant earnings may be applied for the provision of lump-sum or death benefits.

An important aspect of these contracts is that the premiums cannot be withdrawn or the policy surrendered except in the case of death or disability, except by way of pension, and for this reason cannot normally be used as collateral security for a debt, except that certain insurance companies will lend on their own policies, and building societies accept them as security for mortgages.

Example 3.13 Waters started in business on 1 January 1979, and during 1982/83 he takes out a single premium retirement annuity contract with an approved insurance company for £3,000. He was born in 1938 and his income tax assessments were as follows:

1978/79	£5,000—	Capital allowances (see Chapter 7)	£1,500 =	£3,500
1979/80	£15,000—	" "	£1,000 =	£14,000
1980/81	£5,500—	" "	£1,200 =	£4,300
1981/82	£4,000—	" "	£600 =	£3,400
1982/83	£8,000—	" "	£1,400 =	£6,600

Retirement annuity relief is calculated as follows:

1982/83: Premium paid	£3,000			
Allowance 17.5% of £6,600	£1,155			
Balance	£1,845 allowed	1981/82	17.5% of 3,400	595
		1980/81	17.5% of 4,300	753
		1979/80		497

One aspect of the change from being able to carry excess retirement annuity relief backwards rather than forwards since 1980/81, is that purchasing a pension after reaching retirement age, for those without an occupation pension, becomes a very attractive investment.

Example 3.14 Wilson, aged 67 and retired, has investment income of £6,000 and his national retirement pension in 1984/85. It would pay him to purchase a retirement annuity for £5,000 and transfer this money from a building society, where most retired people have their savings. The building society pays 11.79 per cent on long-term investment, or £589, which is subject to basic rate 30 per cent amounting to £176.70 tax and giving a net return of £412.30, or 8.2 per cent on the £5,000 invested.

Purchasing a retirement annuity with *immediate vesting*—that is, obtaining a pension immediately—will give the following result:

Purchase price	£5,000
Less Income tax 30%	£1,500
Net cost	£3,500

This will purchase a pension for life (guaranteed for five years) of £712 p.a., subject to tax at 30 per cent i.e. £213.60, giving a net return of £498.40 or 14.25 per cent, almost double.

The only snag, of course, is that once a pension is purchased, apart from being guaranteed for normally five years, the capital £3,500 disappears whilst in the building society it is retained. This drawback can be met by accepting a tax-free cash payment and a lower pension, resulting in the following:

Purchase price		£5,000
Less income tax 30%	1,500	
Cash payment	1,590	3,090
Net cost		£1,910

Pension £470 less tax 30 per cent £141 = £329. This gives a net return on £1,910 invested of 17.2 per cent for life, guaranteed for five years, compared to the building society return of 8.2 per cent subject to fluctuations.

One word of warning: this investment is attractive only because of the tax relief involved. If a person purchases a pension which does not qualify for tax relief, its attractiveness is much diminished, so before purchasing the pension the maximum tax relief should be checked.

(*m*) **Investment income surcharge.** If *net investment income*, which is income from dividends, interest, rents, etc., after the deduction of annual payments (mortgage interest, Court Order payments, etc.) exceeded £7,100 in the year 1983/84 an additional charge of 15 per cent is made on the excess. Alimony payment received is not regarded as investment income for the purpose of the surcharge. The investment income surcharge was abolished for 1984/85 and subsequent years.

3.11 Higher Rate Bands

As already explained, some taxable income is tax-free (see 3.9) and some (most in fact) is taxed at the basic rate of 30 per cent with the balance at the higher rates as follows for 1984/85 and 1985/86:

	1984/85	*1985/86*
Taxable income	15,401–18,200 (2,800) = 40%	16,201–19,200 (3,000) = 40%
	18,201–23,100 (4,900) = 45%	19,201–24,403 (5,200) = 45%
	23,101–30,600 (7,500) = 50%	24,401–32,300 (7,900) = 50%
	30,601–38,100 (7,500) = 55%	32,301–40,200 (7,900) = 55%
	Over 38,100 = 60%	Over 42,200 = 60%

3.12 Revision Test

Answers	*Questions*
1. Income tax law is made up of Statute Law, the Acts of Parliament and Case Law; the interpretation of the Statute by the Courts.	**1.** Describe what is meant by the legal framework of UK income tax?
2. The term income is not defined in the Statutes. The Acts enumerate sources of income in the five schedules.	**2.** Define income for income tax purposes?
3. Capital receipts, gambling wins, gifts of a personal nature, compensation for loss of office up to £25,000. Interest from National Savings Certificates, National Saving Bank (Ordinary) Account up to £70, Save As You Earn schemes, etc.	**3.** What receipts are not regarded as income for tax purposes?
4. Certain literary and scientific institutions. Non-residents on foreign income. Certain saving banks and pension funds,	**4.** What persons are exempt from income tax?

charities, certain friendly societies and trade unions, etc.

---

5. Certain mortgage and other interest can be deducted and annual payments under Court Order etc. before fixing the total income for income tax.

5. What is meant by the 'Concept of total income'?

---

6. Each individual is entitled to either a single person's allowance or if married with his wife living with him a higher personal allowance. If either spouse reached the age of 65 and total income is under £8,100 in 1984/85 an Age Allowance is due.

6. What tax-free personal relief is every resident individual entitled to?

---

7. Wife's Earned Income Relief is given on wife's earned income up to £2,005 in 1984/85.

7. What allowance is due for a working wife?

---

8. The additional personal allowance is due to a single person looking after a child. For 1984/85 it was £1,150 and should be claimed in place of housekeeper.

8. In what circumstances should an 'Additional Personal Allowance' be claimed?

---

9. The allowance for a single woman claimant is £145 and £100 in other cases. This must be remembered when claiming separate assessment of wife's earnings.

9. Distinguish between the two 'Dependant Relative' Allowances available.

---

10. The allowance is only £55 and a much larger benefit can be secured by means of a 7 year covenant.

10. Can you explain why few people claim the £55 allowance for daughter's services?

11. It has been abolished for policies written after 13 March, 1984, but many people have earlier policies under which premiums are paid and these qualify for relief.	**11.** Life Assurance Relief has been abolished, but can still be claimed. Explain.
12. Retirement Annuity Relief can be claimed by self-employed people and employees not in a pension scheme. It is normally at 17½% and can be claimed for six years back.	**12.** In what circumstances can Retirement Annuity Relief be claimed?

4
The Treatment of Husband and Wife

Section 37 of the Income and Corporation Taxes Act, 1970, reads as follows: 'A woman's income chargeable to income tax shall, so far as it is income for a year of assessment during which she is a married woman living with her husband, be deemed for income tax purposes to be his income and not her income.' Two important consequences flow from this section. First, a married couple is basically taxed as a single unit; the income of husband and wife are added together, and tax is charged, after all deductions and allowances have been made, on the total, as if it were income of one person. Second, it is the husband who must complete the tax return when required, claim all the allowances, including those relating to the wife—for example, if she maintains a widowed mother. The husband must take responsibility for the tax due on both his and his wife's income. This means that for income tax purposes, a married woman living with her husband is treated like an infant, as an **incapacitated person**. There is one exception to this rule: that is, if the wife has the income and will not hand it over to the husband to pay tax on it (which under married women's property law she can legitimately do), Section 40 of the Act provides for the Inland Revenue to collect the tax assessed on the husband, but attributable to the wife's income, from the wife direct.

The reason for the present system is that the **aggregation rule** (adding the wife's income to the husband's) was introduced in 1806, when married women had no property and did very little work outside the home. Even in 1921 less than 10 per cent of married women were gainfully employed, but some 50 per cent were in paid employment in 1981.

4.1 Historical Development

The history has been set out in the Government Green Paper (Cmnd 8093) published in December, 1980 ('The Taxation of Husband and Wife'), and is as follows:

1806 Aggregation rule first introduced.

1894 Wife's Earned Income Relief of £500 introduced. It is £2,205 in 1985/86 (see 3.10).

1909 Supertax introduced, which would make it advantageous for wealthy people not to get married. Supertax became surtax in 1929 and Higher Rates of Tax in 1973/74 (see 3.11).

1914 Right to separate assessment introduced. Section 38 of the 1970 Act provides that either husband or wife can apply for separate assessment. This option does not reduce the total amount of tax paid, but makes both husband and wife responsible for handling their own tax affairs. It enables each to make a separate tax return. The advantage of this election is that the wife does not have to tell her husband about her income, and it releases the husband from the responsibility to make a *correct and complete return* of his wife's income. The tax is also collected from the wife in respect of income which has not been taxed at source. The effect of a claim under Section 38 is shown on page 47.

1918 Higher personal allowance for a married man introduced (see 3.10).

1920 The Royal Commission of Income Tax reported in favour of the aggregation rules in the following terms:

'The aggregation for Income Tax purposes of the income of husband and wife is not dependent upon any mediaeval conception of the subordination of women ... The incomes are aggregate because the law of taxable capacity is the supreme law in matters of taxation, and taxable capacity is, in fact, found to depend on the amount of income that accrues to the married pair, and not upon the way in which that income happens fortuitously to be owned by the members of that union. It is beyond question that in the immense majority of cases where the wife has separate means she contributes to the common purse, either by the actual merger of her income with her husband's or by bearing expenses which in less fortunate households would fall upon the husband.'

1920 Higher personal allowance increased to 1.16 times the lower personal allowance, and wife's earned income allowance increased.

1942 Wife's earned income allowance increased to lower personal allowance to encourage married women to help the war effort.

1944 PAYE introduced.

1948 Working wife given her own reduced rate bands (abolished after 1979/80).

1954 Question reviewed by Royal Commission, which reported as follows:

'We see in the existing rule nothing that embodies an outmoded or unworthy conception of the relations of man and woman in marriage ... It does appear to us ... that marriage creates a social unit which is not truly analogous with other associations involving some measure of joint living expenses and that to tax the income to two married people living together as if each income were equivalent to the income of a single individual would give a less satisfactory distribution than that which results from the present rule.' They saw the wife's earned income relief of 1950 as excessive.

1971 Wife's earnings election introduced (see 4.3).

1978 Wife given the statutory right to receive her own PAYE repayments.

1978 Inland Revenue practice on correspondence with married women was changed. Instead of writing to the husband Inspectors now write to the wife.

4.2 The effect of a claim under Section 38 of the Income and Corporation Taxes Act, 1970 (ICTA)

Under the normal aggregation rule (Section 37, ICTA) the tax is calculated as follows:

Example 4.1

1985/86		£	
Husband's salary		13,000	
Wife's earned income		8,000	
Wife's investment income		5,000	
		26,500	
Less: Higher Personal Allowance	3,455		
Wife's Earned Income Allowance	2,205	5,660	
Taxable income		20,840	
		16,200×30%=	£4,860
		3,000×40%=	1,200
		1,640×45%=	738
Tax due			6,798

£1,738.50 is paid by the wife under PAYE, £1,500 deducted at source and the balance by the husband under PAYE.

Example 4.2 Effect of claim under S.38 ICTA 1970 circumstances of Example 4.1. The claim has to be made by 6.7.1985 but not before 6.1.1985 to be effective.

	Husband	Wife
	£	£
Salary	13,500	8,000
Investment income		5,000
		13,000
Personal Allowance $\frac{13{,}500 \times 5{,}660}{26{,}500}$	2,883	2,777

Taxable income		10,617	10,223
Basic Rate	$\frac{13,500 \times 16,200}{26,500}$	8,253	7,947 at 30%
At 40%	$\frac{13,500 \times 3,000}{26,500}$	1,528	1,472
At 45%		836	804

As a result of the claim the husband pays only £3,463.30 and the wife pays £3,334.70, but the liability of the couple is still £6,798 as before.

Since the present taxation position does not reflect the social changes which have taken place in the status of married women, the Chancellor of the Exchequer published a Green Paper (Discussion paper Cmnd 8093) suggesting that a system under which the assessment for husband and wife is split equally, rather than in proportion to relevant income would have the following advantages:

(*i*) Wives as well as husbands would be able to have a considerable degree of privacy over their affairs. At present the wife does not need to tell the husband her income, but the husband can easily work out that if he gets 45% of the combined allowances, the wife has 55% of the joint income. The only exception to this rule is that the wife must receive at least £2,005 of the allowances in 1984/85. An equal split would prevent this.

(*ii*) Married women would, as at present, if an election is made, make their own tax return, pay their own tax and get their own repayment.

(*iii*) Married women would be able to benefit from exactly the same personal allowances as their husbands, irrespective of income as shown in Example 4.3.

Example 4.3 The same figures as in Example 4.1 with 'Green Paper' option.

1985/86		Husband £	Wife £
Income as per Example 4.2		13,500	13,000
Personal Allowances ½×5,660		2,830	2,830
Taxable income		10,670	10,170
Basic Rate	$\frac{10,670 \times 16,200}{20,840}$	8,294	7,906 at 30%
At 40%	$\frac{10,670 \times 3,000}{20,840}$	1,536	1,464
At 45%		840	460

The result of this would be that the wife would pay £3,164.40 instead of £3,334.70 or £170.30 less tax.

4.3 Effect of Wife's Earnings Election (S.23, FA, 1971)

One result of the *aggregation rule* was that professional women were better off tax-wise if they did not get married, since marriage would make their income when added to the husband's income, liable to pay tax at higher rates. It was shown that this aspect of the tax law not only discouraged well qualified married women to seek employment, but was not in the public interest. S. 23, FA, 1971 remedied this situation and provided that if a husband and wife *jointly* elect (both have to sign the election before 6.4.1987 for the year 1985/86) to have the wife's earnings treated as if belonging to a single woman, and assessed separately.

Example 4.4

1985/86 Figures as for Example 4.1.	Husband	Wife
	£	£
Salaries	13,500	8,000
Investment income	5,000	
	18,500	
Personal Allowance	2,205	2,205
Taxable income	16,295	5,795
Basic Rate	16,200	5,795 at 30%
At 40%	95	

As a result of the election the couple saved £6,798−£6,636=£162

Example 4.5 If the combined income had been less, say investment income £2,000, the position would be different.

(*a*) Position without election:		£
1985/86 Husband's salary		13,500
Wife's salary		8,000
Wife's investment income		2,000
		23,500
Less: Higher Personal Allow.	3,455	
Wife's Earned Income Allow.	2,205	5,660
Taxable income		17,840
		16,200×30%=£4,860
		1,640×40%= 656
Tax due		5,516

(*b*) Position with election:	Husband	Wife
1985/86	£	£
Salaries	13,500	8,000
Investment income	2,000	
	15,500	
Personal Allowance	2,205	2,205
Taxable income	12,295 +	5,795×30%=£6,327

The couple would not make an election, since they would lose £6,327—5,516=811 in tax as a result. This proves that in many cases the election should be reviewed each year, since unless it is withdrawn it continues to be applicable.

The results of an election can be summarised as follows:

(*a*) The wife is taxed on *her earnings* as if she were a single person and these include:

(*i*) Income from employments, whether full-time or part-time,
(*ii*) Any pension from a previous employment, or a National Insurance Retirement pension paid as a result of *her own contributions*.
(*iii*) Income from a trade, profession or vocation carried on by her personally or as an active partner in a partnership. *These earnings do not include any pensions she may receive as a result of her husband's past employment or his National Insurance contributions.*

(*b*) It should be noted also that not only does the husband lose the Higher Personal Allowance, but also the Higher Age Allowance and since the Age Allowance is limited to an income of £8,100 in 1984/85 before it will normally pay to make an election, no Age Allowance will in fact be due.

(*c*) Mortgage interest payments and payments under covenant if they are made by the wife must be set against her income and might affect the Wife's Earned Income Relief due. Mortgage interest paid by the husband or jointly on the jointly owned home is allowed against the husband's income.

One of the suggestions frequently made is that the wife's earnings election should be extended to the whole of the wife's income and include investment income.

The Green Paper estimates that if such an option were introduced some 500,000 married women would benefit compared to the 100,000 benefiting from the present wife's earnings election. It admits also that a potential tax advantage could be gained by transferring investment income from husband to wife, which would be an easy way for wealthy people to reduce their tax burden.

4.4 Equal Opportunities Commission's Response to Green Paper

The main features of the Commission's proposals are:

(*a*) The repeal of Section 37, ICTA, and its substitution by a section declaring that for the purposes of taxation the individual, regardless of sex, is the basic tax unit.

(*b*) The abolition of the higher personal allowance and wife's earned income relief.

(*c*) The deployment of the revenue thus generated to increase child benefit per child by £4.50 per week.

The Commission seek to abolish the idea that a woman on marriage becomes a dependant of her husband. The notion of the dependency of the wife does in fact correspond with reality in families where the children have grown up and the wife does not go to work, and in the present circumstances of high unemployment would find it very difficult to find paid employment. The Commission's proposals would also increase substantially the tax burden of married couples without children where both spouses are working. On the other hand, it would reduce considerably the tax burden of married women with investment income and generally would benefit married couples with high incomes.

4.5 Proposals During the 1983 General Election

Although the Government did not promise to implement any of the suggestions made in the Green Paper, both the Labour and Alliance Parties proposed to phase out the married man's allowance, thus depriving married men of £1,250 for 1985/86 (the difference between the higher and lower personal allowance), and to replace this loss by proportional increases in child benefit allowances, which are tax-free. It was claimed that such a step would reduce the *poverty trap* (see 1.4). As has been explained already, the poverty trap is caused by the low thresholds both for *income tax* and *national insurance contribution* exemption, and any meaningful reform would involve both taxes, which is rather more complicated than the promises in the election manifestoes that the married man's allowance would be abolished.

The abolition of the allowance and replacement with higher child benefit allowances would not help the large number of pensioners whose children have grown up, and it would not help families with children over eighteen attending further education, who do not qualify for child benefit allowances under the existing rules. It is hoped that since the Government and the Opposition parties were committed to changing the way husband and wife are treated for taxation purposes, the complexities of the problem will be explained and suitable solutions found. Professor Atkinson, who advised the House of Commons Select Committee, posed the following questions in his lecture on 26th October, 1983:

(*a*) Under an integrated scheme, would the new tax apply to all income, or just earnings? (National Insurance contributions only apply to *earnings*, but income tax is charged on *investment income* as well.)

(*b*) If it applies only to earnings, how are these to be defined? Would it be as under the income tax? If so, would it include occupational pensions and social security benefits?

(*b*) If it applies to all income, then who will be liable to pay the new rates? Will it apply to all taxpayers, or will there be an exemption for those at present exempt from National Insurance contributions (above minimum pension age) or for those eligible for the age allowance (see 3.10 (*a*)) under income tax (one person 65 or over)?

(*d*) What rate will be charged for the self-employed (see 6.14), taking account of the fact that there are no employer's contributions in this case?

(*e*) Will there continue to be reduced contributions for married women who have retained the option to pay at a lower rate?

(*f*) Will there continue to be contribution conditions for National Insurance benefits? If so, what forms will they take? (Under the existing system a large number of people do not qualify for full benefits, since gaps in their contributions exist, as in the case of married women who are not gainfully employed throughout their working lives and people living abroad for part of their working lives.)

(*g*) If the State Earnings Related Pension Scheme continues, how will the contribution records be maintained? Will there be provisions for contracting out? If these allow a reduced rate of tax to be paid, will this reduction apply to all types of income? (At present it is confined to earnings.)

(*h*) Lastly, the question arises, if the married man whose wife is not working is for income tax and NIC purposes treated as a single person, will he also only get a single person's retirement pension and other National Insurance benefits?

The reader will appreciate that the apparently simple proposal to abolish the higher allowance so dear to politicians is quite complex. This does not mean that these problems cannot be solved, or that the treatment of married women for tax and NIC purposes should not be reformed. It does explain, however, why politicians who advocate radical tax reform before coming into Government lose their enthusiasm when assuming political power.

4.6 The Effect of Unemployment on the Present Situation

The poverty trap has already been mentioned (1.4). The effect of the present taxation and social security rules are such that it will pay the unemployed man with two small children to send his wife out to work and stay at home to look after the children.

Example 4.7 Jones lost his job as fitter in an engineering firm and is offered a post as a shop assistant at a local grocers. His wife could equally do the work and could get the same pay.

(*a*) Assuming husband takes the post:

	£
1985/86 earnings	5,000
Personal allowance	3,455
Taxable income	1,545 at 30% = 463.10

(*b*) Assuming the wife takes the post:

Earnings		5,000	
Less personal allowance	3,455		
Wife's earned income relief	2,205	5,660	
Taxable income		Nil	
Add unemployment benefit, say			£1,000
Total saving			1,463.50 or £28 per week

The implication of the taxation treatment of married women when the husband is unemployed, or the full extent of high unemployment (over 10%) on British living patterns, has not been widely studied. It can, however, not be denied that the gap in living standards between families with both husband and wife working and those experiencing unemployment is widening and may have serious social effects.

4.7 The Use of the Seven-Year Covenant to Save Tax

The simplest tax-saving device for parents with children over the age of 18 in full-time education or for other reasons not having a taxable income of over £2,205 in 1985/86 is the **seven-year covenant** (see 3.9). A specimen document would be drawn up along the following lines:

'I Joe Bloggs of .... covenant to pay my son David Bloggs of .... (the same address) a gross amount of £2,000 (any sum that will not bring the son's income over the threshold of £2,205 in 1985/86) payable on .... (date) for a period of seven years, or for the period of our joint lives (whichever is the shortest period), the first payment to be made on .... (date).

Dated: ....

Signed, sealed and delivered by Joe Bloggs

In the presence of: .... (witness's signature and address)

It should be noted that to be effective the document must have affixed to it a small red seal, next to the signature. This can be obtained from a law stationer for a few pence.

Example 4.8 Assume that Joe Bloggs has an income of £10,000 in 1985/86 and his son is aged 20 and on a full-time course, with no income.

(*a*) Tax position for 1985/86 without a covenant:

Salary	£10,000
Less personal allowance	3,455
	6,545 at 30% = £196.35

(*b*) With covenant:

(*i*) Joe Bloggs' position is the same as under (*a*), but:

(*ii*) Son David can reclaim tax as follows:

Cheque from father £1,500 less tax at 30% £450 = £1,050	
Tax repayment from Inland Revenue, since on £1,500 no tax is due	450
Spendable income	1,500

In other words, Joe Bloggs would have to pay his son another £450 to put him in the same financial position as the covenant has done.

4.8 The Breakdown of Marriage

The tax treatment of getting married has already been referred to in Example 3.9.

(*a*) **Informal separation**. A marriage breakdown quite often starts with an 'informal separation', when the husband still pays for the upkeep of the family home, but no longer lives there. As explained on page 36 the husband can still claim the higher personal allowance (married man's allowance) as long as he *makes voluntary payments substantially maintaining his wife*. How strictly the term 'substantially maintained' is interpreted varies, particularly where the estranged wife has income apart from her husband's allowance. Inspectors tend to argue that if the wife has a job paying more than (£1,250 for 1985/86) the earned income and not the husband's allowance substantially maintains the wife. This interpretation is, of course, more stringent than what is normal in cases of married couples with both spouses working. In all such cases the higher personal allowances is given.

Until the High Court defines the term 'substantially maintaining the wife', it will be advantageous to the taxpayer faced with the Inspector's refusal to give the higher personal allowance on the ground that the wife has other income which maintains her, to enter a *formal* separation agreement from a tax point of view, but before one enters such an agreement a solicitor should be consulted to see what effect this may have on getting an eventual divorce.

(*b*) **Formal separation and divorce**. From the point of view of income tax the treatment of formally separated and divorced spouses is precisely the same:

(*i*) A separated or divorced wife is treated as a single person and is entitled to the full personal allowance (£2,205 for 1985/86); there is no apportionment in the year of separation, when the husband is entitled to the higher personal allowance. Moreover, the payment the husband makes to the wife under a Court Order or Separation Agreement is treated as the wife's income and a charge on the husband's income.

If the alimony payment falls within the term **small maintenance payment**—that is, the amount for the wife does not exceed £33 weekly of £143, or £18 weekly and £78 monthly for each child—the payment is made without deduction of tax. All other alimony payments should be made after tax has been deducted. If the wife has custody of a **qualifying child**—defined as a child under 16, or if over 16 attending full-time education or training (which has to be for 2 years—she is entitled to the additional personal allowance (see page 37).

Example 4.9 Mr and Mrs Connor were divorced on 6 October, 1985, and custody of Peter, aged 10, was given to Mrs Connor. Mr Connor's salary for 1985/86 was £12,000 and he paid £10 per week for the maintenance of the child under a Court Order. Mrs Connor was employed throughout the year, earning £5,000.

(*i*) Tax liability of Mr Connor: Salary		£12,000
Wife's salary		2,500
		14,500
Less Court Order payment 26×£10 =	260	
Higher personal allowance	3,455	
Wife's earned income relief	2,205	5,660
Taxable income		8,840×30%=£2,652

(*ii*) Tax liability of Mrs Connor: salary		£2,500
Court Order payments		260
		2,760
Less personal allowance	2,205	
Additional personal allowance	1,250	3,455
		Nil

Example 4.10 Assume the facts are the same as in Example 4.9 except that his income is £20,000 and he pays £40 per week for the maintenance of the child.

(*i*) Tax liability of Mr Connor: Salary		£20,000
Wife's salary		2,500
		22,500
Less higher personal allowance	3,455	
Wife's earned income allowance	2,205	5,660
Taxable Income		16,840×30%=5,052

(*ii*) Tax liability of Mrs Connor: Salary		£2,500	
Court Order payment		1,040	
		3,640	
Less personal allowance	2,205		
Additional personal allowance	1,250	3,455	
Taxable Income		185×30%=	£55.50
Tax paid on alimony £1,040×30%=£312			312 –
Repayment due			256.50

It will be noted that since the alimony is not a small maintenance payment Mrs Connor received £1,040 less tax £312=728. This was allowed to Mr Connor, by extending the basic rate tax band from £16,200 to £16,840.

Alimony payments fall under Sections 52 and 53 of the ICTA, 1970. Accordingly, if they are paid out of taxable income, Section 52 applies, which means that the payer (husband) is entitled to deduct the tax at basic rate before making payment. Alimony of, say, £3,000 per year in 1985/86 will mean a payment of £2,100. If, however, the payer forgets to deduct the tax before the payment is made and pays the full amount, the wife with no other income cannot reclaim the tax suffered, since no certificate R185 of tax paid will have been issued and the Inland Revenue will collect the tax as shown in Example 4.10.

Moreover, unless the wife returns the £900 tax paid over by mistake, which would regularise the situation, the decision in *Taylor v. Taylor (1938) 1KB320* established that he can deduct the payments from future unpaid instalments in the same tax year but not for earlier years. In these cases the Inland Revenue benefits since it retains the tax repayment which would normally be made to the wife.

(*c*) **Alimony paid in arrears**. It is quite common to find that alimony is paid in arrears and it must be stressed that this can penalise the wife.

Example 4.11 Mr Bannister pays three years' alimony to his wife in 1983/84 at a rate of £2,000 per year. Mrs Bannister has no other income. His income is £15,000.

(i) If alimony had been paid on time, Mrs Bannister's tax position would be as follows:

1981/82 Alimony received	£2,000	
Less personal allowance	1,375	
Tax due	625×30%=	£187.50
Tax deducted at source (R185)	2,000×30%=	600
Repayment due		412.50
1982/83 Alimony received	£2,000	
Less personal allowance	1,565	
Tax due	435×30%=	£130.50
Tax deducted at source (R185)	2,000×30%=	600
Repayment due		469.50
1983/84 Alimony received	£2,000	
Less personal allowance	1,785	
Tax due	215×30%=	£64.50
Tax deducted at source (R185)	2,000×30%=	600
Repayment due		535.50

(*ii*) Three years' alimony paid in 1983/84

Alimony received	£6,000	
Less personal allowance	1,785	
Tax due	4,215×30%=	£1,264.50
Tax deducted at source (R185)	6,000×30%=	1,800
Repayment due		535.50

It will be noted that Mrs Bannister loses tax repayments of £882 as a result of the delay in paying over the alimony. It does not affect Mr Bannister's liability.

(*d*) **Court Order payments made direct to the children**. If the payment of £520 as in Example 4.10, is made in favour of the child, Mrs Connor's income would have been reduced to £2,500, below the threshhold for tax, and the child could have reclaimed the tax of £156.

(*e*) **Mortgage interest relief**. The financial adjustments following divorce or separation often involve the matrimonial home, which is usually subject to a mortgage. If the husband continues to pay the mortgage interest on what was a qualifying mortgage, the interest qualifies for tax relief after the husband has left the home. Moreover, even if the husband purchases another *main residence* with a mortgage, the interest on both mortgages qualify provided the two mortgages together do not exceed the limit of £30,000 for 1984/85 and 1985/86. Tax is usually deducted at source under the MIRAS scheme.

If the mortgage interest is barred from tax relief, the husband can increase the alimony payment and have it made legally enforceable and deduct the increased alimony; the ex-wife can then claim the interest on the mortgage of her main residence.

(*f*) **Life assurance policies**. Section 3.10 explained that a taxpayer can claim 15 per cent tax relief, deducted at source, on whole-life policy premiums on the life of one's self or one's wife. Divorce or separation does not alter this and the relief is due on the premiums on the life of the ex-husband or wife, provided that the policy was taken out when the parties were married.

(*g*) **Pension rights and policies**. Where pension policies provide for provision for a pension for the widow, an arrangement should be considered when the financial settlement of the separation or divorce is being reviewed, since the divorced wife cannot legally become the widow. The matter should therefore be taken up with the pension fund or insurance company.

4.9 Revision Test

Answers	*Questions*
1. It treats the family as one unit, and the wife's income as belonging to the husband.	**1.** Explain the 'aggregation rule'.
2. The result is that the tax liability is split between husband and wife in proportion to their respective incomes. The claim for 1984/85 has to be made after 6.1.1984 and before 6.7.1984.	**2.** What is the effect of a claim for separate assessment and when must it be made?
3. It enables the joint tax liability to be reduced by excluding the wife's earned income from the higher rate bands, but at the same time the difference between the higher and lower	**3.** Explain the effect of an election to have the wife's earnings assessed separately.

personal allowance is lost (£1,250 in 1985/86).

---

4. (*i*) Nothing—existing system reflects general situation and creates no hardships. (*ii*) Extend the earnings election to investment income. (*iii*) Any other suggestion.

4. What do you think should be done to deal with the taxation grievance of married women? Give reasons.

---

5. It pays the husband to stay at home and the wife to seek gainful employment, and creates the house-husband.

5. What is the effect of the present tax-law in conditions of unemployment?

---

6. The wife gets a whole year's personal allowance for part of the year. There is no restriction of the Higher Personal Allowance.

6. What are the taxation effects of a voluntary and formal separation?

---

7. Under voluntary separation the husband receives the Higher Personal Allowance and any payments to maintain the wife are ignored. After a formal separation the husband loses the HPA, but can deduct the maintenance payments to the wife, which are treated as her income.

7. Distinguish between the effects of a voluntary and formal separation?

---

8. The alimony payment is paid 'net' after tax at basic rate has been deducted, but a 'Small Maintenance Payment' is paid gross and is added to the wife's taxable income.

8. Distinguish between alimony payments generally and 'Small Maintenance Payments'?

---

9. If both husband and wife are working and have regular incomes, it will pay them to arrange the separation around 6 October. In this case the husband will qualify for full WEIR and the wife will get her full personal allowance.

9. Is there a good time to arrange a formal separation?

---

10. They are treated as alimony payments and reduce the taxable income of the husband and increase the taxable income of the wife.

10. How are maintenance payments for children, treated?

---

11. It does pay, because the wife's income is reduced by the Court Order payment and the income will belong to the child for tax purposes and thus qualify for a personal allowance.

11. Does it pay to have the main tenance payment made in favour of the child by the Court?

---

12. The 15% deduction is still given, provided the policy on the life of the spouse was taken out before 14.3.1984 and the wife was living with him at the time the policy was written.

12. How is life assurance relief affected by divorce?

5
Income from Land and Property

Income from land and property in the UK is assessable to tax under three schedules:

1 **Schedule A,** which deals with rents, sporting rights and premiums on leases, etc.

2 **Schedule B,** which deals with the occupation of woodlands managed on a commercial basis. If X owns woodlands which are managed commercially he will pay tax under both Schedule A and B, but if he lets the property to Y who manages the estate commercially, then X will be liable to tax under Schedule A and Y under Schedule B.

3 **Schedule D, Case VI**, which deals with income from furnished letting.

5.1 Schedule A

This schedule divides the income into three groups:

(*a*) Rents under any lease and rent charges, such as feu duties etc.

(*b*) Receipts other than rents arising from the ownership of land, e.g. shooting and other sporting rights, wayleave rents, camping sites, etc.

(*c*) Premiums on leases of less than 50 years' duration. Profits on the disposal of longer leases are subject to capital gains tax if appropriate.

5.2 Basis of assessment

Section 67 of the ICTA, 1970, provides: 'Tax ... shall be charged by reference to the rents or receipts to which a person becomes entitled in the chargeable period.' This means that the assessment is based on the income actually receivable during the year. Moreover, the assessment for 1985/86 is based provisionally on the income of the year 1984/85, tax being payable on 1 January, 1986 but if the Inspector is satisfied that the income for 1985/86 will be less than the income for 1984/85, he can reduce the tax payable on 1 January, 1986. In any case, the 1985/86 assessment is adjusted to the actual income receivable in 1985/86 after 5 April, 1986, when the detailed information is available.

5.3 Allowable Deductions

Payments in respect of the following expenses can be deducted from the assessable income:

(*a*) **Repairs**, which includes maintenance and redecoration expenditure.

(*b*) **Cost of insurance and management**. This includes cost of rent collection, advertising, salaries of management, including the owner's wife, legal and accountancy charges.

(*c*) **Cost of services**. This includes the cost of services the landlord is obliged to provide for the tenants under the terms of the lease, but for which he is not reimbursed. The type of expense depends on the terms of the lease, but normally includes the cost of cleaning stairs in blocks of flats, wages of caretakers, costs of lighting, etc.

(*d*) **Rates and taxes.** This includes general and water rates and VAT.

(*e*) **Rents**. This includes rent paid to a superior landlord, ground rent, etc.

(*f*) **Capital allowances**. This includes allowances available (see Chapter 7) in respect of any plant in use, e.g. lifts.

If part of the property is let and part owner-occupied, joint expenses have to be apportioned and only the proportion relating to the let part can be claimed.

Example 5.1 Maxwell owns number 10, 12 and 14 Park Street and the income and expenditure in respect thereof for the year 5 April, 1986 were as follows:

	No. 10	No. 12	No. 14
Income	£	£	£
Rents due	660	800	670
Outstanding 5.4.1985	50	—	30
Balance	710	800	700
Outstanding 5.4.1986	60	50	—
	650	750	700
Dilapidations from tenants	200		
Insurance claim for recovery for flood damage	—	340	—
	850	1,090	700
Expenditure			
Agent's commission 10%	66	80	67
Repairs and maintenance	320	485	220

Insurance	30	50	35
Rates	280	300	230
Professional charges	120	100	50
Interest paid	180	160	
	996	1,175	602

	No. 10	No. 12	No. 14
Repairs and maintenance comprising:	£	£	£
Repairing roof		145	
Repairing flood damage		340	
Redecorating on change of tenant	320		
Redecorating			100
Installing fitted cupboards			120
	320	485	220
Professional charges comprising:			
Accountancy	50	50	50
Valuation for insurance purposes	70	50	
	120	100	50

The interest paid was in respect of a loan from the bank to instal central heating in 1978/79. The terms of letting were: No. 10, full-repairing lease, which means that the tenant is responsible for the repairs; No. 12, non-repairing lease, which means that the landlord is responsible for the repairs; No. 14 is let furnished.

The Schedule A assessment is calculated as follows:

	No. 10			No. 12		
	£	£	£	£	£	£
Rent receivable			660			800
Less expenditure		996			1,175	
Except interest	180			160		
Dilapidations	200					
Insurance recovery		380	616	340	500	675
Net income			44			125

The furnished letting is assessed under Case VI of Schedule D:

	No. 14		
	£	£	£
Rent due			670
Less expenditure	602		
Except fitted cupboards	120	482	
Add concessional allowance (10% of rent less rates in lieu of capital allowances) 10% (670–230) 440		44	526
Assessable income			144

Tax relief for interest paid is explained on page 31. The assessable income from the three properties for 1984/85 is therefore made up of

£44 + 125 + 144 = £363	
Less interest paid	340
(£180 £160)	23

5.4 Conditions Governing Allowances

Expenses can be claimed under Schedule A only if they have not been allowed against business profits or in any other way, and are not recoverable from an insurance company. Normally, payments are to be allowed in the year in which they are made. If, however, the full allowance cannot be claimed in that year because the property was sold or transferred to some other person, so that no rents are available to use up the expenses, the expenses can be claimed for the period the payment became due rather than in the period they were paid. When property accounts are prepared by accountants, it is possible to agree with the Inspector to have expenses allowed on the basis of the accounting year and not the year of assessment (ending 5 April).

5.5 Losses

An excess of expenditure on one property can be set against rents from other properties of the same landlord, provided that the properties in question are let at a *full rent*, where the tenant pays rates but the landlord is responsible for repairs. If this is not possible, the loss can be carried forward to be set against future income from the same kind of lease. If an excess of expenditure occurs on a property let at a *full-repairing lease*, where the tenant is responsible for rates and repairs, the loss can be set off against income from the same kind of lease only.

Some properties are let at less than full commercial rent to relatives or friends, etc. Technically, such occupation is known as **beneficial occupation** and any deficit arising from such a letting can only be set off or carried forward against income under the same lease. In fact, the loss has to be borne by the landlord who lets property below market rate.

Beneficial occupation also arises where living accommodation is provided by the employer, except when it is part of the conditions of employment, when it is regarded as **representative occupation** and no taxable profit arises, because the employee has to live in the accommodation provided and has to give it up when the employment ceases. Examples of representative occupation are tied cottages for farm workers, police houses, flats occupied by bank managers, caretakers, etc.—the most famous example being 10 Downing Street.

The calculation of the taxable benefit arising from beneficial occupation provided by the employer is dealt with in Chapter 10.

5.6 Lost Rent Relief

As explained, the basis of assessment under Schedule A is the sum the landlord is *entitled* to receive by way of rent, but if the tenant defaults or the landlord has waived the rent because the tenant was in financial difficulties, the *lost rent* can be deducted from the assessment.

Example 5.2 D lets a farm at a rent of £1,000 per year on a 21 years' lease. The farmer has a bad year in 1983/84 and cannot pay the rent in December and March. D decides to waive the rent of £500. Under section 87 of the ICTA, 1970, the Schedule A assessment for 1983/84 will be reduced to £500.

5.7 Premiums on Leases

Premiums for the grant of a lease for 50 years or less are taxable on a special basis. The amount to be assessed under Schedule A is the premium reduced by $\frac{1}{50}$ of its amount for each complete period of 12 months, except the first, provided for in the lease. The following items have to be added to the premium where appropriate:

(*a*) The value of any work not paid for which the tenant agreed to do to the property thus enhancing its value.

(*b*) Instalments not yet paid of the premium have to be included in the assessment, except that one can claim to defer the tax in respect of instalments spread over eight years, or the period of instalments if less, where hardship can be shown.

5.8 Other Payments Treated as Premiums

(*a*) Any increase in the value to the landlord of the reversion of a lease which is attributable to an obligation of the tenant to improve the property.

(*b*) Payments in commutation of rent or for the right to surrender the lease.

(*c*) Payments, other than rent, for the variation or waiver of the terms of the lease.

(*d*) Payments for the reassignment of a lease which was originally granted by the landlord at an undervalue.

5.9 Top-slicing Relief in Respect of Premiums

The whole of the taxable part of the premium is assessable in the year of receipt, except that the taxpayer can claim **top-slicing relief**, which enables the taxpayer to claim that the tax on the premium be calculated at the rate of tax which would have applied if he had the premium spread over the period of the lease.

Example 5.3 Watkins owns the freehold of a shop and grants a 14-year lease to

Evans determinable at his option at the end of the seventh year, on 10 April, 1985. The premium of £6,500 was paid on the grant of the lease and the rent payable annually in advance is £2,000 per annum. Watkins' salary during 1985/86 was £16,000. His tax liability will be calculated as follows:

(*i*) Without claiming top-slicing relief:

1985/86 premium	£6,500		
Less $\frac{7-1}{50} \times$ £6,500	780		
	5,720		
Add rent	2,000		
Schedule A assessment	7,720		
Add earnings	16,000		
	23,720		
Personal allowance	2,205		
Taxable income	21,515		
	16,200×30%=	4,860	
	3,000×40%=	1,200	
	2,315×45%=	1,041.75	
Tax due		£7,101.75	

(*ii*) With claiming top-slicing relief:

Assessable part of premium			5,720
Top-slicing relief $\frac{5,720}{.7}$	£ 817		
Add rent	2,000		
Schedule A assessment	2,817		
Add earnings	16,000		
	18,817		
Personal allowance	2,205		
	16,612	16,200×30%=	£4,860
		412×40%=	164.80
			5,024.80

Thus claiming the top-slicing relief saves Watkins £2,076.95 tax in 1985/86, but he pays more tax in succeeding years though probably not at the higher rates. It will be noted that although the lease is for fourteen years, for tax purposes it is treated as a seven-year lease, because of the option to terminate it after seven years.

5.10 Schedule B (Woodlands Managed on a Commercial Basis)

Woodlands managed on a commercial basis are subject to tax under Schedule B (amenity woodlands are exempt). The basis of assessment is one third of the *annual value*, which is the gross annual value for rating purposes and is based on the rent one can obtain from letting the woodlands in the open market, the tenant paying the rates and the landlard paying for repairs, at the relevant date. The basis for rating valuation is the value on 6 April, 1973.

Once Schedule B tax has been charged any profits made from the sale of timber is tax-free. As an alternative to being assessed under Schedule B, the taxpayer can elect to have the profits assessed under Schedule D, Case I (see Chapter 6). The election must extend to all woodlands owned by the same person on the same estate. The reason for making this election is that under Schedule D trading losses can be set against other income (see Chapter 8), but this facility is not available under Schedule B. The election must be in writing, and once made cannot be reversed.

Investment in woodlands is an attractive tax-saving device, since not only is profit from the sale of timber not assessed to income, or capital gains tax (but under Schedule B) but it also receives favourable treatment under capital transfer tax. Moreover, although an election to have Schedule D applied cannot be reversed, one can always form a company and revert to Schedule B.

S. 51 FA 1984 provides that any woodland the use of which commenced after 13 March, 1984, wholly or mainly for the purpose of felling processing or removing timber, or for clearing lands for replanting in connection with a trade carried on by the user, no longer falls within Schedule B, but has to be dealt with under Schedule D as a trade. It reversed a decision by the Courts in 1983 and envisages the felling of trees as a subsidiary of a trading activity. It will take some time before the full implications of the change in the law is realised.

5.11 Revision Test

Answers	*Questions*
1. Rents, sporting rights, camping sites, wayleaves, premiums on some leases.	**1.** What income is assessable under Schedule A?
2. It is based on the rents receivable in the year of assessment.	**2.** What is the basis of assessment under Schedule A?
3. Repairs provided it is not a *full-repairing* lease, cost of insurance, management, services rates and groundrent etc.	**3.** What expenses can be claimed against rent income for tax purposes?
4. There is a concessional allowance for depreciation of furniture etc. of 10% of the gross rent—rates.	**4.** What concessional allowance can be claimed against income from furnished lettings?

5. Losses can be set against surpluses of the same year as long as the income is from the same type of lease. Unallowed losses can be carried forward and allowed against future surpluses of the same kind of leases.

5. How can losses be claimed under Schedule A?

---

6. (*a*) 'Beneficial Occupational' arises where property is let at a rent of less than the market rate.
(*b*) 'Representative Occupation' arises when rent-free property is provided by the employer as a condition of employment (tied cottage).

6. Explain the following terms:
(*a*) 'Beneficial Occupation'
(*b*) 'Representative Occupation'

---

7. A 'full-repairing lease' is one where the tenant is responsible for the repairs of the property and if the landlord pays for them, he cannot claim them for tax purposes.

7. Explain the term 'Full-repairing lease'?

---

8. Since the 'rent receivable' is the basis of assessment, if it is not paid, the amount lost can be claimed as a deduction.

8. Explain the term 'lost rent' and how tax relief is given?

---

9. The 1984/85 Schedule A assessment is provisionally based on the 1983/84 figures payable 1.1.1985. If it is apparent by 1.1.1985 that the 1984/85 income is less than 1983/84 income, the assessment can be reduced.

9. When is tax payable under Schedule A due? Can hardship arise and how?

---

10. There are two kinds of premium
(*i*) Those relating to leases of no more than 50 years duration are taxed under Schedule A.
(*ii*) Those relating to leases over 50 years duration subject to CGT.

10. How are premiums on leases taxed?

11. One takes the premium and reduces it by a formula $\frac{\textit{length of lease} - 1}{50}$ and add it to the rent.	**11.** How are premiums taxed under Schedule A?
12. When the taxable part of the premium if added to other income puts the recipient into higher rates of income tax. 'Top-slicing relief' enables him to spread the taxable part of the premium over the length of the lease.	**12.** Explain in what circumstances 'top-slicing relief' should be claimed?

6
Income of The Self-Employed

The profits from trades, professions and vocations are assessed under Schedule D, Cases I and II. The distinction between the two Cases of Schedule D is historical and no longer of practical significance.

6.1 What Constitutes Trading?

Section 526 of the ICTA, 1970, defines trading: '*trade includes every trade manufacture, adventure or concern in the nature of trade*'. This definition has been framed deliberately wide, to give the Courts extensive discretion in interpretation. Moreover, sums of money not treated as taxable profits for income tax may still be liable to **capital gains tax**. In deciding whether or not a trade is being carried on, the Courts have established certain principles known as the **marks of trading**, of which the most common are:

(*a*) **The existence of a profit-seeking motive**. This arises when an isolated sale at a profit can either be regarded as a change of investment, subject to capital gains tax, or trading, which is subject to much higher income tax. In *CIR v. Frazer (1942) 24 TC 948*, Lord Moncrieff in the Court of Session expressed himself as follows: 'When a man deals with a trading commodity such as whisky in bulk in bond, which he has acquired merely for the purpose of re-sale and proceeds to sell, and there are no further material circumstances in the case, he engages in my view in trade, and in trade only, and not in investment of capital funds.'

This problem often arises when the taxpayer purchases and sells property or stocks and shares, etc., over a period, when other facts have to be considered.

(*b*) **The way the asset was acquired**. Normally, the profit a builder makes from selling houses is trading profit, but if it can be shown that the houses sold were built for letting and not for sale, the profit is to be regarded as a capital gain. This was decided *West v. Phillips (1958) 38 TC 203*.

(*c*) **The nature and quality of the asset acquired**. It was decided in *CIR v. Scottish Automobile & General Insurance Co. Ltd (1931) 16 TC 381* that the buying and selling of shares by an insurance company formed part of its normal trade.

(*d*) **What happens to the asset (purchase) pending sale**. It was held in *CIR v. Livingstone and other (1926) 11 TC 358* that an isolated purchase of a ship by three people—a ship repairer, blacksmith and fish salesman—who converted it and sold it was trading. The judge stated: 'The profit made by the venture arose not from the mere appreciation of the capital value of an isolated purchase for resale, but from the expenditure on the subject purchased of money laid out upon it for the purpose of making it marketable at a profit. That seems the very essence of trade.'

(*e*) **The interval between purchase and sale**. Normally, if the interval is short the transaction will be regarded as trading, but this need not be so. It was held in the case *Wisdom v. Chamberlain (1968) 45 TC 92* that a casual profit on a hedge against inflation, i.e. the purchase and sale of silver bullion, did not constitute trading. Goff J. expressed himself as follows: '... this was not an adventure in the nature of trade, but was what Mr Halpern meant it to be, a security to protect his client against devaluation, and the actual profit realised was fortuitous.'

(*f*) **The way the sale was secured** and the number of transactions involved. There are a number of cases which tend to show that unless good cause can be shown a number of purchases and sales of what are normally regarded as capital assets, it will constitute trading, but not always.

(*g*) **The destination of the profits**. This follows on similar principles to (*f*) if the proceeds of the sale of a house are used to purchase another which in turn is sold and so on, it will tend to establish trading, but not necessarily so.

6.2 What Constitutes a Profession?

Since both trades and professions are treated alike, it is sufficient to define a profession briefly. Generally, a professional person is one who belongs to a professional institute, e.g. the Law Society, British Medical Association, Institute of Chartered Accountants of England & Wales, etc., with a code of conduct for members and disciplinary procedures, and admission restricted to persons who have passed a qualifying examination.

6.3 What Constitutes a Vocation?

The definition of what constitutes a vocation is important since if an activity of a self-employed person can be described as neither trade, profession or vocation it escapes assessment to tax. The term has been defined widely in the case of *Partridge v. Mallandaine (1886) 2 TC 179.* It concerned a bookmaker who claimed that he did not fall within either Cases I or II of Schedule D. Denman J. held he was assessable and expressed himself as follows: 'I think the word vocation ... is a very large word; it means the way in which a person passes his life, and is a very large word indeed. These persons go to races and they systematically bet and for this reason it must be assumed make profits. Does it lie in their mouths to say that they are not to be assessed?'

In practice, keeping a boarding house and similar activities, which are neither trades nor professions, are assessed as vocations.

6.4 What Constitutes a Trading Receipt?

Whether or not a particular sum of money constitutes a trading receipt subject to tax depends on:

(*a*) **Does the receipt arise from the trade?** In the case of *Murray v. Goodhews (1978) STC 207* it was held that a voluntary payment of a brewer to tenants of public houses was not a taxable receipt. On the other hand, a gratuity received by a self-employed taxi-driver is regarded as taxable, and goods taken from stock for private use have to be valued at selling price when crediting them in the accounts in accordance with the decision in *Sharkey v. Wernher (1955) 36 TC 275.*

(*b*) **Does the receipt represent income and not capital?** In the case of *The Glenboig Union Fireclay Co. Ltd v. CIR (1922) 12 TC 427* it was held that the receipt of compensation for being prevented from extracting fireclay under a railway line constituted a capital receipt and not trading income. On the other hand, in the case of *Jeffrey v. Rolls-Royce Ltd (1962) 40 TC 443* it was held that the sale of 'know-how' to the Republic of China was a trading receipt.

The facts of the Rolls-Royce case were unusual, as explained by Pearce LJ (in the Court of Appeal): 'The facts create a strong impression that, in territories where the company could not hope to sell its engines, it was pursuing a wise policy of allowing local manufacture from which it could receive the benefits of advertisement, lump sums and royalties. This was not in substitution for its policy of selling its own engines, in territories where it could do so, but a collateral and supplementary method of trading in territories where it could not do so ... The knowledge sold in this case is not some secret of permanent value sold by an owner who is transferring or terminating his business. Such a sale would clearly be a sale of a fixed asset. The knowledge sold in this case is in the main a transient by-product of advancing engineering science.'

In fact there were cases both before and after this decision in which the sale of **know-how** was treated as a capital transaction. The test is whether it was an isolated transaction as in the case of *Evans Medical Supplies Ltd v. Moriarty (1957) 37 TC 546* or whether it is part of a deliberate policy of licensing others to manufacture engines in countries where Rolls-Royce found it difficult or impossible to export engines of its own manufacture. The cost of know-how is treated as capital expenditure (see 6.6) and qualifies for capital allowances (see 7.8).

6.5 Receipts to be Excluded

(*a*) Receipts of a capital nature.

(*b*) Dividends and interest, etc., taxed at source.

(*c*) Untaxed interest received is assessable under Case III of Schedule D, but certain small sums can be included as trade receipts as a matter of convenience, but not as a matter of law.

(*d*) Rent received for premises not occupied for trading purposes, which are assessable under Schedule A (see Chapter 5).

(*e*) Gifts, which must be distinguished from 'expected gratuities' such as tips to a self-employed taxi-driver. A gift is a completely unsolicited sum of money, but if one denies a taxi-driver his tip, his comments will usually show that he expected to receive it.

(*f*) Lump sums, which are either capital or are covered by special provisions, which enable authors, painters, sculptors, composers and other artists to spread the lump sum received over two or three years, provided the work took more than twelve months to produce. If the copyright is sold after ten years, the lump sum can be spread over six years.

6.6 Allowable Business Expenses

Generally, a business expense can be deducted from the taxable profit, provided:

(*a*) It is specifically authorised by the statutes; or

(*b*) It is, in the circumstances of the particular business, a proper commercial deduction according to accounting practice and it is neither (*i*) capital expenditure nor (*ii*) prohibited by any provision of the statutes.

Section 130 of the ICTA, 1970, provided the general rules about expenses and contains a list of prohibitions, implying that those expenses which are not prohibited are properly allowable. The main provision, Section 130 (a), provides that no sum shall be deducted in respect of *any disbursements or expenses, not being money wholly and exclusively laid out or expended for the purposes of the trade, profession or vocation.*

The main allowable expenses can be summarised as follows:

(*a*) **Normal business expenses**, including cost of materials, stocks for re-sale, wages, rent, interest, repairs, transport, advertising, etc. The list is long and depends on the business.

(*b*) The problem of **defining capital expenditure** recurs and the general principle was laid down in the case of *Atherton v. British Insulated & Helsby Cables Ltd (1926) 10 TC 155*, when the judge expressed himself as follows: 'When expenditure is made not only once and for all, but with a view to bringing into existence an asset or advantage for the enduring benefit of a trade, I think there is very good reason ... for treating such an expenditure as properly attributable not to revenue, but to capital.' (The case concerned the cost of buying pension rights for existing staff on the introduction of a pension scheme. Part of such expenditure can now be claimed, but this does not affect the principle involved).

(*c*) The problem of **defining what is a repair**. The principle was laid down in the case of *Bullcroft Main Colleries Ltd v. O'Grady (1932) 17 TC 93*. Rowlatt J. expressed himself: 'Of course, every repair is a replacement. ... But the critical matter is ... What is the entirety? ... If you replace in entirety it is having a new one and it is not repairing an old one.'

(*d*) **Bad trading debts**, including the provision for specific bad debts, which are unlikely to be received. A provision of, say, 5 per cent of trade debtors is regarded as not *specific* and is not allowable.

(*e*) **Fines**. Many business people incur fines from time to time, particularly parking fines. The principle was laid down by the judge as follows, in the case of *Alexander von Glehn v. CIR (1927) 12 TC 232*: 'The case is of some importance, not so much for the facts of the particular case, but because the arguments of the appellants amount to this, that if a trader in the course of ... business incurs penalties whether it be because he commits breaches of the laws relating to licensed houses ... such a trader is entitled to treat ... his profits as reduced by the penalties which he has to pay ... It would be an extremely serious thing ... if that proposition could be established. It cannot be said that the disbursement in the present case is made for the purpose of the trade ... The disbursement is made ... because the individual who is conducting the trade has ... been guilty of an infraction of the law.'

It follows from this judgement that fines for motoring offences paid on behalf of employees are allowable, since the trader has not himself broken the law.

(*f*) **Legal expenses of a revenue nature**, such as maintaining trading rights, collecting debts, renewing an existing lease, etc., but not preparing a new lease, or taking a disagreement with the Inland Revenue to appeal.

(*g*) **Expenses not incurred as businessman.** This often arises and for this reason has to be subdivided:

(*i*) Damages: This was laid down in the case of *Strong & Co. (of Romsey) v. Woodifield (1906) 5 TC 215*, which concerned the payment of damages to a customer for injuries sustained from a falling chimney, as follows: 'It does not follow that if a loss is in any sense connected with a trade it must always be allowed as a deduction; for it may be only remotely connected with a trade ... To give an illustration, losses sustained by a railway company in compensating passengers for an accident might be deducted. On the other hand, if a man bought a grocer's shop, for keeping which a house was necessary and one of the window shutters fell upon and injured a man walking in the street, the loss arising thereby to the grocer ought not to be deducted ... In the present case, I think that the loss sustained by the appellant was not really incidental to their trade as inkeepers, and fell upon them in their character not of traders but of householders ...'

(*ii*) Cost of travelling from home. The cost of travelling from where one chooses to live to work is regarded as a private expense and not allowable. The problem arises when one travels from home not to the office but to see a customer. This occurred in the case of a builder who worked from home and was decided in *Horton v. Young (1971) 47 TC 60*. Brightman J. expressed himself as follows: 'It seems to me that there is a fundamental difference between a self-employed person who travels from his shop or office or his chambers or his consulting rooms in order to earn profits ... and a self-employed person who travels from his home to a number of different locations for the purely temporary purpose at each such place of there completing a job of work, at the conclusion of which he attends at a different location ... The point is that this trade ... is by its very nature itinerant. ... In my view, where a person has no fixed place or places at which he carries on his trade ... the travelling expenses of that person incurred between his home and the places where from time to time he happens to exercise his trade or profession will normally be wholly and exclusively laid out for the purpose of the trade or profession.'

(*h*) **Duality of purpose.** The principle was laid down in the case of *Caillebotte v. Quinn (1975) 50 TC 222*, which concerned the cost of meals incurred by a carpenter whilst working on building sites. Templeman J. expressed himself as follows: 'In 1971 ... Mr Quinn was a self-employed carpenter. ... His home was the base from which he carried on his business. ... He worked as a subcontractor ... on sites within a forty mile radius of his home. The building sites were too far from his home to allow him to go home for lunch, and when he was working he bought lunch at a public house or cafe. The average cost of a bought lunch was 40p, as compared with his estimated cost of a home lunch of 10p. ... A Schedule D taxpayer, like every other taxpayer, must eat in order to live; he does not eat in order to work.... In these circumstances no part of the cost of Mr Quinn's lunch was *exclusively* ... expended for the purpose of his trade as a carpenter....'

6.7 Expenses Specifically Prohibited

(*a*) Non-business expenses (Section 130 (a), ICTA, 1970).

(*b*) Expenses for the personal maintenance of the trader and his family (Section 130 (b) ICTA 1970). The most common question arises here where the trader, etc., works from home and employs his wife or other members of the family. The principle was laid down by two decisions. In *Copeman v. William Flood and Sons Ltd (1941) 24 TC 50* Lawrence J. said: 'I think it is perfectly true that the Commissioners cannot interfere with the prerogative of the company to pay its directors (all members of the same family) whatever it thinks fit, but they can find ... that sums so paid are not wholly and exclusively laid out for the purpose of the trade.' In *Thompson v. Bruce (1927) 11 TC 607* it was held that alleged payments to the wife for services rendered but not entered in the books could not be treated as a salary.

Inspectors frequently try to oppose the charge of wives' salaries because of the wife's earned income allowance (see page 00) but provided (*i*) the wife can be shown to work in the business and (*ii*) she is paid separately from housekeeping money, and these payments are reasonable for the work done and entered in the books, the Inspector will have to allow it. If the payment is over the threshold of £2,205 for 1985/86 PAYE has to be applied, and the liability to pay Class I National Insurance Contribution, if the income exceeds £1,820 in 1985/86, must not be forgotten.

(*c*) Rent and other expenses relating to premises or part thereof not occupied for the business (Section 130 (c) ICTA). This also commonly arises where a self-employed person works from home and part of his home is used as an office or consulting room, etc. Inspectors frequently try to discourage such claims by pointing out the capital gains tax implications of claiming part of one's home as business premises. Capital gains tax is outside the scope of this book, but it can be stated here that the simplest way to deal with this question is to agree a round sum allowance for the business use of the home covering the cost of light, heat, rates, insurance, etc., rather than agree that a fraction of the premises is used.

(*d*) Charges for repairs of premises, etc., not actually incurred (Section 130(d)). This means that no provision for repairs or other expenses is allowable.

(*e*) Any loss not connected or arising out of the business (Section 130(e)).

(*f*) Cost of capital withdrawn or employed in improvements etc. (Section 130(f) and (g)).

(*g*) Any sum recoverable under a contract of insurance (Section 130(k)).

(*h*) Any sums paid net after deduction of income tax, e.g. certain interest, annuities, royalties and other annual payments (Section 130 (l–o)).

(*j*) Cost of business entertaining, except in the case of overseas customers (Section 411 (1 and 2)).

(*k*) Cost of gifts of food, drink, tobacco or vouchers exchangeable for such items (Section 411(7a)), except that luncheon vouchers issued to employees are allowable, but see Chapter 10.

(*l*) Cost of gifts, except articles incorporating conspicuous advertisement and not costing more than £2 each (Section 411 (7b)). This covers the office diary and ballpoint pen with the firm's name on it. (This has been increased to £10 from 1985/86 onwards.)

6.8 Expenses Specifically Allowed by Statute

(*a*) Fees and expenses incurred in obtaining patent rights, whether the patent is subsequently granted or not (Sections 132 and 382, ICTA, 1970).

(*b*) Payments for technical education related to the business (as decided in the case of *Wickwar v. Berry (1963) 41 TC 33*).

(*c*) Certain expenditure in abortive attempts to win access to mineral deposits (Section 62, Capital Allowances Act, 1968).

(*d*) Premiums on leases for business premises (Section 134, ICTA, 1970). The trader can deduct each year the cost of the premium assessed under Schedule A (see Example 5.3) spread over the term of the lease.

(*e*) Research expenditure, e.g. grants to universities on scientific research related to the trade (Section 99, *Capital* Allowances Act, 1968).

(*f*) Relief for overseas trading by individuals (Section 27, Finance Act, 1978).

The relief consists of a 25 per cent deduction in respect of **qualifying**

days spent abroad, provided at least 30 days were spent absent from the UK on business in the year of assessment. A qualifying day is any day on which the claimant was absent from the UK at midnight. In cases of continuing periods abroad of at least seven days, intervening rest days (week-ends) are ignored and the whole period qualifies. For absences in 1984/85 the allowance is reduced to 12½ per cent and for absences after 6.4.1985 the allowance is abolished.

Example 6.1 Gray regularly visits foreign countries to increase his exports. In 1983/84 he spent 50 qualifying days abroad and his taxable profits were £14,500. Relief would be calculated as follows:

$\frac{50}{365} \times £14{,}500 \times 25\% = £497$, which is deducted from the £14,500

(*g*) Pre-trading expenses. S.39, FA, 1980, provides that expenditure incurred after 31 March, 1980, and within one year before commencement of the trade qualifies for tax relief, if it would have been a properly allowable expense had the trade been in existence at the time. S.50, FA, 1982, extended this relief to expenditure incurred in the *three* years before commencement of the business, provided it was incurred after 31 March, 1980. For both income and corporation tax purposes, the pre-trading expenditure is treated as having been incurred on the day the trade commenced.

In other words, under the new provisions, expenditure which was previously barred by the decision in *Law Shipping Co. Ltd v. CIR (1924) 12 TC 621* can be claimed, if it is incurred after 31 March, 1980 and within three years of the trade starting. On the other hand, capital expenditure, e.g. formation costs of forming a trading company are still not allowable.

6.9 Stock Relief

Stock relief was originally introduced in 1975 to mitigate the effects of inflation on the cash flow of businesses replacing their stocks at increasing prices. There have been several forms of stock relief, the most recent one being contained in Schedule 9, Finance Act, 1976, for accounting periods ending before 14 November, 1980 (when the Chancellor made the announcement) and periods after that date when a completely new system applies. Special rules apply to periods straddling the two and there is transitional relief when one can claim either under the 'old' or the 'new' system.

(*a*) **The 'new' relief** for accounting starting 14 November, 1980. The following rules apply:

(*i*) Relief is based on the opening stock and work in progress at the beginning of the accounting period, which is normally one year.

(*ii*) £2,000 is deducted from the value of the opening stock, to exclude very small traders.

(*iii*) The Department of Industry prepares for the purpose of stock relief an 'All Stocks Index', which records the average price level of stocks, etc., held by businesses in the UK on a sample basis monthly. The percentage increase shown by the index for the month when the trading period commences and ends is then applied to the figure for *opening stock*, etc.

Table 6.1 The All Stock Index.

Month	*1981*	*1982*	*% Increase*
April	204.0	219.7	7.70
May	205.5	220.6	7.35
June	206.4	220.5	6.84
July	206.5	221.1	7.08
August	208.6	221.7	6.28
September	209.9	223.0	6.25
October	211.8	224.3	5.91
November	213.1	225.3	5.73
December	214.5	227.1	5.88
	1982	*1983*	
January	217	229.1	5.58
February	218.6	230.5	5.45
March	218.9	231.4	5.72
April	219.7	233.4	6.24
May	220.6	234.3	6.22
June	220.5	235.4	6.76
July	221.1	235.5	6.67
August	221.7	237.3	7.04
September	223.0	238.7	7.05
October	224.3	238.9	6.51
November	225.3	239.1	6.13
December	227.1	240.3	5.82
	1983	*1984*	
January	229.1	242.6	5.90
February	230.5	244.0	5.86
March	231.4	246.1	6.36

(*iv*) There is no **clawback** of relief already given unless the business has actually ceased, or its operations have become 'negligible' to that in any of the last six years. (The term 'negligible' in this context has not yet been defined by the courts.)

Example 6.2 Black, a self-employed plastics manufacturer, has been in business since 1970. For the year to 31 December, 1981, his opening stock and work in progress figure was £25,320 and his closing stock and work in progress figure was £26,450. His taxable profit was £15,850 less capital allowance (see Chapter 7) of £1,150. The All Stocks Index for December, 1980, was 196.5 and for December, 1981, 214.5. Stock relief is calculated as follows:

Opening value of stock	£25,320
Less	2,000
	23,320

$$23{,}320 \times \frac{214.5 - 196.5}{196.5} = £2{,}136$$

A rise in the index of 9.16%

Assuming that Black claimed the maximum relief, the computation is:

1982/83 Adjusted profit		£15,850
Less capital allowances	1,150	
Stock relief	2,136	3,286
Assessable profit		12,564

(*b*) **The 'old' relief** for accounting periods ending before 14 November, 1980:

(*i*) Relief was based on the increase in *closing stock* over *opening stock*, but was restricted by 10 per cent of taxable profit less capital allowances for individuals and partnerships and 15 per cent for companies.

(*ii*) There was provision for **clawback**—that is, the withdrawal of the relief previously given when the closing stock was less than the opening stock. Relief for 1973/74 and 1974/75 can no longer be clawed back. Stock relief for 1975/76 to 1979/80 were to be written off after the sixth anniversary of the end of the accounting period for which it was claimed.

(*iii*) Clawbacks in periods after 1979/80, but before 14 November, 1980, qualified for a partial referral, subject to special complicated rules.

(*c*) **Transitional relief** for accounting periods ending on 14 November, 1980, or straddling that date—say, the year to 31 December, 1980. Basically, the transitional relief enabled the trader to claim either under the old or new rules, whichever suited him. Since readers qualifying for this relief will have claimed it at the time of reading this book, the way to calculate it has not been included. Stock relief has been withdrawn for accounting periods beginning after 12.3.1984 and no claw-back will be claimed after this.

Example 6.3 The Schedule D, Case I or II, computation: James has been trading as manufacturer's agent for some years and his profit and loss account for the year to 31 December, 1984, was:

	£	£
Gross profit		25,364
Interest on Government securities		410
Premium Bond prize		150
Profit on sale of car		120
		26,044
Less		
Salaries (including wife £700)	11,122	
Light and heat	150	
Rates	320	
Car expenses	500	
Office expenses	130	
General expenses	2,360	
Bad debts	48	
Depreciation	350	
Repairs, etc., to the office	180	
Accountancy	250	
Legal expenses	380	15,790
Net profit for the year		10,254

Notes on the accounts

(*a*) Mrs James acts as book-keeper and works approximately 16 hours per week.

(*b*) Mr James works from home and it has been agreed that one quarter of rates, light and heat, etc., is for the office.

(*c*) It is estimated that Mr James did 15,000 miles motoring in the year, of which 4,000 miles were private. He replaced his car in July, 1984.

(*d*) General expenses were made up as follows:

Staff Christmas party	£100
Entertaining: UK customers	120
Overseas customers	90
UK agent of overseas customer	20
Christmas gifts (overprinted diaries costing £1 each) 200	200
Charitable donations	30
Telephone (10 per cent private use)	80
Premium on retirement annuity policy	700
Bank interest	50
Other allowable expenses	970
	2,360

(*e*) Legal expenses comprise:

Cost of successfully defending a charge of dangerous driving whilst delivering goods	50
Debt recovery	100
Cost of tax appeal	230
	380

(*f*) Bad debts account shows:

Increase in general provision	200
Bad debts written off	100
	300

Less		
Debt recoveries	52	
Specific provision no longer required	200	252
		48

Computation of 1985–86 assessment

		£
Net profit		10,254
Add:		
Cost of tax appeal (see 6.6(*f*))		230
Depreciation (see 6.6(*b*) capital expenditure)		350
Bad debts (increase in general provision)		200
Entertaining UK customers (see 6.7(*j*))		120
Entertaining UK agent (see 6.7(*j*))		20
Private telephone (see 6.7(*j*))		8
Premium on retirement annuity (see 6.7(*a*))		700
Private car expenses (4/15 × £500)		133
Private portion of rates, light (1/3 × £470)		156
		12,171
Less		
Interest on Government securities (see 6.5(*c*))	410	
Premium Bond prize (see 6.5(*a*))	150	
Profit on sale of car (see 6.5(*a*))	120	680
Taxable profit		11,491

6.10 Basis Periods

One aspect of taxing business profits which puzzles people is that the assessable profit is not normally the same as the profit, even after adjustments shown in the accounts, as the following illustration shows.

Example 6.4 Barrett started in business as a jobbing builder on 1 January, 1973, and decided to form a limited company on 1 January, 1983. His adjusted profits were as follows:

Year to 31 December, 1973:	Profit	£1,200
1974:	Profit	1,500
1975:	Profit	2,000
1976:	Profit	2,800
1977:	Profit	4,000
1978:	Profit	5,600
1979:	Profit	7,800
1980:	Profit	10,000
1981:	Profit	12,800
1982:	Profit	16,000
Total trading results (10 years)		63,700

The tax assessments will be as follows:

1972/73:	Period 1 January, 1973, to 31 March, 1973, ¼ × £1,200	£300
1973/74:	Year to 31 December, 1973	1,200
1974/75:	Year to 31 December, 1973	1,200
1975/76:	Year to 31 December, 1974	1,500
1976/77:	Year to 31 December, 1975	2,000
1977/78:	Year to 31 December, 1976	2,800
1978/79:	Year to 31 December, 1977	4,000
1979/80:	Year to 31 December, 1978	5,600

1980/81: Year to 31 March, 1981 (revenue option exercised)
¾ of £10,000 = £7,500 − ¼ of £12,800 = 3,200 = £10,700
1981/82: Year to 31 March, 1982
¾ of £12,800 = £9,600 − ¼ of £16,000 = 4,000 = £13,600
1982/83: Period 1 April, 1982, to 31 December, 1982
¾ of £16,000 = £12,000
Total profits assessed to tax £54,900

Since total profits were £63,700, £8,800 profits escaped assessments. Moreover, assuming that monthly profits continued at the rate of £1,400 per month, it would pay Barrett to cease trading as a builder and transfer his business to the company on 1 May, 1983.

Example 6.5 The figures are the same as in Example 6.4, except that Barrett ceases to trade on 30 April, 1983, and profit for the period 1 January, 1983, to 30 April, 1983, were £5,600.

The assessments would be as follows:

1972/73 to 1979/80—as in Example 6.4.	
1980/81: Year to 31 December 1979	£7,800
1981/82: Year to 31 March 1982: ¾ × 12,880 + ¼ × 16,000 =	13,600
1982/83: Year to 31 March, 1983	
(¾ of £16,000) £12,000 − ¾ of £5,600 = £4,200 =	16,200
1983/84: Period 1 April, 1983, to 30 April, 1983, ¼ × £5,600 =	1,400
Total profit assessed to tax	57,600

This postponing of the date of cessation will increase the profits, which escape taxation by £2,900 (profits £69,300—assessed profits £57,600 = £11,700).

These examples show that the arbitary rules of assessment demand that one year's profit (the profit of the first trading year) is assessed *twice*, whilst on cessation one year is *missed*, which is either the second-last or third-last year's trading. So in order to make sure that one saves tax, one must be careful to ensure on cessation that the profit for the year *missed* is greater than the profit assessed *twice*.

The detailed rules are as follows:

(*a*) The basis of assessment for the year in which the trade is commenced is the profit of that year (Section 116, ICTA, 1970).

(*b*) The second year of assessment is based on the adjusted profit of the first 12 months' trading (Section 116).

(*c*) The third and subsequent years of assessment (normal basis) are based on the adjusted profit of the *accounting year ending within the previous assessment* (Section 115).

To avoid hardship in cases where the second and third year's profit is less than the first year's profit, the taxpayer can claim to have the second and third year's assessment reduced to the actual profits of those years. It should be noted that the claim must be for both years not for only one. (Section 117.)

(*d*) For the year in which the business is *permanently discontinued*, the assessment is based on the profit of that year, and the Inland Revenue has the option to increase the assessments of the *penultimate* and *pre-penultimate* years to the actual profits of those years, as in Examples 6.4 and 6.5 (Section 118, ICTA, 1970).

6.11 Change of Accounting Date

Sometimes it is necessary to change the date to which accounts are made up and with rising profits it may pay traders or partnerships to change their accounting date and save some tax. The detailed rules are referred to in Chapter 9.

6.12 Special Basis Periods for Farmers

Since 1978 a special basis can be claimed by farmers, who are subject to fluctuating profits due to changes in weather or world prices. The farmer is able to claim to average his profits over two years, provided the profits in the low profit year is no more than seventy per cent of the better year, with special provisions for borderline cases.

Example 6.6 Walker, a market gardener, has been in business for a number of years and has the following trading results:

Year to 30 April	1979	1980	1981	1982
	£	£	£	£
Adjusted profit:	12,000	5,000	9,000	14,000

Averaging 1979–80:

Year to 30 April, 1979	£12,000
Year to 30 April, 1980	5,000
Difference	7,000

30% of higher figure: £12,000 × 30% = £3,600

Average $\frac{£17,000}{2}$ = £8,500: therefore revised assessments are:

1980/81 £8,500 (original £12,000)
1981/82 £8,500 (original £ 5,000)

Averaging 1981–82:

Year to 30.4.81	£9,000
Year to 30.4.82	14,000
Difference	5,000

30% of higher figure: 14,000 × 30% = 4,200

Average $\frac{£23,000}{2}$ = £11,500: therefore revised assessments are:

1982/83 £11,500 (original £9,000)
1983/84 £11,500 (original £14,000)

Where the difference is less than 30 per cent but more than 25 per cent **marginal relief** applies.

6.13 The Correct Schedule of Charge

A reader comparing the treatment a taxpayer receives under Schedule E (see Chapter 10) with that under Schedule D described in this chapter, will appreciate Lord Justice Harman's remarks in his judgement in the case *Mitchell & Eden v. Ross (1961) 40 TC 11*: '... the pleasure of life depended nowadays upon the schedule under which man lived.' The case concerned the question whether appointments under the National Health Service Act, 1946, of part-time consultants (specialists) were assessable under Schedule E. The appellants contended that the income as consultants with a hospital board was assessable under Schedule D as part of their professional income and not separately as an employment under Schedule E. The Court of Appeal held that their contention was not correct.

This case has to be read together with the case of *Davies v. Braithwaite (1933) 18 TC 198*, when Miss Lilian Braithwaite, the famous actress, was held to be assessable under Schedule D. In this case it was established that if the contract is for *services* and not *service*, which means that the boss or employer exercises a degree of control over the work being carried out, it usually becomes assessable under Schedule E. Another way of explaining the position is that when a customer employs a builder, he does not exercise control over the way he performs his work and does not pay unless he is satisfied that the work was completed according to the contract. On the other hand, the builder employs people to carry out the work and these people will carry out his instructions and will be paid provided they have attended for work and carried out instructions. The fact that the work was not done satisfactorily is no excuse for withholding payment. In other words, the builder has a **contract for services**, assessable under Schedule D, but his staff hold **contracts of service**, assessable under Schedule E.

The question of **correct schedule of charge** affects a growing number of taxpayers—musicians who teach music part-time, accountants who work part-time for more than one employer, journalists, broadcasters, part-time lecturers. Rowlatt J. put it like this in *Davies v. Braithwaite*: 'It seems to me quite clear that you can have both employment and a profession at the same time. Quite clearly you can have it in different categories ... A man might have the steadiest employment in the world by day, and might do something else entirely different in the evening and make some more money by way of a professional vocation ... I do not see why a man who is a musician, for instance, and holds an office, could not do that. ...'

It is not surprising, however, in view of the tax advantages which flow from being treated under Schedule D, that the Inland Revenue quite often resists claims to fall under Schedule D. In questions of doubt the following factors are relevant:

(*a*) What degree of control is exercised by the employer?

(*b*) Is the work carried out in the taxpayer's home or in premises provided by the employer?

(*c*) Who provides the equipment and capital investment?

(*d*) How many 'customers', 'clients' or 'employers' has the claimant? (If he works for one client exclusively, it is difficult to win a claim that Schedule D should apply.)

(*e*) How is payment made for the work done? (For example, part-time lecturers are not paid if the lecture is cancelled or no students turn up, but a full-time lecturer is.)

(*f*) Is the contract for the hour, the week, the year, etc., and does it give entitlement to redundancy payments, sick pay, holiday pay, notice, and membership of pension funds? (If all these entitlements are included then the chances of a claim for Schedule D succeeding are slim.)

(*g*) Who pays for the electricity, maintenance and raw materials used for work done at the claimant's own premises? (If the customer pays, the Inspector will try to claim that the 'outworker' is really an employee, and the question arises whether he is protected by the legislation, e.g. redundancy pay, sick pay, etc.)

(*h*) What kind of National Insurance Contributions are paid? (If Class 1, involving both employer's and employee's contributions, it will strengthen the Revenue claim, but if Class 2 and 4 is applied dealing with self-employed persons, the taxpayer has a very good claim.)

6.14 National Insurance Contributions

If one is self-employed one may have to pay an earnings-related National Insurance Contribution. This Class 4 contribution is paid in addition to the flat-rate Class 2 contribution. In this connection it should be pointed out that in order to qualify for sickness, unemployment payment and national retirement pension, one must pay National Insurance Contributions as follows:

Class 1—Employed persons receiving income over £1,820 (1985/86)
Class 2—Self-employed persons
Class 3—Non-employed persons

Class 4 contributions are generally assessed and collected by the Inland Revenue together with the Schedule D tax. The Class 4 rate for

1985/86 is 6.3 per cent of the amount by which profits or gains exceed £3,960. The maximum charge is on profits of £13,000, i.e. £569.52, and after 6.4.1985 50% is tax deductible.

The following people are **excepted** (the official word used from Class 4 liability:

(*a*) Man aged 65 or woman aged 60 at the beginning of the year (6 April).
(*b*) Non-residents (for definition see Chapters 10 and 12).
(*c*) Trustees, or executors in some cases.
(*d*) Sleeping partners (see Chapter 9).

It is quite possible to overpay National Insurance Contributions and this commonly arises in the following circumstances:

(*a*) An individual has more than one employment. A claim for deferment should be made on DHSS Form CF 379.
(*b*) An individual who has an employment and carries on a part-time profession, e.g. musician, writer, journalist, gardener, etc. A claim for deferment should be made on DHSS Form CF359.
(*c*) When the taxpayer has reached the *excepted age*, but the matter has been overlooked by the Inspector of Taxes.

If the application for deferment or exception is not made in time, a refund may be due. This is likely to occur, particularly if the taxable earnings from all sources exceed £13,000 for 1984/85. An application for refund should be made to DHSS Class 4 Group if the National Insurance Contributions have been collected with the Schedule D assessment, otherwise to the Newcastle DHSS Headquarters. It must be remembered also that all correspondence must contain the DHSS reference number and not the income tax one.

6.15 Revision Test

Answers	*Questions*
1. It is sometimes difficult to decide whether a surplus from an isolated transaction constitutes a taxable trading profit. The Courts have laid down a number of factors to be considered—the profit motive being the most important.	**1.** What constitutes trading?

2. The definition was given in *Partridge v Mallandaine (1886)* 'the way a person passes his life'.	**2.** What constitutes a vocation?
3. Receipts of a capital nature, dividends, interest, rent, etc.	**3.** What receipts have to be excluded from the adjusted profit for tax purposes?
4. Those specifically authorised, those normally charged according to accounting principles, and not specifically prohibited.	**4.** What expenses can be claimed in arriving at the adjusted profit for tax purposes?
5. Those specified by S.130(a) 'Not wholly and exclusively laid out for the purpose of the trade', which covers all non-business expenses.	**5.** What expenses cannot be claimed?
6. Fees and expenses in obtaining patent rights, payments for technical education of staff, premium on leases, pre-trading expenses.	**6.** What expenses are specifically allowed?
7. In general the treatment is according to accounting principles. Stock is valued at cost or market selling price, whichever is lower. The Special relief for stock increases was withdrawn for accounting period starting after 12.3.1984.	**7.** How is stock treated for tax purposes?
8. The accounting year ending in the previous year of assessment.	**8.** What is the 'normal' basis period of assessment of a continuing business?
9. In the year the trade commenced the basis is the adjusted profit of that year. The 2nd year of assessment is the profit of the first 12 months trading. This means that the first or second year's profit is assessed twice.	**9.** What is the basis period for assessment of a new business?

10. The last year of assessment is based on the profit of that year and the Inland Revenue has the option to increase the assessments of the penultimate year and pre-prenultimate year to the actual profits of those years.

10. What is the basis period of assessment for the last 3 years of a business?

11. If profits are rising and the accounting dates convenient, it pays to change the accounting date.

11. Does it pay a trader to change his accounting date?

12. Farmers' can claim the basis of the average of two years provided the profit in the low profit year is no more than 70% of the high profit year.

12. Explain the special basis of assessment for farmers.

7
Capital Allowances

Capital allowances are a method of standardised depreciation allowances for tax purposes. It has already been explained that *depreciation* provision is not an allowable deduction when adjusting the accountant's profit for tax purposes.

Capital allowances are given as a deduction from the taxable income in accordance with the Capital Allowances Act, 1968. The allowances are given mainly to traders or self-employed persons, but can also be claimed by employees who are necessarily obliged to use capital equipment during their employment, e.g. motorcars, typewriters, wordprocessors, etc. Similarly, capital assets such as central heating, lifts, qualifying buildings, etc., qualify for capital allowances against property income assessable under Schedule A. Moreover, if claimed by a trader, capital allowances can be used to enhance the amount of tax allowable loss (see Chapter 8).

Normally, the allowances are given as deduction from taxable income, but in certain circumstances, they are given by means of tax repayment; for example, on leased industrial buildings, leased plant, or agricultural buildings and patent rights.

7.1 What Assets Qualify?

Capital allowances are given on wasting assets enumerated in the Capital Allowance Act, 1968, and assets not enumerated, however deserving, do not qualify:

(*a*) Plant and machinery.
(*b*) Industrial buildings and structures.
(*c*) Mines and oilwells.
(*d*) Agricultural buildings.
(*e*) UK patents.
(*f*) Dredging.
(*h*) Know-how.
(*j*) Hotels.

(*k*) Crematoria and cemetaries.
(*l*) Small workshops.
(*m*) Enterprise zones.

7.2 Plant and Machinery

The words *plant* and *machinery* are not statutorily defined and for this reason have been defined by Case Law.

(*i*) *Capital expenditure qualifying as plant:*

(*a*) A dry dock (*CIR v. Barclay Curle & Co. (1969) 45 TC 221*).

(*b*) Concrete grain silos (*Schofield v. R & H Hall Ltd (1974) 49 TC 538*).

(*c*) A swimming pool at a caravan site (*Cooke v. Beach Station Caravans Ltd (1974) 49 TC 514*).

(*d*) Movable partitioning (*Jarrold v. John Good & Sons Ltd (1963 40 TC 681*).

(*e*) Books used by a barrister (*Munby v. Furlong (1977) STC 232*).

(*f*) Wallpaper designs (*Mcveigh v. Arthur Sanderson & Sons Ltd (1968) 45 TC 273*).

(*ii*) *Capital expenditure not qualifying as plant:*

(*a*) Animals for breeding (*Derby (Earl of) v. Aylmer (1915) 6 TC 665*).

(*b*) A canopy over petrol pumps (*Dixon v. Fitch's Garage Ltd (1975)*).

(*c*) Water towers (*Maggrett v. Lowestoft Water & Gas Co. (1935) 19 TC 481*).

(*d*) Floating restaurant (*Benson v. Yard Arm Club Ltd (1979)*).

These are a selection of a much longer list of cases, but they establish the principle which was defined by a judge in the following terms: '... there is a clear thread running through the recent cases ... showing that a structure is not plant, if its only purpose is to provide shelter and if it plays no part in what may be termed the *commercial process*. That conclusion is, I think an inevitable result of the application of the *functional test*. In this difficult area of the law it is, in my view, important to stick to the established tests. In his submission the taxpayer's counsel sought to introduce a new test: whether the item in question is commercially desirable or necessary to enable the taxpayer to sell his petrol (*Dixon v. Fitch's Garage Ltd*) to best advantage. That to my mind, is an amenity test as distinct from a functional test and is not a permissable test. The right test is the *functional test*.'

(*iii*) *Basis periods for claims*

As explained already, the person who uses the plant can claim the allowances. Normally it is used for business by the trader or a trading company, but a person who leases plant also qualifies for the allowance if he is responsible for the wear and tear of it; if not, the lessee can claim the allowance.

Basis periods for assessment vary between the schedules:

(*a*) Current year basis under Schedule A for lessors (see Chapter 5).

(*b*) Preceding year basis under Schedule D normally, but current year basis when the business commences and ceases. In certain circumstances, in the periods after commencement and prior to cessation, basis periods overlap or one period misses assessment, when special rules apply.

(*iv*) *First-year allowances* (Sections 41–43, Finance Act, 1971 and Section 67, Finance Act, 1972).

A very generous 100 per cent FYA (First Year Allowance) is available for the basis period, normally the year in which the plant was acquired, with certain restrictions:

S.58 and Schedule 12, FA, 1984 provide that the first year's allowance be progressively withdrawn as follows:

(1) The 100 per cent allowance is reduced to 75 per cent for expenditure incurred after 13 March, 1984 and
(2) Reduced to 50 per cent in respect of expenditure incurred after 31 March 1985, and
(3) Reduced to nil for expenditure incurred after 31 March, 1986. However, the 100 per cent allowance will continue to be available in respect of the expenditure incurred before 1 April, 1987 under a binding contract entered into before 14 March, 1984 and in respect of future expenditure under special arrangements for development areas and also for teletext and viewdata receivers qualifying for special allowances.

Example 7.1 Emerson, who has been trading for some years, makes up his accounts to 31st March each year.

He purchased a word-processor for his office on 20 March, 1983, for £2,000, paying a deposit of £200 and the balance by hire purchase with monthly payments over two years. FYA for 1983/84 is £2,000.

In order to obtain the allowance, the plant purchased need not be new, but if second-hand plant is purchased from a **connected person** (Finance Act, 1971, Schedule 8, Paragraph 3), the allowance is not available. The term 'connected person' is important for many tax purposes and receives special treatment:

(*a*) An individual is *connected* with his wife or with relatives, including their spouses.

(*b*) A trustee of a settlement is *connected* with both the settlor and beneficiary in certain circumstances.

(*c*) A partner is *connected* with his partners and in certain circumstances with spouses and relatives of those partners.

Connected persons also figure in corporation tax, capital gains tax and development land tax, but these concepts are outside the scope of this book.

Another restriction is that the FYA is not available in the year the trade or profession ceased, and the most common exclusion relates to motorcars capable for private use (S41 FA, 1971).

The Finance Act, 1980, introduced further restrictions on the availability of FYA in respect of plant leased. These restrictions were introduced after widespread abuse of leasing was reported. It provided that the FYA would not longer be given unless the plant is leased for a *qualifying purpose* during the *requisite period.*

A *qualifying purpose* is use:

(1) By a lessee for the purpose of trade in circumstances which would have qualified for FYA, if the lessee had purchased the plant himself. This is the most common restriction and stopped thc leasing of expensive cars capable for private use qualifying for FYAs in the tax computations of the lessor.

(2) By a person who obtained a lease for a short term. **Short-term leasing** has been defined as applying where either:

(*a*) The plant is leased to the same person for less than 30 consecutive days, and

(*b*) It will normally be leased to the same person for less than 90 days in any period of 12 months, or

(*c*) The plant is leased to the same person for less than 365 consecutive days, and

(*d*) In the same *requisite period* the aggregate during which it is leased, not qualifying under (*a*) or (*b*), is no more than *two* years.

The **requisite period** for this purpose has been defined as the period when the plant is first brought into use and ends on the date *four years* after it is brought into usc, or the *date of sale* (whichever is the earlier).

(3) By a lessee who is **resident** (defined in Chapter 10) in UK or carries on a trade there of short-term leasing.

(4) By an owner who uses the plant for a trade other than leasing, or

(5) By an owner of a ship let on charter and that activity amounts to a trade in the UK, and the lessor is responsible for navigating and managing the ship throughout the charter and also for paying expenses.

(6) By an owner of an aircraft similar to those under (5).

(7) By an owner of containers similar to those under (5).

(8) By an owner of a vehicle for the disabled, as long as the vahicle is used by an individual in receipt of a mobility allowance.

There are also special rules for allowances on leased television and viewdata equipment.

It is not necessary for a taxpayer to claim the whole of the FYA. If his income is small and expected to rise, it may pay him to claim 50 per cent or not to claim the FYA at all, but to confine himself to the writing-down allowance.

(*v*) *Writing-down allowance* (Section 44, Finance Act, 1971, and Section 39, Finance Act, 1976).

This allowance has been given for many years and is 25 per cent of the cost or *written-down value* of plant in use at the end of the basis period. The WDV is the original cost less all the capital allowances previously given. The cost of an asset is added to the **pool**—that is the total of the written-down values of existing plant—and 25 per cent taken. It is possible to have an alternative or **straight-line basis** (fixed percentage of cost each year) to the *reducing balance method* (25 per cent of written-down value).

The allowance is not due in the first year the plant is used, if FYA is claimed. The full allowances are also not available during periods of commencement and cessation of a trade or profession, when the basis period is less than a year.

It is possible to get the 25 per cent allowance increased if it can be shown that wear and tear has been greater than normal owing to the manner of the use of the plant. If, for example, the Inland Revenue can be satisfied that plant is used by two shifts and worked for 16 hours rather than 8 hours, a higher allowance can be claimed.

Certain assets, however, are not included in the 'pool':

(*a*) A motorcar costing more than £8,000; in such cases the writing down allowance is restricted to £2,000.

(*b*) Where the asset is used partly for private purposes. This usually arises where the trader or professional person uses the business car or furniture (when working from home) privately.

(*c*) Plant which is leased.

(*vi*) *Disposal of plant—balancing allowances and charges.*

If an asset is sold from the pool, the proceeds from the sale are simply deducted from the written-down value, except in the exceptional circumstances in which the sale price exceeds the original cost, when the balancing charge is disposed between connected persons (see page 91) the market value is substituted for the sale price. The market value is also substituted in the following circumstances:

(*a*) The trade continues but the plant is given away or sold below market value.

(*b*) The trade continues but the plant, although retained, is no longer used for the business.

(*c*) The plant (usually a motor car) is transferred from business to private use.

(*d*) The trade is discontinued, but the trader retains the plant.

Section 40 of the Capital Allowances Act, 1968, provides that the taxpayer can claim to have the balancing charge deducted from the cost of the plant it replaces, but no other plant.

Example 7.2 Bingham, a self-employed consulting engineer, replaced his existing car used entirely for business with a new one costing £7,000. The written-down value of his present car was £3,600 and the trading-in value of his old care £4,200. The position is as follows:

1984/85	Written-down value	£3,600	
	Sale	4,200	
	Balancing charge	600	
	New car		Cost £7,000
	Less balancing charge		600
			6,400
	Less writing-down allowance		1,600
	Written-down value		4,800

Bingham has been in business for some years and made his accounts up to 31 March: the exchange of cars took place in June, 1983.

The set-off is not possible if the plant is used partly privately.

(*vii*) *Private use*

Complications arise when plant is used for both business and private purposes. Moreover, the matter is not solved by Section 28 of the Capital Allowances Act, 1968, which provides that the allowances in such cases should be 'just and reasonable'.

The question to be determined first is the extent of the private use. If the Revenue can establish that the car used is more luxurious than required for the business and is used privately, the restriction for private use may be much greater than the relative proportion of private use would justify. In the case of *Chambers G. H. (Northiam's Farm) Ltd v. Watmough (1956) 36 TC 711* it was held that the purchase of a Bentley car by a farmer was partly at least in consideration of Mr Chamber's personal choice rather than business necessity.

Example 7.3 Corteel, an architect, uses his car partly for business and partly privately. His accounts are made up to 31 December and he has been in business since 1970. He purchased a car for £4,000 in June 1978 and the business use agreed was as follows:

Year to 31 December, 1978: 80%
Year to 31 December, 1979; 70%
Year to 31 December, 1980; 75%
Year to 31 December, 1981; 85%

Year to 31 December, 1982; 10%
Year to 31 December, 1983; 20%
In 1982 he purchased a second car for business, which is not used privately and the first car was sold in October, 1983, for £2,000.

The computation is as follows:

	Cost (£)	%	Capital Allowance (£)
	4,000		
1979/80 Writing-down allowance	1,000	80	800
	3,000		
1980/81	750	70	525
	2,250		
1981/82	562	75	422
	1,688		
1982/83	422	85	399
	1,266		
1983/84	316	10	32
	950		
1984/85 Sale	2,000		
Excess	1,050		

The balancing charge is calculated as follows:

Cost of car	£4,000
Sale price	2,000
Net cost	2,000

Average business use for period: $\frac{80 + 70 + 75 + 85 + 10 = 320}{5} = 64\%$

Business use (64% of net cost £2,000)			£1,280
Less allowances given	1979/80	800	
	1980/81	525	
	1981/82	422	
	1982/83	399	
	1983/84	32	2,178
Balancing charge	1984/85		898

Sometimes a private car is introduced into a business; the computation can be illustrated as follows:

Example 7.4 Stockwell, a grocer, decided to offer a delivery service to his customers and brought his private car into the business in January, 1980, after he had been in business 10 years. The car cost £3,000 in June 1976, and the business use was 25 per cent. His accounting period was to 31 March. The car was sold in January, 1984 for £600. The computations are as follows:

	Cost	3,000
1977/78:	Notional (assumed) allowance 25%	750
		2,250
1978/9:	Notional (assumed) allowance 25%	662
		1,688
		1,266

1980/81:	Writing-down allowance 25%	316
		950
1981/82:	Writing-down allowance 25%	238
		712
1982/83:	Writing-down allowance 25%	178
		534
1983/84:	Writing-down allowance 25%	134
		400
1984/85:	Sale	600
Excess		200

Balancing charge 4/7 × £200 = £114, since actual allowances were given in only 4 years.

Example 7.5 Connor has been manufacturing tools for some years. His accounting period is to 30 June. In the year to 30 June, 1982, he purchased the following plant:

Machine A costing £5,000 on 1 March, 1982
Machine B costing £2,000 on 1 April, 1982

A car costing £10,000 is bought on 10 December, 1981, and is used privately 30 per cent. Connor decided to claim only 50 per cent of the FYA.

1983/84:	Machine A cost £5,000 – FYA 50%	£2,500 = Wda			£2,500
	Machine B cost 2,000 – FYA 50%	1,000 = Wda			1,500
	Car cost £10,000				3,500
Less wda (restricted)	2,000	– private use 30%	1,400		
Written down value	8,000	Allowances due	4,900	Pool	3,500
1984/85 wda 25%	2,000	– private use 30%	1,400	wda 25%	875
	6,000				2,625

Provided that no assets are either purchased or sold during the year to 30 June, 1983, Connor receives capital allowances of £2,275 in 1984/85.

The reader will note that FYA and writing down allowances cannot be claimed in the same year.

(viii) Hire purchase

Assets are often acquired on hire purchase, the charges being the excess of the hire-purchase price over the cash price sometimes called interest, (but legally not interest but a hire charge). They are not calculated like interest, as can be illustrated:

Example 7.6 Bertrand, a self-employed insurance broker who has been in business for some years and makes up his accounts to 30 September, purchased a car on HP on 1 August, 1983, details being as follows:

Cash price	£4,000
Less initial rent	400
	3,600
HP charge	864
Balance of rent	4,464

This is payable in 36 monthly rentals of £124 on the 30th day of each consecutive month commencing on 30th August, 1983. Assuming that there is

20 per cent private use, the calculation for 1984/85 is as follows:

Capital allowance	Cost	£4,000
Writing-down allowance 25%		1,000 allow 80% = £800
		3,000

Add hire charge $\frac{£864 \times 2}{36} = £48$ (two payments by 30.9.83) × 80% = £38.

If the car is *hired* but not purchased and costs over £8,000 the hire charge has to be restricted.

Example 7.7 Assume that Bertrand hired a car and the hire charge was £2,800 in the year to 30 September, 1983, and the retail value of the car is £12,000. The allowable hire charge is computed as follows:

$$\frac{£8{,}000 \text{ (maximum) } \tfrac{1}{2}\,(12{,}000 - 8{,}000)}{12{,}000} \times £2{,}800 = £2{,}334$$

7.3 Industrial Buildings and Structures

Section 7 of the Capital Allowances Act, 1968, defines an industrial building as a mill, factory or warehouse attached to manufacture, buildings used for the trade of catching fish, etc. Shop and office premises do not qualify for the allowance, but buildings and sports pavilions occupied by a trader and used for the welfare of employees do qualify. The only explanation one can offer for including sports pavilions but not commercial buildings is that the legislation was introduced in 1945 by a Labour Government, which wanted to encourage industrialists to spend money on staff welfare facilities. Where less than 10 per cent of the building has *non-industrial* use the whole building qualifies, but if more than 10 per cent is used the allowance is restricted to the proportion used for industrial purposes.

(*i*) Basis period of claims, is the same as for *plant and machinery*.
(*ii*) Initial allowance is given to a person, who incurs capital expenditure on the *construction of an industrial building* occupied by him for the purpose of his own trade or that of a lessee. It will be noted that it is not the purchase price, which qualifies but the cost of construction and this means that a second-hand building does not qualify nor does the cost of the site. For expenditure incurred after the 10 March, 1981, 75 per cent. The allowance is reduced to 50 per cent in respect of expenditure incurred after 13.3.84 and to 25 per cent for expenditure incurred from 1.4.1985–31.3.1986, after which the allowance is abolished.
(*iii*) *Writing-down allowance*—S.2, CAA, 1968

The writing-down allowance is computed on the basis of 2 per cent of the original cost if the building was erected before 5 November, 1962, and 4 per cent thereafter. If a building erected before 5 November, 1962, is sold within 50 years (the expected life of the building for purposes of the allowances) the writing-down allowance has to be recomputed. If the building was erected after 5 November, 1968, the period is 25 years. For buildings erected before April, 1958, the old mills and factories allowance could be claimed as an alternative.

(*iv*) *Balancing allowances and charges* (Section 3)

A balancing charge or allowance is made if the building sold either within 50 years of first use (or 25 years if erected after 5 November, 1962) or demolished or ceases to be used. From 11 March, 1981, other changes—e.g. by way of gift—also incur a balancing charge of allowance, even if the building is no longer used as an industrial building by a trader.

The balancing charge is restricted to the total of the capital allowances given (this, of course, also applies to plant), but not after the 50 years' or 25 years' life-span, as may be, has expired.

Example 7.8 A building erected by a trader at a cost of £40,000, excluding land, was first used as an industrial building in December, 1974, and was sold to another trader for £35,000 in February, 1983. The cost of the land was estimated at £3,000. Both vendor and purchaser make up their accounts to 30 June.

(*a*)	Allowances due to vendor: Cost		£40,000
	1975/76 initial allowance 50%	£20,000	
	Writing-down allowances		
	1975/76 to 83/84 × 9 years × 4%	14,400	34,000
	Residue before sale		5,600
	Sale price £35,000–£3,000		32,000
	1984/85 Balancing charge		26,400

(*b*)	Allowances due to purchaser	
	Residue before sale	£5,600
	Add balancing charge	26,400
		32,000

Year of first use 1984/85; 25 years' life-span of building ends 1990/2000 or 16 years after purchase; therefore the writing-down allowance is $\frac{£32,000}{16}$ = £2,000 per annum.

It is important to make sure when purchasing an industrial building to discover the original cost of erection and the date of erection and to agree with the vendor a figure for the cost of the site, since if the cost of site is not mentioned in the contract a long and costly dispute can ensue. Moreover, unless one finds out the original cost one may discover later that the allowances one assumed to be entitled to were too optimistic.

7.4 Mines and Oilwells (Sections 51–66, Capital Allowances Act, 1968)

Until recent years few people were concerned with these allowances because coal and iron ore were mined by nationalised industries and oil was imported. This has, however, changed. The allowance is based on the **royalty value:**

First 10 years of working source	50% of royalty value of output
Next 10 years of working source	25% of royalty value of output
Thereafter	10% of royalty value of output

Royalty value is defined as reasonable royalties on output in basis period. On sale or when the mine or well ceases to be worked balancing charges or allowances are available.

7.5 Agricultural Buildings (SS. 68–69, CAA, 1968)

If the owner or tenant of agricultural or forestry land incurs expenditure of a capital nature on the construction of farmhouses, farm or forestry buildings, cottages, fences etc. an allowance of 10% is granted for each of the ten years after the year of assessment (income tax year) in which the expenditure was incurred unless some other basis period is agreed with the Inspector, usually the accounting period. The maximum allowance on farmhouses is *one third* of the expenditure.

(*i*) Initial allowance—S.33, FA, 1978.
Capital expenditure incurred after 11 April, 1978 qualifies for an intial allowance of 20% in addition to the 10% allowance. This initial allowance is abolished for expenditure incurred after 1.4.1986 when 10% allowance becomes a straight-line allowance of 4%.

(*ii*) Sale of farm and cessation of tenancy.
No balancing charge or allowance arises, but any unallowed allowance is given to the person taking over the farm.

Example 7.9 A farmer erected a farmhouse costing £20,000. In the three months to 31 October, 1978, some cowsheds costing £1,800 and a garage costing £800. The garage is used 50% for business. He sold the farm on 5.1.1983.

(*a*) The allowances due to the vendor are:

	Cost	Qualifying expenditure
Farmhouse	£21,000 × ⅓	£7,000
Cowsheds	1,800	1,800
Garage	800 × ½	400
		9,200

1979/80 Initial Allowance 20% £1,840

Writing down allowance 10%	920
1980/81 & 1981/82 2 × 10%	1,840
1982/83 Sale 5.1.83 ¾ × 10%	690
	5,290

(b) Allowances due to purchaser:

1982/83: ¼ × 10%	£230
1983/84 to 1986/87	920 per annum

7.6 UK Patents (Section 378, ICTA, 1970)

Expenditure incurred in the purchase of UK patent rights qualifies for a writing-down allowance. The allowance is 1/17, starting with the basis period in which the purchase was made. (The reason for this fraction is that UK patent rights are granted for 16 years.)

There is no initial allowance but balancing allowances and charges and if one makes a profit on the sale of a patent right, the surplus is subject to income tax. If one makes a profit on the sale of any other asset such a surplus is subject to capital gains tax, which is outside the scope of this book. The computation will take into account the following:

(*a*) If the rights come to an end without being revived, a balancing allowance equal to the unallowed expenditure is due.

(*b*) If the whole of the rights are sold, a balancing charge or allowance is made equal to capital expenditure still unallowed less the selling price.

(*c*) If a part of the right is sold for less than the unallowed expenditure, the sale price is deducted from the unallowed expenditure before further allowances are given.

(*d*) The balancing charge is restricted to allowances given (as with other assets) and the capital profit is assessed under Section 380, ICTA, 1970, in six equal instalments, starting in the year in which the right is sold, unless the sale is to a non-resident, when it is assessed in one sum.

Example 7.10 Barnes acquires the rights of a band new pump in the accounting year to 31.3.1978 for £10,000 and sells a licence to manufacture it for £3,500 in June 1981 and sold the rights for £9,000 in August, 1982.

The computations are as follows:

Cost		£10,000
Writing-down allowances 1978/79–1981/82	$\frac{10,200}{17} \times 4$	2,400
Written down value		7,800
1982/83 sale of licence		3,500
		4,800
Writing-down allowances	$\frac{4,800}{17}$	283

Written down value	4,517
1983/84 Sale	9,000

Balancing Charge restricted to allowances given £2,400 + £283 = £2,683.

Schedule D assessment under Case VI £12,500 − 10,200 = £2,300 assessed in equal six instalments starting in 1983/84. This system will be replaced by a 25% writing down allowance for patents granted after 1.4.1986.

7.7 Scientific Research (S.90, CAA, 1968)

Capital expenditure on scientific research for the purposes of the trade is wholly allowed in the year it is incurred. Revenue expenditure on scientific research can be claimed as a normal trade expense if incurred by the trader, or if the sum is paid to an approved research association, university, college or similar institution.

7.8 Dredging (S.67, CAA, 1968)

Capital expenditure on dredging in connection with a trade consisting of maintaining or improving the navigation of a harbour, estuary or waterway or connected with a dock qualifies for capital allowances.

(*i*) Initial allowance of 15 per cent is available for capital expenditure incurred after 15.4.1958 (10 per cent before that date).
(*ii*) Writing-down allowance of 4 per cent is available for dredging first used after 5.11.1962 (2 per cent before that date) until 25 years have expired or the expenditure is written off, whichever is earlier.
(*iii*) Balancing allowances and charges only arise on permanent cessation of the trade. The mere sale of the dock etc., involves the transfer of the remaining writing-down allowances to the purchaser. This system will be replaced by a writing-down allowance of 4 per cent 'straight-line' for expenditure incurred after 1.4.1986.

7.9 Know-How (SS. 386–387, ICTA, 1970)

Know-how is defined as 'any industrial information and techniques likely to assist in the manufacture or processing of goods or materials, or in the working of a mine, oil-well or other source of mineral deposits, or in the carrying out of any agricultural, forestry or fishing operations.'

(*i*) A writing-down allowance of *one sixth* is available on expenditure not otherwise allowed.
(*ii*) Balancing allowances are available if the trade ceases before the full cost has been allowed, in the year of cessation. If the know-how is sold sums received are treated as trading receipts. This system will be

replaced by a writing-down allowance of 25 per cent for expenditure incurred after 31.3.86.

7.10 Hotels (S.38, FA, 1978)

(*i*) Initial allowance of 20 per cent is available on the cost of building an hotel. This allowance is not given on the purchase price of a second-hand hotel. This allowance is withdrawn for expenditure incurred after 1.4.1986.
(*ii*) Writing-down allowance of 4 per cent is available in the same way as an *Industrial Building Allowance*.
(*iii*) Balancing allowances and charges are calculated in the same way as for industrial buildings.

To qualify as an hotel, the building has to have 10 letting bedrooms, be open for at least four months in the year, include the provision of breakfast and have been built as a hotel.

7.11 Crematoria and Cemetaries (Section 141, CAA, 1968)

(*i*) Cost of land, including cost of levelling and draining, sold for interments is treated as a trade expense.

(*ii*) Residual capital expenditure in proportion to spaces sold and number for sale can be claimed as a trade expense.

(*iii*) No balancing allowances or charges arise; if there is a sale the new owner takes over the allowances.

7.12 Small Workshops (Section 75, FA, 1980 and Section 73, FA, 1982)

(*i*) An initial allowance of 100 per cent is available on expenditure incurred after 26 March, 1980, and before 27 March, 1983. For this purpose a **small workshop** is an industrial building with a gross internal floor space of 2,500 square feet. After 27th March, 1983, but before 26 March, 1985, the allowance has been extended to the *very small workshop*, which has been defined as having an internal floor space of 1,250 square feet.

(*ii*) It the claimant does not claim the whole of the initial allowance in the first year, he can claim a writing-down allowance of 25 per cent calculated on a straight-line basis as for industrial buildings allowances.

Example 7.11 A manufacturer started in business on 1 January, 1982, in a newly constructed small workshop costing £15,000 and decided to claim only 50 per cent of the initial allowance.

The computation is as follows:

1981/82: Cost		£15,000
Less 50% initial allowance	£7,500	
Writing-down allowance	938	8,438
Written down value		6,562
1982/83: Writing-down allowance 25%		3,750
Written down value		2,812
1983/84: Writing-down allowance		2,812
Written down value		Nil

7.13 Enterprise Zones (Section 74, FA, 1980)

Seven Enterprise Zones were designated in 1980—and were added to since—to be given special treatment:

(*i*) An initial allowance of 100 per cent but if not claimed in full.

(*ii*) A writing-down allowance of 25 per cent on original expenditure until used up (as in Example 7.11). All buildings, including offices and shops, qualify, but not dwelling houses.

7.14 Revision Test

Answers	*Questions*
1. Plant and machinery, industrial buildings, mines and oil wells, agricultural buildings, UK patents, scientific research, dredging, know-how, hotels, crematoria and cemetaries, small workshops and enterprise zones.	**1.** What assets qualify for capital allowances?
2. A number of Court decisions established the principle of the 'functional test', i.e. to be plant an asset has to have a function. If it merely supplies a setting e.g. a canopy in the case of a petrol filling station, it does not qualify.	**2.** Define the term 'Plant and Machinery'.
3. The asset is regarded as purchased when the contract begins and the principal sum qualifies for capital allowances. The hire charge is a revenue expense and has to be charged in accordance with accounting principles. In case of	**3.** How is 'hire purchase' treated for capital allowances?

motorcars costing more than £8,000 the allowable hire charge is restricted, as it is for private use.

---

4. It reduced the allowance from 100 per cent to 75 per cent for expenditure incurred under contracts entered into after 13.3.1984. For expenditure after 31.3.1985 it is 50 per cent and for expenditure incurred after 31.3.1986 it is abolished.

4. What changes did the FA, 1984 make to the First Year Allowance?

---

5. It includes a mill, factory and warehouse attached to manufacturing. It also includes sports pavilions for the welfare of employees, but not offices and shops.

5. Define the term 'Industrial Building'?

---

6. The Initial Allowance has been reduced from 75 to 50 per cent for expenditure on contracts signed after 31.3.1985 and for expenditure incurred after 31.3.1986 it is abolished.

6. What changes have been made to the Industrial Building Allowances by FA 1984?

---

7. The initial allowance of 20 per cent is abolished for expenditure after 31.3.1986 and the writing down allowance is reduced from 10 to 4 per cent.

7. What changes did the FA1984 make to the Agricultural Building Allowances?

---

8. The system of writing off UK patent rights over 17 years is replaced for patents granted after 31.3.1986 with a writing down allowance of 25 per cent as for plant.

8. What changes has the FA1984 made to capital allowances on the cost of UK patents?

---

9. The initial allowance of 15 per cent is abolished for expenditure incurred after 31.3.1986.

9. What changes has the FA 1984 made to capital allowance on the cost of dredging?

---

10. The initial allowance of 20 per cent been withdrawn for expenditure

10. What changes has the FA 1984 made to capital allowances on

incurred after 31.3.1986.

hotels?

---

11. The existing 1/6th writing-down allowance is replaced by a reducing balance allowance of 25 per cent for expenditure incurred after 31.3.1986.

11. What changes has the FA, 1984 made to the allowances on know-how?

---

12. The writing down allowance on plant, industrial buildings etc. is given for the trading period, on assets in use at the end of the accounting period which forms the basis period for assessment.

12. What is the basis period for writing down allowances.

8
Business and Other Losses

The losses for which some form of income tax relief is available are of two kinds:

(*a*) **Trading losses,** including certain payments made under deduction of tax and capital allowances.

(*b)* **Non-trading losses.** These arise under Schedule A (Chapter 5) and under Case VI of Schedule D (page 000).

A **trading loss** occurs when expenses exceed income during the trading period. For income tax purposes the trading loss is arrived at the same way as a trading profit, i.e. it is not the figure shown in the profit and loss account, but the adjusted figure for tax purposes (see Example 6.3).

8.1 Loss in Trade Set Against Other Income (S. 168, ICTA, 1970)

Any trading loss sustained can be set against the trader's other income of that year and any unrelieved balance may be carried forward for *one* subsequent year. In calculating the qualifying loss capital allowances and stock relief may be used to augment the loss. There is a time limit for making this claim and it is *two years from the end of the year of assessment* for which the claim is made. In other words, if one makes a loss in the trading year to 31.12.1985, the S.168 claim must be lodged by 5.4.1988.

(*a*) **Basis period.** S. 168 provides that the loss should be the loss of the year of assessment, which is the year to 5 April, but in practice the Inland Revenue accepts the loss of the accounting year ending in the year of assessment, except in the following circumstances:

(*i*) The first three years of assessment of a new business.

(*ii*) The fourth year of business, where the second and third years have been based on the actual profits (see Section 6.10).

(*iii*) Any year which immediately follows a year for which the relief as calculated on the *statutory basis*, or (*iv*) Where the taxpayer desires it.

Example 8.1 Carter has been trading since 1970 and his recent trading results as adjusted for tax purposes were as follows:

Year to 31.12.1981	Profit	£5,000
Year to 31.12.1982	Loss	6,000
Year to 31.12.1983	Profit	4,000

If he claims S.168 relief in respect of the loss, the assessments will be as follows:

1982/83 Profit year to 31.12.1981	£5,000
Less: S.168 relief—Loss incurred in trading period ending 82/83	6,000
Loss available for carry-forward £1,000	Nil
1983/84 Year to 31.12.1982 Loss	Nil
1984/85 Year to 31.12.1983 Profit	£4,000

The balance of the loss is not available under S.168, since it can only be claimed in the years 1982/83 and 1983/84, but it can be claimed under S.171, ICTA, 1970.

If Carter is entitled to capital allowances the position is:

Capital Allowances 1982/83 £500, 1983/84 £450 and 1984/85 £600

1982/83 Profit	£5,000
Less: Capital allowances	500
	4,500
Less S.168 relief £6000 450	6,450
	Nil

1983/84 Nil, 1984/85 £4,000—CAS £600 = £3,400

(*b*) **Trader with other income**

Example 8.2 Assuming that Carter (Example 8.1) receives rents and War Loan interest of £800 each year, the position is as follows:

1982/83 Profit year to 21.12.1981	£5,000	
Less: Capital allowances	500	
Schedule D, Case I	4,500	
Investment Income	800	
Total Income	5,300	
S.168 Relief Loss CAs	6,450	Loss c/f £1,150
	Nil	
1983/84 Loss year to 31.12.1982	Nil	
Investment income	800	

Carter could claim S.168 relief for 1983/84, but since the £800 investment income is covered by his tax-free personal allowances, no tax liability arises therefore no claim is made.

1984/85 Profit year to 31.12.1983		£4,000
Less CAs	£600	
Loss (s171)	1,150	1,750
		2,250

(*c*) **Trader who is married**

Example 8.3 Assuming that Carter (Example 8.2) is married and his wife has a salary of £6,500 and investment income of £500, the position is as follows:

1982/83 Profit year to 31.12.1981		£5,000
Less: Capital allowances		500
		4,500
Investment income (self)	800	
Earned income (wife)	6,500	
Investment income (wife)	500	7,800
Total income		12,300
S.168 relief loss—CAs		6,450
		5,850
Less: Higher personal allowance	2,445	
Wife's earned income relief	1,565	4,010
Tax due		1,840 × 30% = £552
1983/84 Schedule D		Nil
Wife's salary		6,500
Investment income (self)		800
Investment income (wife)		500
		7,800
Less: Higher personal allowance	2,795	
Wife's earned income relief	1,785	4,580
		3,220 × 30% = £966
1984/85 Schedule D, Case I £4,000—CAs 600		= £3,400
Wife's salary		6,500
Investment income (self)		800
Investment income (wife)		500
		11,200

If the wife's salary is £3,000 it will pay Carter to claim to have the loss relief restricted under S.168(3).

Example 8.4

1982/83 Profit year 31.12.1981		£5,000	
Less: Capital allowances		500	
		4,500	
Investment income		800	
		5,300	
Less: S.168 Relief		6,450	Loss c/f £1,150
		Nil	
Wife's income—salary		3,000	
Investment income		500	
		3,500	
Less: Higher personal allowance	2445		
Wife's earned income relief	1565	4,010	
		Nil	
1983/84 Schedule D		Nil	
Wife's salary		3,000	
Investment income (self)		800	
Investment income (wife)		500	
		4,300	

Less: Higher personal allowance	2795	
Wife's earned income relief	1,785	4,580
		Nil
1984/85 Profit less CAs		3,400
Less: Loss relief (S171)		1,150
		2,250
Investment income (self)		800
Investment income (wife)		500
		3,550

(*d*) **Order of set-off**

It is important to remember that a loss under S.168 is set off against other income in the following order:

First—Against the earned income of the individual making the loss.
Second—Against the investment of the individual making the loss.
Third—Against the earned income of the spouse.
Last—Against the investment income of the spouse.

The order of set-off affects the calculation of the Investment Income Surcharge up to 1983/84 and wife's earned income relief.

8.2 Loss in Early Years of a Business (S.30, FA, 1978)

A *trading loss* arising in (*a*) the first year of assessment, or (*b*) any of the next *three* years of assessment qualifies for relief. The relief is given by carrying back the loss against the claimant's income for *three* years of assessment immediately preceeding the year of assessment in which the loss was incurred. The loss is first set off against the earliest of those three years and if not wholly used the balance is then carried forward for set-off against later years. The first year for which the relief is available is 1978/79.

Example 8.5 Bloggs, who has been employed for many years and made redundant in 1982, started in business on 1.6.1982 and made a loss of £10,000 in the year to 31.5.1983. His remuneration for recent years was:

1978/79	£4,600
1979/80	5,000
1980/81	5,400
1981/82	6,000

1982/83 Period 6.4.1982 to 31.5.1982 £1,200

His wife's investment income is £2,000, but she has a small child and has no earned income. The computations are as follows:

Schedule D loss

1982/83 Period 1.6.1982 to 31.3.1983 10/12th of loss 10,000 = £8,333

Assessment for 1982/83 salary	£1,200
Wife's investment income	2,000
	3,200

Less: higher personal allowance	2,445	
Tax due	755 × 30% = £226.50	

Bloggs could claim S.168 Relief which would reduce the tax liability to nil, but affect his loss relief:

Salary 1982/83	£1,200	
Less: S.168 Relief (excluding wife's income)	1,200	
	Nil	
Wife's investment income	2,000	
Less: Higher personal allowance	2,445	
Tax due	Nil	
S.30, FA, 1978 relief as amended: 1978/79	Loss £8,333	
S.30 relief (excluding wife's income)	4,600 to	
1978/79 Assessment Wife's investment	3,733 c/f	
income	£2,000	
Less: Higher personal allowance	1,535	
Tax due	465 × 25% = £116.25	
1979/80 Salary	£5,000	
Less: S.30, FA, 1978 relief balance of loss	3,733	
	1,267	
Wife's investment income	2,000	
	3,267	
Less: Higher personal allowance	1,815	
Taxable income	1,452	
	750 × 25% =	£187.50
	702 × 33% =	231.66
Tax Due		419.16

1980/81 £5,400 assessed in the normal way.
1981/82 £6,000 assessed in the normal way.
1982/83 as shown.
1983/84 Nil (wife's investment income covered by personal allowance).
1984/85 Nil (based profit for year to 31.5.83).
1985/86 Profit—Year to 31.5.1983 less loss b/f 10,000 − 8,333
= £1,667

8.3 Loss in Aggregation

It is possible to have the loss in one of the first trading years allowed more than once for tax purposes.

Example 8.6 John commenced to trade after retiring from the police and has the following trading results:

Six months 30 June, 1982:	Loss	£6,000
Year to 30.6.1983:	Profit	£9,600

Capital allowances were agreed as follows: 1981/82, £500; 1982/83, £550; 1983/84, £480; and 1984/85, £420. The computation is as follows:

1981/82 Period 1.1.1982 to 31.3.1982 Loss (½ of £6,000)	£3,000	Nil
1982/83 Year to 31.12.1982 Loss (6 months to 30.6.82)	6,000	
Profit (6 months to 31.12.82)	4,800	
Loss	1,200	Nil

1983/84 Year to 31.12.1982 as for 1982/83			Nil
1984/85 Year to 30.6.1983 Profit		9,600	
Less: Capital allowances 81/82 to 84/85		1,950	
Assessment		7,650	

No loss relief is due, since the whole of the loss of £6,000 has been allowed in *aggregation*. This is not always the case as can be illustrated.

Example 8.7 Bob commenced to trade on 1.1.1981. The agreed trading results were as follows:

6 months to 30.6.1981:	Profit £5,000
Year to 30.6.1982:	Loss 4,000
Year to 30.6.1983	Profit 6,000

Capital allowances were: 1980/81, £600; 1981/82, £800; 1982/83 £700; 1983/84, £525; and 1984/85, £450.

1980/81 Period 1.1.1981 to 31.3.1981 Profit	£2,500		
Less: Capital allowances	600	1,900	
1981/82 Year to 31.12.1981			
(6 months to 30.6.1981)		5,000	
Loss (6 months to 31.12.1981)		2,000	
Profit		3,000	
Less: Capital allowances		800	2,200
1982/83 Year to 31.12.1981 Profit		3,000	
Less: Capital allowance		700	2,300
1983/84 Year to 30.6.1982			
Loss £4,000, CAs £525 c/f			Nil
1984/85 Year to 30.6.1983 Profit		6,000	
Less: Capital allowances 1983/84	£525		
1984/85	450		
Loss b/f 'S171)	2,000	2,975	3,025

Readers will notice that only half the loss £2,000 has been allowed in *aggregation* and for this reason the loss for the period 1.1.82 to 30.6.82 can be carried forward and claimed.

8.4 Trading Losses Carried Forward (S171, ICTA, 1970)

Trading losses can be carried forward and set against profit of the *same trade* indefinitely. The Inland Revenue enforces the rule strictly to the extent that if a business man wishes to sell his business on the basis that there are unallowed losses available to be set against future profits, the new owner carrying on the business cannot claim these losses since both the trade and the trader must be the same. The losses are in fact personal. Even if the trader dies and his wife takes over, she cannot claim the accumulated losses of her husband.

In the case of a company the position is rather different and certain reliefs are possible, but corporation tax is outside the scope of this book. A word of warning, however: companies who advertise their tax losses as the only assets for sale should be looked at most carefully and no purchase of shares should be undertaken without the fullest professional advice.

8.5 Terminal Losses (S.174, ICTA, 1970)

On the **permanent discontinuance** of any trade, profession or vocation losses *sustained in the year ending on the date of cessation*, so far as not otherwise allowed, may be carried back to the penultimate year and the two years preceding that year. The relief is calculated as follows:

(*a*) The loss sustained in the year of assessment in which the trade is permanently discontinued.

(*b*) The relevant capital allowances for that year of assessment.

(*c*) The loss sustained in part of the preceeding penultimate year of assessment, beginning 12 months before the date of discontinuance.

(*d*) The same fraction of the relevant capital allowances for the penultimate year.

Example 8.8 Bill has carried on business as a tailor since 1965, but on 30 June, 1983, he permanently discontinued. The adjusted profits and losses for tax purposes have been:

	Profit	Loss
	£	£
Year to 30 June, 1979	1,800	
Year to 30 June, 1980		500
Year to 30 June, 1981	1,200	
Year to 30 June, 1982	900	
Year to 30 June, 1983		1,600

There were no purchases of assets between 1.7.1982 and 5.4.1983, and the capital allowances due were:

	£
1980/81	200
1981/82	150
1982/83	112

On 5 April, 1983, the written-down value of fixtures and fittings was £336 and on 29 June 1983, were sold for £200.

The calculations are as follows:

(*a*) *Cessation adjustments*
1983/84 Period 1.4.1983 to 30.6.1983 Loss £400 + Balancing allowance £336 − 200 = £136
1982/83 Year to 30.6.1981 Profit £1,200
1981/82 Year to 30.6.1980 Loss 500 Nil.

Revenue option under S.118, ICTA, 1970, to change the basis of assessments for the years 1981/82 and 1982/83 is not exercised. Therefore assessments are as follows:

	£
1980/81 Year to 30.6.1979 Profit	1,800
Less: Capital allowances	200
	1,600
Less: S.168 Relief 1981/82 Loss 500+CAs150	650
	950
1981/82 Year to 30.6.1980 Loss	Nil

1982/83 Year to 30.6.1981 Profit 1,200—Capital allowances 112=£1,088

(b) *Terminal loss calculation*		£
The loss sustained in 1983/84		400
Capital allowances for 1983/84		136
Period 1.7.1982 to 31.3.1983		1,200
Capital allowance ¾ of 82/83 already allowed		
Qualifying loss		1,736
Allowed 1982/83	1,088	
1981/82	Nil	
1980/81	648	

8.6 Loss of Trader who Becomes Company Director (S.172, ICTA, 1970)

As has been explained, normally a loss suffered by one individual cannot be carried forward and utilised by another person, but if the business is transferred to a company and the individual receives shares in the company for the business which has been transferred, the loss can be allowed.

To qualify for the relief under S.172, the sole or main consideration of the individual's business is an allocation of shares, and the beneficial ownership must be throughout the year for which a claim is made. The claim is available only against the income *derived from the company*. The set-off must first be against salary and any unrelieved balance can be set against dividends.

Example 8.9 Vera carried on a business as a hairdresser until 31.3.1982, when she transferred the business to a limited company, the purchase price being satisfied solely by means of a transfer of shares in the company. The unrelieved losses at the time of the transfer were £1,500. Vera received director's fees of £800 and dividend plus tax credits of £200 in 1982/83, and director's fees of £1,000 and dividends plus tax credits of £200 in 1983/84. S.172 relief will be calculated as follows:

1982/83 Director's fees	£800
Less: Loss b/f	800
Dividend	200

Less: Loss b/f	200
Tax repayment (Tax credits) 200 × 30% = £60	
1983/84 Director's fees	£1,000
Less: Loss b/f	500
	500
Dividend	200
Taxable income	700

8.7 Relief for Losses on Unquoted Shares in Trading Companies (S.37, FA, 1980)

This is a loss on the disposal of **qualifying shares**, which from 1980/81 is available for income tax relief (before it was an allowable loss for capital gains tax purposes only). The loss is computed in the same way as a capital loss for capital gains tax purposes.

A qualifying share is broadly one in a trading company that has always been resident in the UK but never quoted on a stock exchange, and has traded for at least six years. Moreover, the shares must have been subscribed by the individual, thus excluding shares he has purchased or acquired through inheritance. If the shares have been subscribed, other than by an *arm's-length* contract, the market value is substituted for their cost. The relief is also restricted to individuals and is not available to trustees. An arms-length contract is between persons who are not related or connected in any way.

Finally, the relief takes precedence over any other loss relief, (e.g. S.168, ICTA, 1970 and S.30, FA, 1978). Just as in the case of S.168 relief, the income of the spouse can be excluded from the claim, which can be made in either the year of loss or in the subsequent year and must be claimed within two years of the year for which it is incurred. The first available year is 1980/81 and in calculating the loss the time of acquisition of the shares is ignored.

Since 31.3.1981 this relief is available to investment companies, provided that the investment company subscribed for the shares but does not control the trading company, nor must it be part of the same group as the trading company.

Example 8.10 Fitzgerald sold qualifying shares in company A, a UK-resident private trading company, for £500 in June 1983. He subscribed £1,450 for these shares in 1976. The market value of the shares, in accordance with S.19, Capital Gains Tax Act, 1979, was £800. The computation is as follows:

Market value (since more than sale price)	£800
Less cost	£1,450
Allowable loss	650

which can be claimed either in 1983/84 or 1984/85

8.8 Annual Payments (SS.173 and 175, ICTA, 1970)

These payments, already referred to in Chapters 3 and 4, reduce the amount of loss relief available and if the payment is made by a trader—say a royalty payment under deduction of tax—this payment, which cannot be deducted from the gross income, can be added to the loss or made to create a loss, which is treated as a trading loss and can be carried forward in the same way as a normal trading loss under S.171, ICTA, 1970.

8.9 Revision Test

Answers	*Questions*
1. Yes; a trading loss is the only tax loss that can be set against non-trading income.	**1.** Are trading losses treated differently to other losses?
2. Yes; if the business is continuing, the profit of the year to 31.3.1984 is assessed for 1984/85 and the loss for the year to 31.3.1985 was incurred in the year 1984/85.	**2.** Is it possible for a trading loss of the accounting year to 31.3.1985 to be set against the profit of the accounting year to 31.3.1984?
3. The order of set-off is: (*i*) Against individual trading income. (*ii*) Against individual's investment income. (*iii*) Against spouse's trading income. (*iv*) Against spouse's investment income. It may affect WEIR.	**3.** Describe the order of set-off on loss relief under S.168 and why is this important?
4. When such a claim results in a loss of tax-free personal allowance.	**4.** In what circumstances should one exclude the spouse's income from a S.168 claim?
5. A trading loss arising in the first 4 years of assessment can be carried back and relieved during the three years immediately preceding the year of loss.	**5.** What loss relief, if any, is available in the early years of a business?

6. This usually occurs when a loss occurs in the first 12 months of trading and is effectively allowed twice due to the rules of assessment.	**6.** Explain the term 'loss in aggregation'.
7. Indefinitely.	**7.** How long can a trading loss be carried forward and set against trading profits of the same trade carried by the same trader?
8. This is a loss which occurs in the last 12 months of trading plus capital allowances for the same period. It is relieved in the penultimate year and the two years preceeding it.	**8.** Explain the term 'terminal loss' and how is it relieved?
9. This is possible when the business has been transferred to a private limited company in return for shares.	**9.** In what circumstances can a trader carry his loss forward and set it against future salary?
10. This relates to shares in a private company resident in UK and carrying on trading for at least 6 years.	**10.** In what circumstances can a loss on share dealings be allowed against income?
11. Annual payments, e.g. patent royalties are paid under deduction of tax and may give rise to a S.53 assessment, in which case they are added to the trading loss.	*11.* How do annual payments affect loss relief?
12. If the trader dies, or sells his business or ceases to trade and has unallowed losses they cannot be relieved.	**12.** In what circumstances can a genuine trading loss fail to get allowed.

9
Setting up in Business and Forming a Partnership

9.1 Tax Treatment of Employee Starting a Business

With the decline in many of Britain's traditional manufacturing industries, many redundant persons consider setting up in business. They are often urged by politicians and others to do so, extolling the virtues of enterprise and explaining that Tesco and Marks & Spencer, to name two famous examples, were started by small market traders. One must warn readers, however, that starting a business with redundancy money is quite a risky matter and should not be engaged in without the most extensive professional advice. The fact is that although some small businesses succeed the greater number fail.

From a tax point of view setting up in business in the service sector from home is a good idea. The reasons are the following:

(*a*) If one was subject to PAYE before, as soon as one commences in business one qualifies for a tax repayment.

(*b*) For 18 months or more the new trader enjoys a 'tax-free holiday'.

(*c*) Losses in the first four years of assessment of business qualify for tax relief against tax paid under PAYE (see Section 8.2).

Example 9.1 Bodger, a married man, was made redundant from his post with the district council on 30.9.1984. Tax-free redundancy pay was £10,000 and the P45 (see Chapter 10) gives the following information:

Pay to time of leaving	£4,000
Tax deducted	480

He starts as a 'freelance gardener' from home on 1.10.1984. As soon as possible he should send P45 (Parts 2 & 3) to HM Inspector of Taxes with a letter informing him that he would not be seeking employment during 1984/85, but had set up as self-employed gardener. The tax repayment will be calculated as follows:

1984/85 Salary	£4,000
Less: Higher personal allowance	3,155
Taxable	845 × 30% = £253.50

Tax paid under PAYE	480
Repayment due	226.50

Assuming that he makes up his accounts to 30 September, 1985, it will take until, say, December 1985 before the tax liability for the years 1984/85, 1985/86 and 1986/87 can be agreed with the Inspector. This means that the earliest Bodger can get his final tax bill for the years 1984/85 and 1985/86 under Schedule D will be January or February, 1986.

Inspectors sometimes make estimated assessments and ask for payment on account, before February 1986, but this does not alter the fact that from an income tax point of view businesses are treated favourably.

9.2 Basis Period for a New Business

The general principles of basis periods for assessment under Schedule D have been already outlined in Section 6.10 but when commencing in business the accounting date chosen for the first trading period is particularly important.

Assume that Bodger's trading result for the year to 30.9.1985 as adjusted for tax purposes shows a profit of £6,000 but during the three months to 31.12.1985 his gardening business only produced £600. The effect of choosing 31 December as accounting date rather than 30 September can be illustrated.

Example 9.2 (*i*) Profit for year to 30.9.1985, £6,000; (*ii*) profit for 15 months to 31.12.1985, £6,600.

(*i*) The assessments would be:

1984/85:	Period 1.10.1984 to 31.3.1985 6/12th × £6,000	= £3,000
1985/86:	Year to 30.9.1985	= 6,000
1986/87:	Year to 30.9.1985	= 6,000
		15,000

(*ii*) The assessments would be:

1984/85:	Period 1.10.1984 to 31.3.1985 6/15th × £6,600	= £2,640
1985/86:	Year to 30.9.1985 12/15th × £6,600	= 5,280
1986/87:	Year to 31.12.1985 12/15th × £6,600	= 5,280
		13,200

So by delaying his accounting date to 30 December Bodger saves £1,800 of assessable or 1,800 × 30% or £540 in tax.

Example 9.3 Assume that Bodger's profits for subsequent periods are:

(*i*) Year to 30.9.1986: £5,000
Year to 30.9.1987: £5,000

(*ii*) Year to 31.12.1986: £5,400
Year to 31.12.1987: £5,200

A claim under S.117, ICTA, 1970, would be appropriate as follows:

(*i*)	1985/86 Year to 31.3.1986	6/12 of £6,000 = £3,000	
		6/12 of £5,000 = £2,500	£5,500
	1986/87 Year to 31.3.1987	6/12 of £5,000 = £2,500	
		6/12 of £5,600 = £2,800	£5,300
	1987/88 Year to 30.9.1986		£5,000
	1988/89 Year to 30.9.1987		£5,600
			£21,400
(*ii*)	1985/86 Year to 31.3.1986	9/15 of £6,600 = £3,960	
		8/12 of £5,400 = £1,350	£5,310
	1986/87 Year to 31.3.1987	9/12 of £5,400 = £4,050	
		3/12 of £5,200 = £1,300	£5,350
			£10,660
	1987/88 Year to 31.12.1985		£5,400
	1988/89 Year to 31.12.1986		£5,200
			£21,260

compared to £21,400 a small saving of £140 × 30% = £42.

9.3 Basis Period when Closing a Business

Just as it is important to choose the most advantageous accounting date when commencing to trade, it is equally important to choose the most advantageous date, from a tax point of view, when to retire from business, when to transfer a business to a company and when to sell the business.

Example 9.4 Purple, a builder, has decided to form a joint stock company with limited liability and he can cease trading either (*i*) on 31.3.1984 or (*ii*) on 30.4.1984. His adjusted trading profits for tax purposes were:

Year to 30.6.1980:	£12,000
Year to 30.6.1981:	14,000
Year to 30.6.1982:	18,000
Year to 30.6.1983:	20,000

Since 1.7.1983 the profits have been at the rate of £2,000 per month. The calculations are as follows:

	(*i*)	(*ii*)		
Year of cessation	1983/84	1984/85		
1983/84 Year to 31.3.1984 9 × 2,000 =		18,000	Period 1.4.84 to 30.4.84	
+ 3/12 of £20,000 =		5,000	1984/85	2,000
Total		23,000	1983/84 as for (*i*)	23,000
1982/83 Year to 31.3.1983 Revenue option				
9/12 × 20,000 = 15,000				
3/12 × 18,000 = 4,500		19,500	as for (i)	19,500
1981/82 Year to 31.3.1982			1981/82 Year to 30.6.1980	
9/12 × 18,000 = 13,500			(py)	12,000
3/12 × 14,000 = 3,500		17,000		
		59,500		56,500

It clearly pays Purple to cease trading a month later, since he will be assessed on £56,500 in place of £59,500—or, having earned £2,000 more and saved tax on £3,000, he saved tax on £5,000 profits.

9.4 Changing the Accounting Date

In times of rising profits it may pay one to change the accounting date and save some money. One cannot do this too often. In fact, it usually works only once in the life-time of a business. The Inland Revenue normal practice in such cases has been laid down in Inland Revenue Leaflet 26, issued in 1974, from which the following is an extract:

(*i*) Under S.115 (2b), ICTA, 1970, the Board of Inland Revenue normally decide that the assessment is to be based on the profits of the period of 12 months ending on the new accounts date in the preceding income tax year.

(*ii*) The question then arises whether there is to be any adjustment for the preceding income tax year under S.115 (3) to the profit of the corresponding period (year ending on the new accounting date). Such an adjustment may increase or decrease the liability, according to the trend of profits.

(*iii*) The considerations which the Board have in mind in determining the question are as follows:

Where there is a permanent change of accounting date, then whether or not revision under S.115 (3) is ordered, one of two things must, in the ordinary course, happen:

(*a*) If the new date is later in the income tax year than the old, the profits of some period will not come into assessment at all;

(*b*) If the new date is earlier in the income tax year than the old, the profits of some period will come into assessment twice. If the profits of the period omitted were relatively low, or the profits of the period coming in twice were relatively high, the Revenue would gain. Conversely, if the profits of the period omitted were relatively high, or the profits coming in twice were relatively low, the taxpayer would gain. The Board attempts to secure that the profits to be assessed twice, or to be omitted from assessment, as the case may be, are 'average' profits. As a rule this object can be secured neither by straightforward revision nor by non-revision, but only by taking for the year to which S.115 (3) applies some figure intermediate between the revised and unrevised figure. That intermediate figure is computed by reference to a consideration of:

(1) The profits of all the accounting periods of which any part enters into either the basis year under S.115 (2) or the 'corresponding period', under S.115 (3), the 'relevant accounting periods' and

(2) The number of years for which the assessments are based in whole or in part on any of the profits of the 'relevant accounting periods' referred to as the 'relevant years'.

Small Differences. Where the 'average' computation brings out an 'aggregate profit' which exceeds or falls short of the sum of the unrevised assessment for the preceding year and the assessment of the other 'relevant year' by a relatively small amount, it is not the Board's normal practice to take any action by way of 'average' adjustment. For this purpose the Board would normally regard as relatively small a difference that was less than ten per cent of the current and preceding years' assessment and also less than £1,000.

Example 9.5 Morgan, an insurance agent, had been in business for 10 years when profits began to improve and he considers whether changing his accounting date would be beneficial. His recent trading results were:

Year to 31.3.1980 Profit	£ 6,000
Year to 31.3.1982 Profit	10,000
Year to 31.3.1983 Profit	20,000

Since profits are still rising he is considering changing his accounting date to 30 June, and the profit for the 15 months to 30.6.1983 was £26,000. The question is, would it pay him to change the accounting date?

(*i*) Assessments without change:	1981/82 Year to 31.3.1981	£6,000
	1982/83 Year to 31.3.1982	10,000
	1983/84 Year to 31.3.1983	20,000
	1984/85 Year to 31.3.1984	24,000
(*ii*) Assessment with change:	1981/82 Year to 31.3.1981	6,000
	1982/83 Year to 31.1.1982	10,000
	1983/84 Year to 30.6.1982 (S.115 (2b))	
	9/12 × £20,000 =	7,500
	3/12 × 20,000	5,000
		12,500
	1984/85 12/15 × 26,000	20,800

In accordance with Inland Revenue practice 1982/83 has to be considered for revision under S.115 (3). The 'corresponding period' is the year to 30.6.81:

9/12 × £6,000 = £4,500 + 3/12 × £10,000 = £2,500 total £7,000

The profits of the accounting periods which enter, in whole or in part, into the basis periods for the 1982/83 'corresponding period' and 1983/84 and 1984/85 are:

12 months to 31.3.1981	£6,000
12 months to 31.3.1982	10,000
15 months to 30.6.1983	26,000
39 months	38,000

Since the *relevant years* are 1981/82 to 1984/85 (four) the *aggregate profit* is:

$\frac{48}{39} \times £48,000 = £46,769$

This sum must be compared with assessments of the *relevant years* without revision under S.115 (3):

1981/82	£6,000
1982/83	10,000
1983/84	12,500
1984/85	20,800
	49,300

(*a*) *Significance test.* Since £49,300 is more than £1,000 different from the aggregate profit of £46,769, the difference is significant.

(*b*) *Intermediacy test.* Revision under S.115 (3):

1981/82 Year to 31.3.1981	£6,000
1982/83 Year to 30.6.1981 (CP)	6,500
1983/84 Year to 30.6.1982	12,500
1984/85 Year to 30.6.1983	20,800
	45,800

Since £46,769 is intermediate between £45,800 and £49,300, the final adjustment is made:

Aggregate profit		£46,769
Less: 1981/82	£6,000	
1983/84	12,500	
1984/85	20,800	39,300

The revised 1982/83 assessment is £7,469, which is more than £1,000 less than the previous assessment of £10,000.

Summary of position

Year	Without change	With change
	£	£
1981/82	6,000	6,000
1982/83	10,000	7,469
1983/84	20,000	12,500
1984/85	24,000	20,800
Total	60,000	46,769

As a result of the change of accounting date Morgan reduced his assessable profit for the four years by £13,231.

9.5 Forming a Partnership

Partnerships are normally formed where the sole trader has neither the capital nor the time or experience to expand his business and therefore wishes to share the responsibility with one or more other persons.

There are two major disadvantages in forming a partnership compared with forming a *joint stock limited liability company:*

(*a*) In the case of a partnership, each partner is *jointly and severally* liable to pay the debts incurred by the partnership. This means that except in the case of a limited partner (who must not take any active part in the running of the partnership, but provides money and is entitled to a share in profits) each partner is liable with his whole private wealth to pay any debts which another partner may have incurred in the course of the business.

Because of this *unlimited liability* of individual partners it is often said that a partnership is a linking of money with experience and it sometimes results in the man with the money gaining experience by losing his money.

(*b*) Because a partnership must be dissolved on the death, retirement or admission of a partner, it lacks continuity.

In practice, partnerships are mainly found among professional people, e.g. doctors, solicitors, accountants, where unlimited liability of the partners is a safeguard for the public.

9.6 What Constitutes a Partnership?

A partnership is not a separate entity in English law, but according to S.1 of the Partnership Act, 1890, it is 'The relation that subsists between persons carrying on a business in common with a view to profit'.

Whether in fact a partnership exists or not can be material in income tax cases. For example, a successful trader can take his wife into partnership and save considerable tax by claiming separate assessment of wife's earnings under S.23 of the Finance Act, 1971 (see 4.3). Whether a partnership exists or not is a question of fact to be decided by the Commissioners in accordance with the above definition. The Revenue will accept a partnership between husband and wife only if the claimants can prove that both spouses are in fact acting as partners. A partnership involves an agreement of the partners to act together. This agreement, in order to be lawful, does not need to be in writing, but a written agreement, or even partnership deed, is usually a good idea to prevent argument later.

Moreover, the existence of an agreement itself does not establish a partnership—the agreement must also be acted on. In the case of *Dickenson v. Gross (1927) 11 TC 614*, which concerned a farmer who entered into a deed of partnership with his three sons to reduce his tax liability, but kept control of the business, the learned judge expressed himself as follows: 'The partnership deed here, of course, was a deed perfectly good according to its tenor, and if it had been what really governed the relations of the parties it would have effected the object of those who purported to enter into it ... A partnership of course is a legal position and a legal result but like every other legal position it depends on facts, and what the Commissioners are saying here it ... although there was the deed they are not acting on it ... They go on treating the undertaking as though it were still the sole and uncontrolled property of the one person, the father.'

Whenever a trader wishes to take his wife or any other member of his family into partnership, he must have regard to the following considerations, which the Revenue will look at. An acting partner would have normally some or all the following qualifications:

(*a*) Have a share of the capital of the business.
(*b*) Have his name on the letter-heading of the business.
(*c*) Have the power to draw cheques on the business bank account.
(*d*) Have a definite task to perform in the business.
(*e*) Have a title to the assets of the business.

9.7 Assessment of Partnership—Share of Partners

S.152, ICTA, 1970, provides that the partners shall be assessed in one sum, although for other purposes, as has been pointed out, the partnership is not a legal entity. The reason for assessing the partnership in one sum is to make the tax liability of each individual partner a partnership debt, thus making all the partners *jointly and severally liable* for the whole tax of the firm.

Although the partnership is assessed in one sum, the tax liability of the partnership is made up of the total individual tax liability of the partners and will depend on the circumstances of the individual partners.

Basis of assessment. The partnership is normally assessed on the profit of the accounting year ending in the preceding year of assessment, but the profit has to be divided among the partners in accordance with each partner's share of the assessment. This means that the assessable share of the profit may have little relation to the actual income received in the year.

Example 9.6 Jones & Co. is a partnership of Jones, Williams and Evans, who have agreed to share the profits as follows: Jones, one half; Williams, one third; and Evans, one sixth. In addition, each partner receives interest on capital of 6 per cent and a salary. The interest and salaries for the years to 31.3.1984 and 31.3.1985 were as follows:

Partner	*Interest*		*Salaries*	
	1983/84	1984/85	1983/84	1984/85
Jones	200	220	5,000	5,500
Williams	100	110	6,000	6,600
Evans	100	110	4,000	4,400

The adjusted profits for the years to 31.3.1983 and 31.3.1984 were £42,000 and £36,000 respectively. Each partner's share would be computed as follows:

1983/84 Year to 31.3.1983		Profit£42,000		
Less: Interest	400			
Salaries	15,000	15,400		
		26,600	Jones' share ½	£23,000
			Williams' share ⅓	8,867
			Evans' share ⅙	4,433

Allocation	*Jones*	*Williams*	*Evans*	*Total*
	£	£	£	£
Salary	5,000	6,000	4,000	15,000
Interest	200	100	100	400
Share of profit	13,300	8,867	4,433	26,600
	18,500	14,967	8,533	42,000

1984/85 Year to 31.3.1984		Profit £36,000		
Less: Interest	£440			
Salaries	16,500	16,940		
		19,060	Jones' share ½	£9,530
			Williams' share ⅓ 6,353	
			Evans' share ⅙	3,177

Allocation	*Jones*	*Williams*	*Evans*	*Total*
	£	£	£	£
Salary	5,500	6,600	4,400	16,500
Interest	220	110	110	440
Share of profit	9,530	6,353	3,177	19,060
	15,250	13,063	7,687	36,000

It will be noted that the profit of 1983/84 forms the basis of assessment of 1984/85, but not the salaries and interest, which are taken from the year 1984/85.

9.8 Change in Partnership

Whenever a partner dies, retires or a new partner is admitted, the partnership automatically comes to an end and a new one is formed. For income tax purposes, where at least one of the persons carrying on the trade before the change in the constitution of the partnership continues in the new firm, an election can be made under S.154, ICTA, 1970, for the business to be treated as continuing, but *only if all old and new partners give written notice* to the Inspector claiming that the partnership should be treated as a continuing business. The reason why all the old and all the new partners must give this written notice is that the election may reduce the tax liability of the firm as a whole, but not of each individual partner. A partner adversely affected should ask the partners who benefit to make commercial restitution of his loss, before signing the claim. The election must be made within *two* years of the date the change took place. The Revenue applies this time limit strictly, so delay in preparing the accounts and making the claim can be quite expensive in tax.

The Chancellor in 1985 promised that legislation would be introduced for 1985/86 and after to alter the basis of assessment applying following a change in the membership of a partnership. In the income tax year in which the change takes place and the three following tax years the assessment will be on the actual profits arising in each of those years.

Example 9.7 Priest and Church have been in partnership for a number of years drawing salaries of £4,000 per year each and dividing the balance of profits 60 per cent to Priest and 40 per cent to Church. On 30 June, 1983, Church retired and Priest took in Pater and Novice. The three partners were to draw salaries of £4,000 each and profits would be shared. Priest one half and Pater and Novice a quarter each.

The profits adjusted for tax purposes were:

	£
Year to 30.6.1979	14,000
Year to 30.6.1980	8,000
Year to 30.6.1981	13,000
Year to 30.6.1982	11,000
Year to 30.6.1983	12,000

The estimated profit for the year to 30.6.1984 is £16,000.

(*a*) Assessments if an election under S.154(2) ICTA, 1970, is made by 30 June, 1985:

Basis period	*Old firm* £	*New firm* £
1980/81 Year to 30.6.1979	14,000	
1981/82 Year to 30.6.1980	8,000	
1982/83 Year to 30.6.1981	13,000	
1983/84 Year to 30.6.1982 (change 30.6.1983)	2,750	8,250
1984/85 Year to 30.6.1983		12,000
1985/86 Year to 30.6.1984 (estimated)		16,000
Total	23,750 +	36,250 = £60,000

(*b*) Assessments if no election is made:

Basis period	*Old firm* £	*New firm* £
1981/82 Year to 31.3.1982 Revenue option exercised under S.118 (2), ICTA, 1970	11,500	
1982/83 Year to 31.3.1983 (£9,000 + 2,750)	11,750	
1983/84 Period 1.4.1983 to 30.6.1983	3,000	
1983/84 Period 1.7.1983 to 31.3.1984		12,000
1984/85 Year to 30.6.1984 (estimated)		16,000
1985/86 Year to 30.6.1984 (estimated)		16,000
	26,250 +	44,000 = £70,250

Clearly the firm benefits to the tune of unassessed profits of £10,250 by making the election, but Priest and Church benefit at the expense of Pater and Novice, who are assessed to income in 1983/84 on profits in which they did not share.

9.9 Partner Residing Abroad

S.152, ICTA, 1970, provides 'Where any trade or business is carried on by two or more persons in partnership, and the control and management of such a trade or business is situated abroad, the trade or business shall be deemed to be carried on by persons resident outside the United Kingdom.'

The effect of this section is that if a person living in the UK is a partner in, say, a farm in Australia, he can only be assessed on a **remittance** basis (see Chapter 12), because the partnership is controlled and managed abroad. In practice, whether part of the business is carried on in this country or whether part of a resident partnership's business is controlled and managed abroad is a difficult question of fact.

Moreover, what constitutes *control and management* in a partnership whose business is international, with some partners living in this country while others live abroad, is a difficult question outside the scope of this book.

9.10 Partnerships Involving Companies (S.155, ICTA, 1970)

This involves corporation tax and therefore is outside the scope of this book.

9.11 Revision Test

Answers	*Questions*
1. The following advantages accrue: (*i*) One can claim a tax repayment under PAYE (*ii*) One enjoys a tax-free holiday for at least a year before the first Schedule D tax is payable. (*iii*) Losses in the first 4 years assessment can be set against previous income.	**1.** What income tax advantages accrue to an employee starting in business?
2. Since the first trading period forms the basis of at least two	**2.** Why is it important to choose the accounting date carefully?

year's tax assessments and possibly more, it is important to arrange one's affairs so that the first accounting period includes low profit months.

---

3. Since on cessation one year's profit escapes taxation, it is important to fix a date which ensures that the profit which escapes is a high one and the Revenue option does not apply.	**3.** Why is it important to consider the income tax implications when permanently ceasing to trade?
5. Usually the advantages are business advantages and not tax advantages, but if one wishes to share profits with one's family forming a partnership is a way to reduce tax liability provided responsibility as well as profits are shared.	**5.** What are the advantages of forming a partnership?
6. Yes there are. A partnership is assessed in one sum and the individual partner's tax liability is a firm's debt.	**6.** Are there any disadvantages in forming a partnership from a tax point of view?
7. Yes, partners' salaries are not true salaries, but allocations of the firm's profits. They are added to the profit assessed and affect each partner's share.	**7.** Are partners' salaries treated differently from other salaries?
8. The Partnership Act, 1890 defines a partnership as 'the relationship that subsists between persons carrying on a business in common with a view to profit.' Each partner is jointly and severally liable.	**8.** Define a partnership.
9. A change in the number of partners constitutes the cessation of trading of the firm, and the formation of another.	**9.** How does a change in the number of partners affect the tax assessment?
10. Since cessation and	**10.** When should an election under

commencement provisions involve extra liability it usually pays to make an election. It has to be made within 2 years of the date of change and signed by all new and old partners.

S.154 be made to treat the partnership as a continuing business?

---

11. If partners reside abroad the question arises, whether 'the control and management of the trade' is carried on abroad and if so the remittance basis applies.

11. If some of the partners reside abroad how is the liability dealt with?

---

12. The death of a partner is treated like any other change and the executors can sign the election under S.154.

12. What effect on the tax position has the death of a partner?

10
Taxation of Employees

Most taxpayers—probably some 25 million—pay tax under PAYE. The Inland Revenue has admitted in its evidence to the House of Commons Public Accounts Committee that 27 per cent of all the cases examined in a random sample of 43 tax offices in 1979/80 were incorrect. If one adds to this that only some 25 per cent of PAYE taxpayers receive a return to complete each year, and many do not claim all they are entitled to, it is quite possible that between 9 and 10 million taxpayers overpay tax each year, although the amount of overpayment may be small in most cases.

10.1 Schedule E (SS.181-207, ICTA, 1970)

The Schedule is divided into three cases:

Case I covers the employee who is both *resident* and *ordinarily resident* in the UK (see Chapter 12) and does not perform the duties of the office or employment *wholly* outside the UK, provided his earnings are not *foreign emoluments*. An individual is liable on all his or her earnings under Case I.

Case II covers the employee who is either *not resident* or if resident, *not ordinarily resident*. Such an individual is liable to UK income on all his UK earnings, and *foreign emoluments* are charged at 50 per cent.

Case III covers the employee who is *resident* in the UK although working wholly abroad, when he may well be regarded as also resident abroad. Such an individual is liable to UK tax only on income *remitted* to the UK. This case normally now applies to individuals not *domiciled* in the UK.

Questions of **residence**, **ordinarily resident**, and **democile** are fully discussed in Chapter 12, but it can be stated that Case I covers some 90 per cent of Schedule E taxpayers.

10.2 Foreign Emoluments (Para. 3, Schedule 7, FA, 1977)

Foreign emoluments are defined as income where in any year of assessment:

(*a*) The duties of the office or employment are performed *wholly outside* the UK and

(*b*) The employment is with a person, body of persons or partnership *resident* outside the UK, and the individual is not *domiciled* in the UK.

The 50 per cent deduction has been withdrawn from 13.3.1984 for individuals, who have been resident in the UK in *nine of the preceding ten years* and is reduced to 25 per cent for those resident for less than *nine years*, from 1987/88, and no relief is given after 6 April, 1989.

Example 10.1 A is teacher of French, who teaches English at a school in France during the academic year 1983/84 (September to July, and returns for Christmas holidays and after July, 1984, to his home in Sussex. His income in France was £5,000.

B is a journalist with a national newspaper and is appointed Washington correspondent for three years from 1 January, 1983. His salary for 1982/83 and 1983/84 was £20,000 and £22,000 respectively.

Both A and B would not qualify under the *foreign emolument* rules, since neither is *domiciled* outside the UK.

10.3 Earnings from Overseas Employments (SS.181 and 184, FA, 1974 and S.31, FA, 1977)

Since 1977/78 certain *special deductions* are available as follows:

(*a*) 100 per cent for an employee who works abroad for a *continuous period* of 365 days or more. The journalist in example 10.1 would qualify for this deduction.

(*b*) 25 per cent for an employee who works abroad for a period of 30 days in the year of assessment, not continuous. In calculating the number of days of absence from the UK, a qualifying day is any day on which the individual is not in the UK at midnight. Other conditions are:

(*i*) The period is substantially devoted to the performance outside the UK of that and other employments, or

(*ii*) Which is one of at least *seven* consecutive days on which the employee is absent from the UK for the purpose of the performance of such duties and which are substantially devoted to such duties (which means that non-working weekends are included), or

(*iii*) On which the individual concerned is travelling for the purpose of the performance of such duties outside the UK.

Seafarers and aircrew employed on journeys between the UK and abroad qualify for the 25 per cent special deductions. Moreover, employees under a separate contract with duties performed wholly abroad can claim the cost of travelling and the cost of accommodation if provided by the employer. Finally, where an employee works abroad for a *period of at least 60 days*, the reimbursement by the employer of the costs of the spouse and children travelling to the country of employment and back are tax-free up to a maximum of two return journeys in any one tax year. Visits to the UK are disregarded in calculating the continuous period of 365 days, provided they do not exceed 62 consecutive days or a total of more than one sixth of the total period of absence. From 6.4.1985 this deduction is abolished and it has been reduced to 12½ per cent for 1984/85.

Example 10.2 Traveller is the European manager of a Canadian trading company with an office in London and a director of the company based in Montreal. His income for the year 1983/84 was:

London office	£18,000
Car benefit	650
Fuel benefit	650
	19,300

He spent 40 qualifying days abroad and received £3,000 director's fees from Canada on which he paid £600 Canadian tax.

Traveller is married and his tax position would be as follows:

1983/84 Salary including benefits in kind	£19,300	
Special Deduction $\frac{40}{365} \times 19{,}300 \times 25\% =$	529	
	18,771	
Add 75% of director's fees	2,250	
	21,021	
Less: Higher personal allowance	2,795	
Taxable income	18,226	
	14,600 × 30%=	£4,380
	2,600 × 40%=	1,040
	1,026 × 45%=	461.70
		5,881.70
Less: Double tax relief—Canadian tax suffered		600
Tax due		5,281.70

10.4 Pensions

All pensions, including the state retirement pension, except those specifically mentioned in Section 3.6 (page 28), are taxable under Schedule E.

10.5 Foreign Pensions and Annuities

(*a*) Since 1974/75 persons *resident*, *ordinarily resident* and *domiciled* in the UK are liable to income tax on 90 per cent of the pension from overseas whether remitted to the UK or not, except

(*b*) Pensions payable under the law of the Federal Republic of Germany or of Austria to the victims of Nazi persecution are taxed on 50 per cent. The pensions are not disability pensions, exempt from German and Austrian tax, which are also exempt in the UK. All foreign pensions are assessed under Case V of Schedule D, the basis periods for which are explained in Chapter 12.

10.6 Employments with International Organisations

A small but growing number of people are employed by the United Nations and their agencies, the EEC Commission, the European Assembly, OECD and similar organisations. Such people are not employed by an employer resident in the UK, as in the case of a British diplomat working in Paris, nor is the employer resident in the foreign country, since these bodies are not employers in those countries. They are not *foreign employments*, since the employer is not liable to foreign tax. In fact salaries paid by these bodies are *tax-free*. The only way this anomaly is tackled is that appointments on the staff of the European Commission contain a salary less a tax factor, which is deducted and the net amount is paid tax-free.

The same applies of course, to pensions paid by these bodies.

10.7 The Difference between Schedule D (Case I and II) and Schedule E

This was already referred to in Section 6.13 and applies particularly to the growing number of people with part-time jobs.

10.8 Meaning of the Term 'Emoluments of Office or Employment'

Any amount derived from the office, provided it is *money's worth*, is included as taxable income. The principle was established in the case *McLoughlin v. Machon (1926) 11 TC 83*, in the following terms: 'If a person is paid a wage with some advantage thrown in, you cannot add the advantage to the wage for the purpose of taxation unless the advantage can be turned into money. That is one proposition. But when you have a person paid a wage with the necessity—contractual necessity if you like—to expend that wage in a particular way, then he must pay tax on the gross wage.'

The case concerned an attendant of an asylum who had been paid a salary with free board and lodgings, etc. He was assessed only on his salary, but when his salary was raised and he had to pay for his board and lodgings out of the increase, he was assessed on the increased salary, since it clearly had become 'money's worth'.

In the case of *Wilkins v. Rogerson (1961) 39 TC 33* it was held that the employer who had provided a suit for his employee, provided 'money's worth' to the extent of the second-hand value of the suit, but not its cost, and the second value was part of the employee's assessable income.

On the other hand, gifts of a *personal nature* by way of testimonial are tax free, but tips received by waiters, taxi-drivers, etc., are regarded as not of a personal nature but received by everybody in that particular employment.

Similarly, awards given to employees on passing a professional examination are tax-free. This was held in the case of a bank employee passing the Institute of Bankers Examination (*Ball v. Johnson (1971) 47 TC 155*). The judge commented as follows: 'The Commissioners went on ... We accordingly hold that the reason for the payments was the appellant's personal success in passing the examinations and the payments were not remuneration for his services with the bank. In my judgement the Commissioners applied the right legal principles.'

10.9 Basis of Assessment

Normally there are two legitimate bases of assessment:

(*a*) The statutory or **earnings basis**, which means any bonus paid late is related back to the period in which it was earned.

(*b*) The **accounts basis**, which is concessional and convenient in the many cases of employees, particularly senior ones, who earn commission and bonuses which are not determined until the accounts of the company have been prepared. In this case the income is not apportioned into income tax years, but the income earned in the accounts year ending in the income tax year is treated as income of that year. This concession enables the Inland Revenue to agree the tax sooner than on the earnings basis. Once the concessional basis has been adopted and the assessment has become *final and conclusive*—that is after the appeal period of 30 days has elapsed (see 2.12)—one cannot ask for the assessment on the accounts basis to be re-opened to apply the earnings basis.

Example 10.3 The following director's remuneration has been voted for Cole:

Accounting year to 31.12.1980: £8,000 paid on 15.4.1981
Accounting year to 31.12.1981: £10,000 paid on 20.4.1982

Accounting year to 31.12.1982: £9,000 paid on 25.4.1983
Accounting year to 31.12.1983: £9,600 paid on 10.5.1984

Year	*Earnings (statutory) basis*		*Accounts basis*
		£	£
1979/80	¼ of £8,000 =	2,000	Nil
1980/81	¾ of £8,000 = 6,000		
	¼ of 10,000 = 2,500	8,500	8,000
1981/82	¾ of 10,000 = 7,500		
	¼ of 9,000 = 2,250	9,750	10,000
1982/83	¾ of 9,000 = 6,750		
	¼ of 9,600 = 2,400	9,150	9,000
1983/84	¾ of 9,600 = 7,200		
	¼ estimated 2,500	9,700	9,600
Total		39,100	36,600

Clearly it pays Cole to accept the accounts basis, but if the remuneration is falling or the appointment comes to an end, it will be the reverse.

Example 10.4 Assume Cole terminates his directorship on 31.12.1983. In this case, he will claim the statutory basis for 1983/84 and the Inspector, provided the 1982/83 assessment has not become final, will apply the statutory basis for that year producing the following results:

1980/81	As before	£8,000
1981/82	As before	10,000
1982/83	Earnings basis	9,150
1983/84	Earnings basis	7,200
		34,350

Under PAYE the income is taxed when it is received and unless it is the same as was earned it is not the proper basis.

10.10 Directors and Higher-Paid Employees

Although the principle that what is *money's worth* should be assessed applies to all employees, special provisions apply to directors and higher-paid employees, defined as employees who, before any allowance of expenses, receive emoluments including all expense payments and benefits in kind at the rate of £5,000 p.a. or more up to 1977/78, £7,500 for 1978/79 and £8,500 for 1979/80 and subsequent years.

S.196, ICTA, 1970, provides that benefits in kind provided by the employer in the form of living accommodation, cost of entertainment, cost of domestic services and other benefits of whatever nature are regarded as taxable emoluments (but see Section 5.5: 'representative occupation' is not assessable).

10.11 Exclusion of Certain Directors

The general effect of the provisions of S.72 of the Finance Act, 1976, is to exclude directors of unincorporated bodies or non-profit making bodies from the requirements under Section 10.8, provided the individuals concerned are neither higher-paid (receive more than £8,500) nor hold a material interest (defined as more than 5 per cent of the ordinary share capital in the company) in the body employing them. Similarly, directors of charities who are neither higher-paid nor hold a material interest are also excluded.

10.12 Dispensation for Payment of Allowable Expenses (S.70, FA, 1976)

In order to avoid the need to submit details of routine expenses, expenses payments and benefits that would clearly involve no extra tax, the Inspector will grant a dispensation from the application of PAYE, if he is satisfied that it is appropriate.

Dispensations are normally given for payment of travelling and subsistence expenses on an approved scale for absences on business journeys in the UK. They are not normally given for round sum allowances or entertaining expenses of employees in trading concerns.

All allowances and benefits in kind have to be included in a special return Form P11D, which the employer has to make at the end of the year for each director or higher-paid employee.

10.13 Fringe Benefits

As has been explained already, this is a wide term and includes 'money's worth' for everyone, **beneficial occupation** (see 5.5) and a lot more for directors and higher-paid employees.

Table 10.1. Benefits in kind.

Benefit	*Employee*	*Director or higher-paid employee*
Private use of employer's car	Tax free if used for business	See Table 10.2
Employer's house rent free	Taxed on gross rateable value, unless *representative occupation*	As for other employees
Special clothing	Tax-free	Tax-free

Suits, etc.	Taxed on second-hand value	Taxed on full cost
Medical insurance	Tax-free	Taxable
Beneficial loans	Interest tax-free	Taxable, if benefit exceeds £200
Cash vouchers and credit	Taxable	Taxable
Luncheon vouchers	Taxable on sum exceeding 15 pence	Taxable on sum exceeding 15 pence
Season tickets	Taxable	Taxable
Assets given for employee's use	Tax-free	Taxable: Valued at 20% annually.

Travelling and entertaining expenses are not taxable, provided the expenses are reimbursed by the employer and incurred in performing the duties of the employment (but see Section 6.7 regarding entertaining).

Where the employer provides living accommodation and pays for the cost of heating, lighting, cleaning, repairs, maintenance etc., plus domestic furniture and equipment assessed at 20% of cost annually, the whole charge is restricted to 10 per cent of net emoluments, after allowable expenses and capital allowances have been deducted from gross emoluments.

S.21, FA, 1983, provided that from 1984/85 an additional charge applies to houses costing more than £75,000, or if purchased more than 6 years previously, worth more than £75,000 when first occupied by the employer after 30.3.1983. The additional benefit is subjected to current rate of interest. In other words, if the house is valued at £85,000, the additional benefit for 1984/85 is £85,000 − £75,000 = £10,000 × 12% (the current rate of interest) = £1,200.

10.14 Scale Charges for Directors' and Higher-Paid Employees

Table 10.2 Scale charges for cars. The rates will apply for 1985/86 (1986/87 in brackets)

Cars with a recognised cylinder capacity	Age of vehicle at end of year of assessment			
Cars with original value up to £17,500 (£19,250)	Under 4 years		4 years or more	
	£		£	
1300cc or less	410	(450)	275	(300)
1301cc–1800cc	525	(575)	350	(380)

More than 1800cc	825 (900)	550 (600)
Cars with original market value		
£17,501 (£19,251–£26,000 (£29,000)	1,200 (1,320)	800 (875)
Over £26,500 (£29,000)	1,900 (2,100)	1,270 (1,400)

If business mileage is *insubstantial*, that is 2,500 or less, or if the car is a second company car, the taxable benefit is 1½ times the scale charge. If business mileage is *predominant*, that is 18,000 miles or more the scale rate is halved. The taxable benefit is reduced pound for pound if the employee is required to contribute for private use.

Table 10.3 Fuel Benefit. The rates which apply for 1985/86 (1986/87 in brackets)

Cars with a recognised cylinder capacity	Cash Equivalent
	£
1300cc or less	410 (450)
1301cc–1800cc	525 (575)
More than 1800cc	825 (900)

If business mileage is 18,000 or more the rate is halved. There is no increase if the business mileage is less than 2,500. The charge is cancelled if employee is responsible for *all* private petrol.

10.15 Scholarship income

Where the educational costs of an employee's child are met by a scholarship fund provided by the employer, the employee is taxed from 1983/84 on the benefit, measured by the cost to the employer, but not if the scholarship was awarded before 15 March, 1983, and the child remains at the same educational establishment.

10.16 Share option and share incentive schemes

The principle that shares given to directors and employees at below market value are taxable in respect of the benefit obtained was laid down in the decision in *Weight v. Salmon (1935) 19 TC 174*. This principle was amended when the option to purchase shares by employees at favourable terms, over a period of years was introduced. Each scheme has to be approved by the Inland Revenue and up to 1983/84, a taxable benefit arose under Schedule E in the year in which the option was exercised. From 6.4.1984 the exercise of an option granted under a newly approved scheme is no longer taxable under Schedule E, but becomes liable to capital gains tax, when the shares are sold. The capital gain is calculated in the normal way. Options exercised under non-approved schemes are still subject to tax under Schedule E.

10.17 Profit sharing schemes

From 6.4.1979 a company can establish a profit sharing scheme with approval of the Inland Revenue, whereby money is allocated to trustees to purchase shares in the value of £1,250 or 10 per cent of salary for any employee subject to an overall maximum of £5,000. In order to qualify the shares have to be held for 2 years before they can be transferred to the employee. When the shares are sold by the employee income tax is chargeable depending upon how long they were held:

Years held	*% of original value taxable*
2–3	100
4	75
5	50
6	25
Over 7	Nil

There is also an allowance of £20 deductible from the original value until disposal with a maximum of £140. The Finance Act, 1985, reduced the period during which the shares must be held from 7 to 5 years, if an income tax assessment is to be avoided.

10.18 Expenses (S.189, ICTA, 1970)

A deduction for expenses is allowed provided a very stringent rule is complied with. This reads as follows: 'If the holder of an office or employment of profit is necessarily obliged to incur and defray out of the emoluments thereof the expenses of travelling in the performance of the duties of the office or employment ... or otherwise to expend money *wholly, exclusively and necessarily in the performance* of the said duties there may be deducted from the emoluments ... the expenses so necessarily incurred and defrayed.' It will be noticed that S.189 is much more stringent than S.130 dealing with allowable expenses under Schedule D (see 6.6) in that not only have expenses to be *wholly and exclusively* incurred in earning the profits, but *necessarily and in the performance* of the duties as well.

(*a*) Cost of travelling between home and work was held not to be allowable on the ground that the taxpayer was not performing his duties as employee when travelling to work, since the duties did not commence until reaching the office (*Ricketts v. Colquhoun (1926) 10 TC 118*).

(*b*) The cost of meals and subsistence incurred by an airline pilot when away from home was held to be allowable in *Nolder v. Walters (1930) 15 TC 380*. The judge expressed the principle as follows: 'Some offices involve the duty of travelling. It is not a question of getting to the place of employment, but the employment is actually to travel, therefore expenses under this head are deductible'. This case must be distinguished from the decision in *Sanderson v. Durbridge (1955) 36 TC 239*, when the cost of a meal in the case of a borough surveyor was not allowed, since he was not performing his technical duties whilst he was eating.

(*c*) Costs of books, etc., to students are not deductible. This was held in *Blackwell v. Mills (1945) 26 TC 468*, when the judge stated: 'The duties of his employment were as a student assistant in the research laboratories of the GEC. It seems to me impossible to say that when he was listening to the lecture at the Chelsea Polytechnic, he was performing the duties of a student assistant at the laboratories of the company.'

(*d*) Subscriptions to professional societies (but not trade unions) related to the employment can be claimed under S.192, ICTA, 1970.

(*e*) Cars used partly during the employment and partly privately qualify to an agreed proportion.

10.19 Terminal Payments (SS.187–188, ICTA 1970; S.43, FA, 1982)

New rules regarding 'golden handshakes' became effective after April, 1982. The first £25,000 is still exempt, but the next £25,000 is charged at half the marginal tax rate and the next £25,000 is charged three quarter of the marginal rate. Any sum in excess of £75,000 attracts the full rate.

Example 10.5 John, a married man, is made redundant on 31.8.1985 and receives a lump sum compensation payment of £30,000. His other income during 1985/86 including earnings is £18,000. The computation is as follows:

1985/86		*Before lump sum*	*Including lump sum*
		£	£
Other income		18,000	18,000
Lump sum (£30,000–25,000)			5,000
		18,000	23,000
Higher personal allowance		3,455	3,455
		14,545	19,545
Income tax: 14,545 × 30%		4,363.50	4,363.50
	1,655 × 30%		496.50
	3,000 × 40%		1,200

345 × 45%	155.25
	6,215.25

Tax on lump-sum ½ (£6,215.25–£4,363.50) = £925.87. Final liability for 1985/86 £4,363.50 + 925.87 = £5,289.37.

10.20 Pay As You Earn (S.204, ICTA, 1970)

PAYE would be better described as 'Pay as you are paid', since it is the most common example of **taxation at source** (see 2.13). It is the employer's duty to deduct tax from the pay of his employees, unless a 'NT' (no tax) code number has been issued by the local Tax Office. Officers of the Inland Revenue Department are empowered by law to make inspections of employer's records from time to time in order to satisfy themselves that the correct amounts of tax and National Insurance contributions are being deducted and paid over to the Department.

(*a*) **Inspection by Audit Centre.** Normally the relevant audit centre selects on a random basis the firms to be inspected and arranges for a visit. The following records have to be produced:

(*i*) Wages and salaries books or equivalents.
(*ii*) Cash books or equivalents and cheque stubs.
(*iii*) Petty cash books or equivalents and petty cash vouchers.
(*iv*) PAYE documents.

It has been stated that some 60 per cent of records inspected were found faulty and if this arises the employer has to pay the tax he should have deducted from employees who have left his employ, without being able to recover the tax from the employees. It is possible, although it will not occur very often, that tax which should have been deducted under PAYE is paid twice—by the employer following an inspection and by the employee who makes a correct tax return. It is possible also that the employer is made to pay tax he should have deducted if no **code number** was available because the employee had been unemployed and would in fact not have been liable to tax. It is important to realise that the Revenue does not check up on its records of the employees who were not subjected to PAYE, whether in fact they were liable. Small firms with temporary employees or a large turnover of staff are particularly vulnerable and more training in the operation of PAYE should be given. Lastly, failure to operate PAYE correctly makes the employer liable to penalties. In fairness, the Inland Revenue usually compromise the issue and will settle without starting penalty proceedings.

(*b*) **Documents required.** To operate PAYE the employer requires (*i*) Deductions working sheets (form P11) or equivalent (see Example 10.6).

(*ii*) Codes for employees which reflect the tax allowances to which they are entitled.

(iii) Tax tables: Tables A (Free Pay Tables) and Tables B–D (Taxable Pay Tables).

(*iv*) End of year returns for each employee (Form P14).

(*v*) Form P46 to be issued when employee is leaving.

(*vi*) Form P15 to be issued when new employee cannot produce P45.

Example 10.6 The Form P11 (tax deduction working sheet) for a single person with a basic salary of £7,200 per year for 1983/84 would look as follows:

Month	*Gross pay*	*Total gross pay*	*Tax free pay*	*Taxable pay*	*Tax due*	*Tax deducted*	*Tax repaid*
	£	£	£	£	£	£	£
1	600	600	149.09	450.91	135.00	135.00	
2	600	1,200	298.18	901.88	270.00	135.00	
3	nil (sick)	1,200	447.27	752.73	225.60		44.70
4	630	1,830	596.36	1,233.64	369.90	144.30	

It can be seen that the system works on a cumulative basis and by the end of the year the amount of tax due should be broadly the same as the amount deducted.

The form P11 also provides a record of National Insurance contributions under Class 1 (see 6.14) which both employer's and employee's contribute to.

(*c*) **Code Numbers.** The employer, in order to deduct the right amount of tax, needs to be supplied with a code number for each employee well before the beginning of the tax year (6th April). Each employee's code number is determined by the Tax Office and is amended by the Tax Office as the employee's circumstances change. The Code is notified to the employee on Form P2, which shows all tax-free allowances, and any restriction of these allowances due to subsidiary income, over allowance of previous year, underpayment of previous year, etc. It does not show superannuation contributions or mortgage interest paid to building societies covered by MIRAS (Mortgage Interest Relief At Source).

It must be remembered that the employee's circumstances depend on the information supplied in the Annual Tax Return. The subsidiary income (e.g. interest received in 1982/83) will be disclosed in the Tax Return for 1983/84 issued in April, 1983, but the Code Number for 1983/84 will have been issued to the employer in March or earlier, which means that it is based on the information contained in 1982/83 Tax Return showing the 1981/82 income. It is clear, therefore, that unless the bank interest assessable in 1983/84 is the same as for 1981/82 and 1982/83, which is not very likely, the Code Number will be incorrect, not because the Tax Office has made a mistake but because the system works in three-year cycles—1983/84 code depending on 1981/82 income.

It is not surprising, therfore, that when the Inland Revenue made a random sample check and reported to the House of Commons Public Accounts Committee in 1979/80 it found that 27 per cent of all assessments were wrong. It involved, of course, underpayment as well as overpayment of tax, and the individual amounts underpaid were higher than those overpaid, who were more in number. In fact, when one remembers that the Tax Office does not issue a tax return each year to PAYE taxpayers and that many people fail to claim all the allowances they are entitled to, it is clear that the 27 per cent understates the true position. This is particularly true in the case of the growing number of pensioners in receipt of an occupational pension as well as a national retirement pension. In these cases the Inspector will include in the Code Number for the occupation pension, which is subject to PAYE, the estimated figure for the National Retirement Pension. This will be estimated in March, 1985 to take account of the increase in pension to take effect on 22 November, 1985, before it is known to include it in the 1985/86 Code Number.

There are certain letters issued with the Code Number:

(*i*) Prefix D or F. Codes which consist of a prefix D followed by 0–4 indicate tax at the higher rate, i.e. D0 = 40%, D1 = 45%, etc., F followed by a number usually means that the non-taxed income exceeds the tax-free allowances and PAYE is operated at a rate higher than 30 per cent. It applies to people with two or more employments.

Example 10.8 Green a married man is a non-executive director receiving director's fees of £1,000 yearly. His other income for 1984/85 was estimated in the sum of £22,000. The directorship has been coded D1, which means that the table D1 taxes the £1,000 × 45% = £450.

(*ii*) Codes with suffixes H, L, P, T or V indicate the place in Table A. H, for example, means Higher Personal Allowance and L, Lower Personal Allowance, P and V involve pensioners.

(*d*) **Tax Tables.** Table A gives the tax-free pay. Tables B–D provide Taxable Pay Rates.

Example 10.9 A single person without any dependants in 1984/85 has a Code Number 200 which means that he is entitled to a tax-free personal allowance of £2,005. The tax-free pay for month 1 from Table A is £167.42 or £2,009 for the year. In other words, £167.42 is as close a possible to 1/12 of £2,005.

(*e*) **Procedure at the end of the year.** At the end of the year the employer is obliged to issue each employee a Form P60, which is part of the P14, is one item of the procedure making the end of year return. The P60 is the certificate of pay and tax deducted for the year, and includes tax and pay of a previous employment during the year.

At the same time the employer makes a return on Form P35 together with Forms P11D and final payment for the Collector of Taxes.

(*i*) When receiving the P60 the taxpayer should check the amount of tax deducted to see whether he or she has overpaid tax. Overpayment of tax is not uncommon, since the Code number may be out of date or changes in circumstances may have taken place during the year.

(*ii*) If the check shows an overpayment the taxpayer must request a notice of assessment to be issued (S.205, ICTA, 1970) and enclose form P60 with the request. In due course a tax repayment will be received together with the notice of assessment.

(*iii*) If the taxpayer has underpaid tax and the Inspector of Taxes makes an assessment, the underpayment is usually coded in to take effect in the Code for the next full year. Thus an underpayment for 1982/83 which will arise on an assessment issued say in August, 1983, will be taken into account in the Code Number for 1984/85 (once again the three-year cycle). An underpayment of £60 appears as a deduction from the allowances on Form P2 as £200, since £200 taxed at 30 per cent produces £60 of tax.

(*f*) **Change of employment.** When a person changes his employment, on leaving the employee is issued with Form P45, Parts 2 and 3. Part 1 of the form is sent to the local tax office. On obtaining a new post, the employee hands in the P45, Parts 2 and 3, to the new employer, who keeps Part 2 as his authority for operating PAYE, and after completing Part 3 sends it to his local Tax Office, who forwards it to the Tax Office named on the back which holds Part 1 with a request to transfer the file. The old Tax Office checks Part 1 and 3 to make sure that they belong to the same set, in order to prevent fraud, notes its records to indicate where the file has gone and then transfers it. In this way the file follows the employee whenever he changes his job.

The procedure adopted when a new employee does not produce Parts 2 and 3 of the P45 has already been outlined in Section 2.5.

(*g*) **Pay as defined for PAYE.** With the exception of certain superannuation contributions (those agreed with the Inland Revenue) the tax deductions must be calculated by reference to the **gross pay** before any deductions are made (e.g. in respect of employee's National Insurance contributions or trade union subscriptions).

(*i*) *Items treated as 'pay'*

(1) **Statutory Sick Pay** (SSP). As from 6.4.1983 the employer is responsible for paying Statutory Sick Pay in certain circumstances for up to eight weeks of sickness absence in a tax year. These payments are

treated as ordinary pay; no National Insurance sickness pay is due and the normal National Insurance contributions have to be paid.

(2) **Holiday Pay.** Tax is deductible in the normal way, but where more than one week's pay is paid in one week, with no pay in subsequent weeks, because the employee is on holiday, the Tables are operated as if the pay would be received each week. In the construction industry, voluntary deductions are made from an employee's pay to be repaid when he goes on holiday, known as 'Holiday Stamps'. The deductions are ignored for PAYE and no tax is deducted when the 'Holiday Stamps' are cashed.

(3) **Christmas boxes in cash.** No tax is deductible from gift vouchers, National Saving certificates given at Christmas or Christmas hampers, but these benefits may still be taxable and have to be included on the forms P9 and P11D at the end of the year. Payments on an employee's marriage or other personal testimonials are not subject to tax (see 10.8).

(4) **Tool allowances** for manual workers. The actual cost of the tools can, of course, be claimed as an expense, and employees should keep receipts of such purchases for claim under S.189.

The Revenue has published the allowances agreed with the trade unions in Revenue Pamphlet IR 1. The allowances for 1980/81 (the latest figures available) are given in Table 10.3.

It will be noted that the list is by no means complete and people affected should do two things: (*i*) consult their trade union and discover what allowance is due and when the allowance had been agreed. It is quite likely that the allowance may be out of date. (The writer discovered recently that one agreement between a trade union and the Inland Revenue had not been changed for 20 years.) (*ii*) Keep detailed records of tools purchased, including overalls, and their cost. Add to this the cost of laundering the overalls and repairing the tools and compare the cost with the agreed allowance. If the cost is more than the allowance make the claim and agree with the Inspector a higher allowance which should be revised whenever it is inadequate.

(5) **Employees' income tax borne by the employer.** This is calculated as follows:

Example 10.10 An employee receives a salary of £500 free of tax. The employee's code is 178L. The employee has no other income.

Pay in month	£500
Free pay (Table A-Month 1)	149.09
Nominal Taxable Pay	350.91

Refer to Table B and find the point where the difference between *total taxable pay to date* and *total tax due to date* amounts to £350.91. Taxable pay column £501 less tax £150.30 = £350.70.

(6) **Payments in respect of the cost of travelling** between the

Table 10.3. Tools etc., allowances from 1980/81.

Industry	*Occupation*	*Allowance* £
Agriculture	All workers	40
Forestry	All workers	40
Vehicles	(*a*) Builders, railway wagon, etc. repairers	65
	(*b*) Railway vehicle painters and letterers, etc.	35
	(*c*) All other workers	25
Precious metals	All workers	40
Electric and electrical supply	(*a*) Those workers incurring laundry costs only	15
	(*b*) All other workers	55
Textiles	(*a*) Carders, carding engineers, etc.	50
	(*b*) All other workers	35
Clothing	(*a*) Lacemakers, hosiery bleachers, dyers, scourers and knitters, etc.	30
	(*b*) All other workers	20
Textile prints	All workers	35
Printing	(*a*) Electrical engineers, etc., in letterpress section	65
	(*b*) Bench hands, compositors, readers, etc.	20
	(*c*) All other workers	40
Glass	All workers	35

employee's home and his normal place of work. This does not apply to travel allowances for travel undertaken during the employment (see 10.18) and payments for time spent in travelling.

(*ii*) *Items from which tax is not deductible*

(1) **Living accommodation** provided for the benefit of the employee, if the employee has to reside there becaue of the nature of his duties, i.e. **representative occupation** (see 5.5), but if it is **beneficial occupation**, tax is due.

(2) Meal vouchers which comply with certain conditions:

(*a*) The vouchers are not transferable.

(*b*) Where any restriction is placed on their issue to employees they are available to the lower-paid staff.

(*c*) The value of the vouchers issued to an employee does not exceed 15p (the value has been unchanged since 1948) for each full working day.

(3) **Payments in lieu of notice** (but see 10.19 regarding terminal payments).

(4) **Benefits under the Workmen's Compensation Acts.**

(5) **Removal expenses** borne by the employer where the employee *has* to change his residence on first taking up the employment, or on transfer to another post within the employer's organisation, provided the expenses are reasonable in amount.

10.21 Purchasing Pension Rights

Reference has already been made to the fact that many people who change pensionable jobs cannot transfer their pension rights and as a result lose substantial benefits. Partial remedy of this situation is that many pension schemes allow late entrants to purchase past pension rights which will not only secure a better pension, but increase the tax allowable part of the superannuation payment.

10.22 Revision Test

Answers	*Questions*
1. 'Foreign Emoluments' are remuneration, where in any year of assessment (*i*) the duties of the office or employment are performed wholly outside the UK, and (*ii*) the employment is with a person resident abroad, and (*iii*) the individual is not domiciled in UK. It has been withdrawn after 13.3.84 for most residents in UK.	**1.** Define the term 'Foreign Emolument' and how has the FA, 1984 changed its tax treatment?
2. The 25% deduction was reduced to 12½ for 1984/85 and is abolished after 5.4.1985.	**2.** What changes has the FA, 1984, made to the 'Special Deduction'?
3. Resident and domiciled individuals in UK are taxed on 90% of their pension.	**3.** How are foreign pensions taxed?
4. A benefit is taxable, if it is 'money's worth' and can be turned into money e.g. season ticket.	**4.** Define a taxable 'benefit in kind'.
5. Salaries are assessed on either (*i*) the 'earnings basis', i.e. money earned in the tax year or	**5.** How are salaries assessed?

(*ii*) the accounts basis earned in the accounting year ending in the tax year.

---

6. Any director or senior employee earning £8,500 or over including benefits is liable to tax on a specified number of benefits from the employer, which may or may not be 'money's worth'.

6. What special rules exist for directors and higher-paid employees.

---

7. Yes, directors of unincorporated bodies, or non-profit making bodies, are excluded provided they receive less than £8,500 nor hold a material interest (over 5% of ordinary shares) in the body employing them.

7. Are certain directors excluded from the special rules?

---

8. Where the educational costs of any employee's child are met by a scholarship fund provided by the employer, the employee is taxed on the benefit, if the scholarship was awarded after 13.3.1984.

8. In what circumstances is scholarship income provided through the employment taxable?

---

9. S.189 provides that the expenses qualifying for allowance have to be incurred 'wholly, exclusively and necessarily in the performance of the duties'. The Schedule E rule including the words 'necessarily in the performance' is more stringent.

9. Compare the expenses rule under Schedule E with the one under Schedule D.

---

10. Terminal payments up to £25,000 are exempt, the next £25,000 tax is taxed at 50% of the rates, the next £25,000 at 75% of the rate and any sum over £75,000 is taxed at the full rate.

10. How are 'Golden Handshakes' treated for tax purposes?

---

11. The tax is due on the basis of earnings of the year, but is taxed at source, when payment is made, which may be in a later year.

11. Pay As You Earn is a misnomer. It should be called 'Pay As You Are Paid'. Explain.

---

12. The Code Number for 1985/86 is issued by January, 1985 based on the information contained in the 1984/85 Tax Return, giving the 1983/84 income and allowances due in April, 1984. If circumstances have changed since then, the Code Number is incorrect.

12. The Code Number is often incorrect. Can you explain why?

11
Treatment of Taxed and Untaxed Interest Dividends and Other Income

Interest, annuities and other annual payments are assessable under Case III under S.109, ICTA, 1970.

11.1 Interest-Paid Government Securities and Debentures (S.93, ICTA, 1970)

Interest is paid net after income tax at 30 per cent (basic rate) has been deducted and is deducted by the Bank of England and paid over to the Treasury under Schedule C.

Certain Treasury Stock interest is tax-free if held by owners who are not ordinarily resident in the UK under S.99 (see Table 11.1).

Table 11.1 UK Government Securities exempt under S.99, ICTA, 1970

3½% War Loan, 1952	9% Conversion Stock, 2000
3% Treasury Stock, 1982	9% Treasury Loan, 1994
5½% Funding Stock, 1982/84	9% Treasury Loan, 1992/96
5½% Treasury Stock, 2008/12	9½% Treasury Loan, 1999
5¾% Funding Loan, 1987/91	12½% Treasury Loan, 1993
6% Funding Loan, 1993	12¾% Treasury Loan, 1995
6½% Funding Loan, 1985/87	12¾% Treasury Stock, 1992
6¾% Treasury Loan, 1995/98	13% Treasury Stock, 1990
7¾% Treasury Loan, 2012/15	13¼% Treasury Loan, 1997
7¾% Treasury Loan, 1985/88	13¼% Exchequer Loan, 1996
8% Treasury Loan, 2002/06	13¾% Treasury Loan, 1993
8¼% Treasury Loan, 1987/90	14½% Treasury Stock, 1994
8½% Treasury Loan, 1984/86	15¼% Treasury Loan, 1996
8¼% Treasury Loan, 1997	15½% Treasury Loan, 1998

Local authority securities issued for foreign currency shall, if the Treasury so directs, be issued with interest free of income tax if paid to non-residents, under S.416, ICTA, 1970, which extends the relief given on Government stock to local authority loan stock.

11.2 Assessments under Case III of Schedule D (S.109, ICTA, 1970)

Income paid without deduction of tax and assessed on the recipient includes:

(*a*) Interest on Government securities held on the Post Office register, e.g. War Loan, Development Bonds.

(*b*) Any interest whether yearly or otherwise. This includes on private loans such as mortgages, bank deposit interest, interest from savings banks, including interest from the National Savings Bank (Ordinary Account) where the interest exceeds the £70 exemptions (see 3.6). The most common omission from annual tax returns is untaxed interest—usually the wife's untaxed interest—and this can give rise to long correspondence and the imposition of penalties (see 2.11). In this connection it should be remembered that any bank or financial institution paying more than £15 per annum in untaxed interest is obliged to inform the Inland Revenue, stating name, address and amount concerning the person credited with the interest. From 6.4.1984 bank interest including Giro bank interest, but not National Savings Bank interest, is paid after deduction of the *composite rate* like building society interest.

(*c*) Discounts on Treasury and Trade Bills, which in effect is another form of interest.

(*d*) Small Maintenance Payments. These are payments under a Court Order to a divorced wife, or for the benefit of a child. The payments are up to £33 per week or £143 per month for the wife and £18 per week or £78 per month for each child. If the payments exceed these amounts they are treated as alimony payments and paid *net*.

(*e*) Certain investment income under the **tax avoidance provisions**, etc., which are outside the scope of this book.

11.3 Basis of Assessment (SS. 119 and 120, ICTA, 1970)

(*a*) **In the first year** in which the income arises, the assessment is on the income arising in that year.

(*b*) **In the second year** of assessment, the assessment is based on the income arising in that year, unless it first arose on 6th April of the preceding year.

(*c*) **In the third and subsequent** years of assessment, the assessment is based on the income of the preceding year, except that where the income in the *third year* is less than the income of the *second year*, the assessment can be reduced to the actual income of that year. This option must be exercised within *six* years of the end of the third year of assessment.

(*d*) **The last year** of assessment. In the year in which the Case III source ceases, the assessment is on the income of *that year* and not the *preceding year* and the Inland Revenue has the option of increasing the assessment of the *penultimate year* to the *actual* income, if it exceeds the existing assessment based on the income of the preceding year (S.121, ICTA, 1970).

Readers will notice that the cessation provisions apply only when the source ceases—that is, the War Loan has been sold or the bank deposit account closed. However, if the bank fails to pay interest or the private borrower defaults on his loan obligation, then provided a claim is made within two years after *six years* without income, the last year of income can be treated as *the year in which the income ceased to be received.*

Moreover, if the source producing no income is disposed of after *two years* without income, then the claim to have the last year of income treated as the year of cessation can be made, without waiting for the six years to elapse.

Example 1.1. Hart opened a bank deposit account in July, 1977, and closes it on 31.12.1983. The following interest was credited:

Income		Assessments		
Year to 31.12.1977	£20	1977/78	£20	
Year to 31.12.1978	55	1978/79	55	
Year to 31.12.1979	35	1979/80	35	(reduced to actual)
Year to 31.12.1980	24	1980/81	35	
Year to 31.12.1981	30	1981/82	24	
Year to 31.12.1982	40	1982/83	40	(Revenue option increase to actual)
Year to 31.12.1983	45	1983/84	45	
Total	249		254	

It can be seen that Hart received interest of £249, but was assessed on £254.

11.4 Transferring Untaxed Interest to Taxed Interest

It sometimes pays to transfer National Savings bank deposits to a building society. This is particularly so if higher rates of taxes are involved.

(*a*) Due date for payment of the tax on untaxed interest is 1st January—that is, the tax for 1985/86 has to be paid on 1st January, 1986 unless the amount of interest is too small for separate assessment in which it is taxed under PAYE, by deduction from the Code Number (see 10.20) and is quite often wrongly taxed during the year 1985/86, starting in April, 1985.

(*b*) Due date for payment of higher rates of tax and investment income surcharge for 1984/85 is 1 December, 1985.

Example 11.2 Lever has an income of £20,000 salary in 1985/86 and a Case

III assessment of £650, based on National Savings bank interest received in the year to 31.12.1984. It is suggested to him that closing his bank deposit account in December, 1984 and transferring the money to a building account in December, 1984 and transferring the money to a building society would be beneficial. He is married and the bank interest for the year 1983 was £550 and his taxable income for 1984/85 was salary £19,000 and Case III, Schedule D £550.

The computations are as follows:

(a) No change		*(b) Transfer to building society*	
1984/85 Salary	£19,000	Salary	£19,000
Case III	550	Case III	650
	19,550		19,650
HPA	3,155	Case III £650 × 40 = £260	
	16,395	payable on 1.1.1985	
15,400 × 30% =	4,620	Tax on interest £550 × 40%	
995 × 40% =	398	= £220 payable 1.1.1985	
	5,018		
1985/86 Salary	£20,000	Salary	£20,000
Case III	650	Case III	Nil
	20,650		20,000
HPA	3,455	plus BSI	1,036
	17,195	(gross)	21,036
16,200 × 30% =	4,860	HPA	3,455
995 × 40% =	398		17,581
	5,258	1381 × 40% =	552,40
		Less 1,036 × 30% £310,80	310.80
		Higher Rate Tax	241,60

So by switching the investment one has increased the net return on £10,000 invested from £650—260 = 390 or 3.9% (net) to £1,036 − 414.40 = £621.60 or 6.2%. Moreover, since the tax on the higher rate is not due until 11 months later, the £103.60 would earn interest of say, £10, making the net return 6.3, or 2.4% better—an increase of 61%.

11.5 What Constitutes a New Source under Case III

This question was decided in the case *Hart v. Sangers (1957) 37 TC 231*. Sangster contended that the £2,000,000 put into his existing deposit account was not a new source for basis of assessment under Case III. It was held that this was not so, which means that every time one makes a lodgement in a deposit account—or a withdrawal for that matter—the commencement provisions and cessation provisions, as the case may be, should be applied. In practice, unless the tax involved is material the Inland Revenue will not regard small lodgements and withdrawals as affecting the treatment of the account as a continuous source.

Example 11.3 Ward purchased £1,000 3½% War Loan in May 1979, and another £2,000 in August, 1980. The computation of Case III is as follows:

Interest received	1.6.1979	£17.50
	1.12.1979	17.50
	1.6.1980	17.50
	1.12.1980	17.50
	1.6.1981	17.50
	1.12.1981	52.50
	1.6.1982	52.50
	1.12.1982	52.50
	1.6.1983	52.50
	1.12.1983	52.50

Case III assessments:	1979/80	£35 (CY)
	1980/81	35 (CY)
	1981/82	35 (PY) + £35 (CY) = £70
	1982/83	35 (PY) + £70 (CY) = 105
	1983/84	105 (PY)
	1984/85	105 (PY)

11.6 Taxed Interest, Annuities, Alimony, etc., Paid in Arrears

These payments are covered by SS.52 and 53, ICTA, 1970, and are treated differently if *made out of profits or gains brought into charge* (S.52) and *not made out of profits or gains brought into charge* (S.53).

(*i*) *Taxed annuities etc., paid in arrears and out of profits brought into charge (S.52).*

Example 11.4 Graham had his property purchased by the District Council under compulsory purchase legislation in March 1978. Compensation was disputed, the Council offering £10,000 at the time, which was not accepted. Two years later the offer was increased to £14,000, but payment was not made until 10.5.1983. Under the Land Compensation Act interest was payable for the period March 1978 to May 1983 and subject to deduction of tax. The interest was £9,950 less tax at 30% (£2,985), i.e. £6,965.

Although the interest paid in arrears accrued over five years under S.528(3), ICTA, 1970, it is income of the year 1983/84 and Graham, assuming that he is married with a salary of £10,000 in 1983/84, will be taxed as follows:

1983/84 Salary	£10,000	
Taxed interest	9,950	
	19,950	
Less: Higher personal allowance	2,795	
Taxable	17,155	
	14,600 × 30% =	£4,380
	2,550 × 40%	1,020
Investment Income Surcharge	9,950	
Less: Exemption	7,100	
	1,850 × 15% =	277.50
		5,677.50

Less: tax deducted interest	2,985 +	
PAYE	2,161.50	5,146.50
Tax due		531.00

If the income had been spread over the years it accrued, neither the higher rate nor the Investment Income Surcharge would have been due.

The most common example of payment in arrears is, of course, alimony payments and this has already been referred to (see 4.8). It has been explained that under S.52 the payer is *entitled* to deduct tax, which means that if he omits to deduct tax for whatever reason, he cannot recover it legally.

(*ii*) *Taxed annuities, etc., paid in arrears, not out of profits brought into charge (S.53).*

In such cases the Inland Revenue has to make an assessment on the interest or alimony paid in order to recover the tax which has been deducted from the payment of interest, etc. The deduction of tax in this case is *mandatory* and if not deducted can be recovered by the payer.

Example 11.5 Blue was divorced in April and remarried. In 1983/84, he paid five years' alimony payments of £2,200 (gross), his income being £8,000. The calculations would be as follows:

S.52 assessment: Salary	£8,000 × 30% =	£2,400
Less: tax retained 1979/80	2,200 × 30% =	660
1980/81	2,200 × 30% =	660
1981/82	2,200 × 30% =	660
1982/83	2,200 × 30% =	660 (which more than covers

the tax due, therefore normal assessment £8,000
Less: Higher personal allowance 2,795
Taxable 5,205 × 30% = £1,561.50
(which includes the £660 deducted from the alimony payment)
S53 assessment—Alimony paid £11,000 − 8,000 = £3,000 × 30% = £900
Less: Extra statutory concession 16 £3,000 × 30% 900

The concession reads: 'Where annuities, etc., are paid in a later year than the due year, but in the due year could have been paid wholly or partly out of taxed income, an allowance is made, in fixing the amount to be paid over under Section 53, for the tax which the payer would have been entitled to deduct and retain under Section 52, if the payment had been made at the due dates.'

The divorced Mrs Blue will have to pay tax on the whole £11,000 as received in 1983/84. No allowances lost can be carried forward by concession, but there is no investment income surcharge on alimony payments.

11.7 Dividends

Since the **imputation system** of corporation tax was introduced from 1973/74, dividends are paid net and the company pays **Advance**

Corporation Tax, which appears as tax credits, being $^3/_7$th of the dividend paid.

11.8 Capital Distributions Made in Cash and Scrip Dividend Options

Since 1975/76 if shareholders receive option to purchase shares in place of dividends, the profit made from exercising the option is treated as dividend income. Similarly, if a dividend is declared out of a capital profit—say, a profit made from selling the office building—such dividend is taxable and subject to $^3/_7$th tax credits.

11.9 Miscellaneous Income—Case VI of Schedule D (S.109, ICTA, 1970)

This covers all the income which judges think should be taxed, but which is not mentioned in any other case of Schedule D, or any other Schedule. The more common income assessed under this heading includes:

(*a*) Copyright royalties of authors, composers, etc., where these do not form their main income assessable under Case II of Schedule D.

Unlike patent royalties, copyright royalties are paid gross, but S.389 and 390, ICTA, 1970, give special reliefs to authors and on artists' receipts.

S.389 provides that where an author receives a lump sum for the sale of serial rights, film rights, etc., he can spread the payment over two years, half in the year in which it is received and half in the year before, provided that the work took more than 12 months to prepare. If the preparation of the book took more than 24 months the lump sum can be spread over three years with one third being assessed in the year it was received and one third in each in the two previous years.

S.390 provides that where an author of an established work assigns the copyright therein wholly or partially for at least two years, *ten years* after first publication, the lump sum can be spread *forward* in equal instalments for up to *six* years, starting with the year of assessment in which the sum is received. (This is similar to the assessment of the capital profit on the sale of a patent right—see 7.6).

(*b*) Recovery of allowances given in excess. This arises when a dependent relative dies, no tax return has been issued and it is not discovered until later that the allowance has been carried forward by mistake. Similar cases can arise with other allowances.

(*c*) Certain 'anti-avoidance' assessments, e.g. tax reliefs obtained from artificial formation and liquidation of companies, etc.

(*d*) Income from furnished lettings if this income does not form part of a boarding house, when Case II would apply. This is probably the most common Case VI assessment found (see Example 5.1).

(*e*) Certain underwriting and insurance commissions—casual income not assessable under Case II.

(*f*) Income from guaranteeing loans and dealing in futures.

(*g*) Post-cessation receipts (SS. 143–151, ICTA, 1970). This arises where a business account has been prepared on the *receipts* (or cash) basis and not the normal earnings basis. In other words, there are no debtors, since credit is not given. This particularly applies to barristers, who under their rules do not sue for their fees and therefore have no debtors. The client does not deal with the barrister direct, but through a solicitor who sends out the bill. If there is default in payment, no legal action follows, but readers should not assume that there are no sanctions for non-payment, since once defaulted a person will find it most difficult to find a barrister to act for him in the future.

For tax purposes fees earned but not paid are excluded from the account and fees paid after the barrister ceased to practice were not taxable until these sections were introduced. It was possible therefore for a barrister to cease practice and accept a directorship in a large company and his post-cessation receipts from the practice would be tax-free. What happens now is that post-cessation receipts can either be added to the Case II assessment during the year of cessation or be assessed in the year they are received under Case VI; the taxpayer has the choice in each case.

11.10 Furnished Holiday Letting (S.50 and Schedule 12, FA, 1984)

The new provision enables income from letting furnished holiday accommodation be treated as trading income with effect from 6.4.1982. The advantage is, of course, that trading income is *earned income*, which for 1982/83 and 1983/84 may otherwise be liable to investment income surcharge, and from 1984/85 onwards it still qualifies for WEIR (Wife's Earned Income Relief), also perhaps most important, a trading loss can be set off against other income under S.168. Lastly, such income also qualifies for capital allowances and retirement annuity relief. It is assessed under Case VI on the current year's basis, but the tax is payable in two instalments on 1 January and 1 July each year.

The following conditions must be met for the income to qualify:

(*i*) The accommodation must be available for letting to the public, generally as holiday accommodation, on a commercial basis for at least 140 days per year, not necessarily consecutively; and
(*ii*) Must be let for at least 70 days; and
(*iii*) For a period comprising at least 7 months (which need not be

continuous, but must include the 70 days mentioned in (*ii*) above) during which it is not normally in the same occupation for a continuous period exceeding 31 days.

11.11 Basis Period for Case VI (S.125, ICTA, 1970)

Under S.125 the assessment *shall be computed either on the full amount of the profits arising in the year of assessment or according to an average of such period, not being greater than one year, as the case may require and as may be directed by the Inspector*. The actual wording of the section has been given to show that the Inspector has wider powers under Case VI than under any other Case or Schedule. This power is, however, subject to appeal to both General or Special Commissioners and the *Commissioners shall have jurisdiction to review* the Inspector's decision under this section.

In practice, where income is casual the basis of assessment adopted is the current year, and where the source is continuous—e.g. a furnished letting where the owner is overseas for a number of years—the previous year's basis will be more convenient and, during an inflationary period, advantageous to the taxpayer.

The due date of payment of Case VI tax for 1983/84 is 1.1.1984.

11.12 Case VI Losses (S.176, ICTA, 1970)

Case VI losses can be set against Case VI income of the same year and any balance can be carried forward.

Example 11.6 Melchett has gone abroad for five years and lets his house furnished. He agreed with the Inspector that PY basis should apply:

Income	£	*Assessment*	£
Year to 31.3.1979	500	1978/79 CY	500
Year to 31.3.1980	650	1979/80 PY	500
Year to 31.3.1981 Loss	800	1980/81 PY	650
Year to 31.3.1982	750	1981/82 PY Loss	Nil
Year to 31.3.1982	900	1982/83 £750—loss £750	Nil
Year to 31.3.1984	850	1983/84 PY 900—loss £50	850
		1984/85 PY	850

The loss cannot be carried back nor set against non-Case VI income.

11.13 Claw-back of Life Assurance Reliefs (S.7, FA, 1975)

Life assurance relief was mentioned briefly under Section 3.2(j), but since an endowment policy qualifies if taken out before 14.3.1984 for life assurance relief and is a form of saving out of untaxed income, its use must be restricted. The conditions for a policy to qualify are as follows:

(*a*) The policy must be for a term of at least 10 years.

(*b*) The premium must be paid by the claimant or his wife.

(*c*) Premiums paid in any one year must not be more than *twice* the total amount payable in any other year.

(*d*) The contract must be with an insurance company, underwriter or registered friendly society, legally established within the Commonwealth or Eire, or lawfully carrying on business in the UK.

(*e*) Premiums qualifying for relief must not exceed *one sixth* of the total income of £1,500, and the capital sum insured must not be less than 75 per cent of the total premiums payable.

If the qualifying policy is surrendered within four years, the Inland Revenue will claw-back some or all of the tax relief previously given, subject to a ceiling.

Table 11.1 Tax relief claw-back

Time of surrender	*Claw-back*	*Ceiling*
In the first two years	15%	Surrender value less 85%
In the third year	10%	Surrender value less 90%
In the fourth year	5%	Surrender value less 95%

The life assurance company deducts the claw-back subject to the ceiling from the surrender value and pays it over to the Inland Revenue.

11.14 Chargeable Event on Non-qualifying Policies and Bonds

If a life policy does not fulfil the requirements under Section 11.13:

(*a*) No 15 per cent relief is given on the premiums, and

(*b*) A charge is made on the *gain*, which is the excess of the surrender value over the premiums paid. This charge is at the higher rates only and not at the basic rate. In other words, the basic rate taxpayer is not affected.

(*c*) Top-slicing relief is available (see 5.9). Under this provision the gain can be spread over the period of the policy.

Example 11.7 Hartley, a married man, purchased a bond in April 1978 for £10,000 and cashes it in May, 1985 for £14,000. His salary in 1985/86 was

£9,000 and his investment income £3,000. The position would be as follows:

Salary	£9,000
Investment income	3,000
Chargeable gain	4,000
Total income	16,000
Higher personal allowance	3,455
	12,545

There is no liability to higher rates or tax, therefore the chargeable gain is not charged at all.

Example 11.8 Assume that Hartley's investment income is £9,000. His total income becomes £21,000—HPA = £17,545. He is liable at 40%, which can be avoided by applying for top-slicing relief:

Salary	£9,000
Investment income	9,000
⅕ chargeable gain	800
Total	18,800— HPA £3,455 = £15,345—Exempt

11.15 Revision Test

Answers	*Questions*
1. War Loan, Treasury Stock, Funding Loan, and Conversion Stock.	**1.** What securities are exempt under S.99, if held by 'not ordinarily resident individuals'?
2. Bank deposit interest is no longer normally, paid gross. The 'composite rate' (CRT) about 26% is paid by the banks as it has been for many years by building societies. The individual's net income is grossed up at 30% for the purpose of the Return. No repayment of the tax deducted is possible. The CRT does not apply to non-residents, companies, clubs, etc.	**2.** Bank deposit interest is treated differently, after 6.4.1985. Explain.
3. The difference occurs in the third year of assessment and in the penultimate and pre-penultimate year of assessment. In effect the accounting period is not relevant in Cases III–V.	**3.** What are the differences in the basis periods comparing Cases I and II and Cases III–V?

4. Hart v. Sangster (1957) 37 TC 231 established that each lodgement in the National Savings Bank etc., represents a new source, but this rule is not applied if the figure is small.	**4.** What constitutes a new source under Case III of Schedule D?
5. Yes, the most frequent case is that of alimony paid in arrears, which can result in the recipient losing one or more years personal allowances.	**5.** When an annual payment is late, can a loss of allowances result?
6. Copyright royalties paid to authors, composers, etc., are normally not paid under deduction of tax. Lump sums paid to authors qualify for special relief.	**6.** How are copyright royalties treated compared with patent royalties?
7. It is either the current year or the preceding year whichever is more convenient.	**7.** What is the basis of assessment under Case VI?
8. Furnished Holiday Letting can be treated as trading income assessable under Case VI on a current year basis, provided certain conditions are met.	**8.** Furnished Holiday Lettings are treated differently from 1982/83 onwards. Explain?
9. They normally arise in the case of barristers, but can apply to other people, who receive income after the trade has been discontinued. They can be assessed under Case VI in the year of receipt or as trading income in the last year of trading.	**9.** Post-cessation receipts. How do they arise and how are they taxed?
10. If the policy is surrendered within 4 years of being taken out. The 'claw-back' is on a sliding scale.	**10.** In what circumstances does a 'claw-back' arise when a qualifying life insurance policy is surrendered?

11. The 'chargeable event' occurs when an 'income bond' matures or is surrendered. These bonds do not suffer income tax on interest when it is accumulated.

11. What is meant by the 'chargeable event'?

---

12. The charge is made on the gain—excess of value over cost at time of surrender. It is taxed on higher rates only, the basic rate taxpayer being exempt. The taxpayer can claim top-slicing relief.

12. How is the 'chargeable event' taxed?

12
Treatment of Foreign Income and Non-Residents

Foreign income of UK residents (to be defined later) is subject to UK income tax in the following ways.

12.1 Income Assessed Directly on the Recipient (S.109, ICTA, 1970)

(*a*) Case IV of Schedule D applies to interest on overseas securities, other than those where tax is deducted from the interest at source.

(*b*) Case V of Schedule D applies to income from overseas possessions, which covers all income not covered by Case IV, and dividends which have tax deducted at source and salaries and wages which are taxed under Schedule E (see 10.1).

The distinction between Case IV and V has ceased to be of practical importance, and income falling under either Case IV is treated in the same way.

12.2 Basis of Assessment (S.122, ICTA, 1970)

Normally the basis of assessment is exactly the same as for Case III Schedule D (see 11.3), except if the recipient is (*a*) an individual not *domiciled* in the UK or (*b*) a British subject, or citizen of the Republic of Ireland, not *ordinarily resident* in the UK, the assessment is on the *remittance* basis, except that income from whatever source in the Republic of Ireland is assessed on the *arising* basis (as for Case III).

Table 12.1 Basis of Assessment—Case IV and V.

Year of assessment	*Arising basis*	*Remittance basis*
1	Actual income	Amount remitted in year
2	Actual income	Amount remitted in year

Year of assessment	*Arising basis*	*Remittance basis*
3	Income of preceding year with option to reduce to actual income.	Remittances of preceding year with taxpayer's option to reduce to actual remittance.
4 and subsequent	Income of preceding year.	Amount remitted in preceding year.
Penultimate year	Income of preceding year with Revenee option to increase to actual.	Amount remitted in preceding year with Revenue option to increase to actual.
Final year	Actual income	Amount remitted in year.

The following further deductions apply, which are not available under Case III:

(*a*) Income from trades carried on and controlled abroad qualify for a 25 per cent deduction (S.122, FA, 1974). This allowance was reduced to 12½ per cent for 1984/85 and abolished after 5.4.1985.

(*b*) A self-employed individual trading partly abroad qualifies for a 25 per cent deduction, provided more than 30 days are spent abroad (see 6.8). The allowance is calculated on a time basis in the same way as under Schedule E (see 10.3). This allowance was reduced to 12½ per cent for 1984/85 and abolished after 5.4.1985.

Example 12.1 Wilson, an import and export trader, spends 60 days abroad in 1983/84 on business. His accounts for the year to 31.12.1982 have been agreed with the Inspector and the assessment for 1983/84 under Case I of Schedule D is as follows:

Taxable Profit		£35,000
Less: Stock relief (see 6.9)	£1,350	
Capital allowances	4,500	5,850
		29,150

Overseas trade relief $\frac{60}{365} \times 29{,}150 \times 25\% = £1{,}198$

1983/84 assessment £29,150 − 1,198 = £27,952

It will be noted that the allowance is based on travel in the year 1983/84 and not travel in the year to 31.12.1982 (the accounts year).

(*c*) Foreign pensions qualify for 10 per cent deductions (see 10.5) unless the 50 per cent deduction applies.

(*d*) Income on an arising basis, which cannot be remitted because of restrictions imposed by the overseas country (S.148, ICTA, 1970).

(*e*) No tax arises on income where remittance is delayed (S.419).

Under this provision, if the taxpayer can show that part of the income remitted arose in an earlier year, when it could not be remitted in spite of *reasonable endeavour*, the income can be treated as income of the year in which it arose. The time limit for a claim under S.419, ICTA, 1970, is *six years* after the end of the year of assessment in which the remittance occurred.

12.3 Double Tax Relief (SS. 497–518, ICTA, 1970)

The UK has entered into agreements with other countries to prevent the same income being taxed in both countries. Thus rent received by a UK resident from letting property in the USA will be liable to income tax in the USA and to UK income tax under Case V of Schedule D. In these circumstances the tax is confined to the higher of the two taxes, and any excess is given as **double taxation relief.**

Certain other overseas income of UK residents is exempt in the country of origin on a reciprocal basis, e.g. German and Austrian pensions (under S.12.1(c)) are not subject to tax abroad. Similarly, foreign employees working in the UK who are resident in the overseas country but not resident in the UK and not physically present in the UK for more than 183 days (which would make them resident), are exempt from UK tax on earnings from an overseas employer. In case of doubt the actual Double Taxation Agreement should be examined.

Example 12.2 Jones, a married man his UK earnings in 1984/85 were £15,000 and foreign income from property of £1,200 on which £300 foreign tax was paid. He is *resident, ordinarily resident* and *domiciled* in the UK. The computation is as follows:

(*a*) *Tax on total income*		
Salary	£15,000	
Income from property	1,200	(foreign tax £300)
	16,200	
Personal allowance	3,155	
Taxable income	13,045 × 30%	= £3,912.50
(*b*) *Tax on UK income alone*		
Salary	£15,000	
Personal allowance	1,155	
Taxable income	11,845 × 30%	= £3,553.50
Difference		360.00

Therefore the final liability to UK tax is £3,913.50—foreign tax £300 = £3,613.50. If the foreign tax had been £400, the allowance would have been £360 (£3,913.50 − 360 = £3,553.50).

12.4 Double Tax Relief on Dividends Paid Through an Agent

As explained under Section 12.2, dividends from foreign companies are subject to UK tax under Case V of Schedule D on the arising basis, if the recipient is *resident* and *domiciled* in the UK. Double tax relief is usually given by the paying agent, e.g. the British branch of a foreign bank.

Example 12.3 The agent receives from a company in the USA a dividend gross £50. The voucher issued to the shareholder in 1984/85 will be:

Dividend declared	£50
Less: US withholding tax at 15 per cent	7.50
Received by agent	42.50
Less: UK tax at 30% less provisional tax	
Credit relief: £42.50 grossed at 15% (30–15)	7.50
Received by shareholder	35.00

The agent assumed that the *net UK effective rate* is more than 15 per cent and has effectively allowed the lower of the two taxes suffered. A sharcholder who is exempt from UK tax will be able to claim back the UK tax paid £7.50, but not the US tax of £7.50. Similarly, if the taxpayer is liable at the higher rate, he will be charged further UK tax in due course.

Example 12.4 AC, a married man with a salary of £18,000, received dividends from an American company of £1,000 paid through an agent.

Dividends	£1,000		
Less: US withholding tax 15%	150		
Received by agent	850		
Less: UK provisional tax			
(after DTR) 15%	150		
Received by shareholder	700		
Tax position for 1984/85 Salary		£18,000	
US dividend		1,000	
		19,000	
Less: Personal allowance		3,155	
Taxable income		15,845	
		15,400 at 30% =	£4,620
		445 at 40% =	178
			4,798
Less: American tax suffered			150
Tax due			4,648

12.5 Unilateral Relief (S.498, ICTA, 1970)

Foreign taxes can also be repaid even if no bilateral agreement exists between the UK and the country where the income of a UK resident is taxed. This relief is on the same lines as the treaty relief. For individuals there is practically no difference, and such differences as exist fall outside the scope of this book.

12.6 Alimony

The Inland Revenue have granted an Extra-Statutory Concession A12 (see Revenue Leaflet IR1) to give *double tax relief* where alimony or small maintenance payments are paid under a UK Court Order or agreement, the income arises from a UK source, regardless of the country of residence of the payer. Notwithstanding that the source is in law a UK source, relief by way of credit is, however, allowed, where:

(*a*) The individual making the payments has left the UK and become resident in an overseas country.

(*b*) The payments are made out of that individual's income in that country and are subject to tax there.

(*c*) UK income tax, if deducted from the payments, has been duly accounted for.

(*d*) The recipient is resident in the UK and effectively bears the overseas tax.

12.7 Residence (SS.49–51, ICTA, 1970)

S.49 and S.50 deal with individuals living in the UK and going abroad, whilst S.51 deals with overseas visitors coming to live in the UK. S.49 provides that a temporary absence abroad does not affect the UK resident status of the individual going abroad. 'Temporary' is defined as occasional. This statutory definition would make it difficult for a UK resident to shed his residence for the part of the year in which he leaves the country. Extra-Statutory Concession 11, however, provides that if he ceases to reside in the UK if he has left for permanent residence abroad, liability to UK tax which is affected by residence is computed by reference to the period of his residence here during the year. In other words, if an individual emigrates on 1.1.1984, he will be resident not for the whole year, 1983/84 but only for the period 6.4.1983 to 31.12.1983, and *non-resident* for the period from 1.1.1984.

S.51 provides that a **temporary visitor** to the UK is not liable to UK tax unless he has spent *six months* in any income tax year in the country. The term 'temporary' was defined in the case *Loewenstein v. De Salis (1926) 10 TC 424*, when it was held that a Belgian subject who visited the UK each year and occupied a hunting box belonging to a company of which he was a director and owned 90 per cent of the shares was resident. In no year was he in the UK for a total period of six months. In other words, an individual who keeps an abode in this country for his use becomes resident in any year in which he visits this abode. However, Extra-Statutory Concession 11 provides that where an individual (*a*) *comes to the UK to take up permanent residence or to stay for at least three years*, or (*b*) *comes to the UK to take up* *employment which is expected to last for a period of at least two years*, liability to UK tax which is affected by residence is computed by reference to the period of his residence here during the year. In other words, if a German comes to London to take up three years' employment on 1.8.1983 he will be treated as *resident* from 1.8.1983 and not for the whole of 1983/84.

The meaning of 'temporary' in S.51 was the subject of the decision in *Lysaght v. CIR (1928) 13 TC 511*, which concerned a director of a company who sold his house in England and went to live in Ireland, but returned to England each month for directors' meetings, remaining for about a week's stay in hotels. He was held to be *resident*, since his regular visits were not temporary, but part of his life style.

In practice the Inland Revenue interpret the meaning of *temporary* in the light of the case law, that if an individual visits the UK for *four* years in succession spending more than *three months* but less than *six months* in the country, each year his visits will be regarded as no longer temporary in the *fifth* year, when he will be treated as resident.

To summarise the position, an individual is **regarded as resident** in the UK for income tax purposes unless:

(*a*) He visits the UK for some *temporary* purpose only.

(*b*) He visits the UK without intending to maintain or establish a place of abode (home).

(*c*) He stays in the UK for less than *six months* in the year of assessments.

In order to be treated as **non-resident** and escape UK tax liability on foreign income all three tests have to be satisfied. Residence, moreover, is determined for each person separately, and a husband can be non-resident while the wife is resident.

12.8 Ordinarily Resident (S.122(2), ICTA, 1970)

'Ordinarily resident' means habitually resident in a country. It is possible for an individual to be ordinarily resident but not resident in the UK, for example, when going for a trip up the Amazon for eighteen months. More common is the case where the individual is resident but not ordinarily resident in the UK, which arises whenever an overseas visitor stays in the UK for more than six months. The matter of ordinarily resident has limited significance and is important only in respect of a British subject or citizen of the Republic of Ireland, who if not ordinarily resident pays tax under Case IV and V on the remittance basis.

Readers will appreciate that it is quite possible to be resident for tax purposes in more than one country, but that one can be ordinarily (habitually) resident in only one country.

12.9 Domicile

An individual's domicile is essentially the country which he looks on as his natural homeland. This is quite distinct from legal nationality and from residence. Together with the concept of residence, domicile has considerable effect on tax liability. It enables many wealthy people who have lived in the UK treating it as a tax haven. Paul Getty, reputedly the most wealthy person in the world at the time, lived permanently in the UK. As an American by birth, he was not domiciled in the UK and liable only to UK taxes on the remittance basis. Moreover, provided he ensured that he only transferred capital sums and not income, he could have lived quite comfortably in the UK without paying any UK income tax.

Domicile is the country one regards as one's natural home; it is the country to which one wishes to return after long absences. Each individual has only one domicile' even though one can have two or even more nationalities.

(*a*) **Domicile of birth.** Each person starts with a domicile of birth, which is normally his father's domicile at the time of birth. In the case of an illegitimate child it is the domicile of the mother at the time. The domicile of origin is not easily shaken off and the fact that an individual is resident for some years in the UK does not establish the fact that he exercised his choice and assumed a domicile of choice.

(*b*) **Domicile of choice.** This is acquired by an adult who leaves his country of birth for another country in which he resides and wishes to make his permanent home. The leading case is the decision in *CIR v. Cohen (1937) 21 TC 301*, in which the taxpayer contended that although he was born in England in 1860, he had lived in Australia between 1878 and 1910 and had acquired a domicile of choice. After 1911 he came back to England and travelled widely in Europe for health reasons, making England his headquarters, but living in hotels and not establishing residence in the UK for any length of time. It was held that the taxpayer's contention was not correct. The learned judge expressed himself as follows: 'I base my decision upon the view that his domicile of origin was English and there is not enough to satisfy the onus, admittedly a heavy onus, which rests upon him to show that the domicile of origin was lost.'

(*c*) **Derived domicile.** Certain dependent individuals are regarded as incapable of choosing their domicile and for this reason infants (children under 18) assume the domicile of the father if legitimate and domicile of the mother if illegitimate. Before 1.1.1974 a married woman assumed the domicile of the husband on marriage and this still applies to all marriages before that date. After that date the Domicile and Matrimonial Proceedings Act, 1973, applies and the wife's domicile is ascertained separately, *by reference to the same factors as in the case of any other individual capable of having an independent domicile.* Moreover, an American woman who married a husband with UK domicile before 1.1.1974 is treated as if the marriage had taken place after 1.1.1974 as provided in the Double Taxation Agreement. Lastly, a widow retains her husband's domicile unless she acquires a different domicile of choice.

Table 12.2. The Effects of Domicile and Residence

Income	*Basis of assessment*
Schedule D, Cases I and II	75% arising basis before 5.4.84
Case III	100% unless exempt for non-residents
Case IV and V	Arising basis; remittance basis if not domiciled
Employments (foreign)	75% arising basis 50% if not domiciled before 5.4.1984
UK income	Subject to S.27 Relief if received by non-resident
Foreign Pension	90% of arising basis, but if not domiciled remittance basis.

12.10 Husband and Wife

It has already been stated that a wife's residence is independent of that of her husband and if the husband is employed full-time, say, in the Middle East and his wife goes with him, but returns before she has been away for a complete year to live in their family home, she will remain resident in the UK for that year, but the husband will be non-resident. In this situation husband and wife are treated as separate individuals, unless this is to their disadvantage. Normally, it means that the wife's investment income is not added to the husband's, but assessed separately on the wife, who is entitled to the Lower Personal Allowance £2,005 for 1984/85. In fact it pays for the husband to transfer bank deposit accounts, etc., in his name to the wife before undertaking a lengthy foreign employment and this should also be done with deposit accounts, etc., in their joint names.

12.11 Taxation of Non-residents

The basic rule is that a non-resident individual is taxable on UK income, but not entitled to tax-free personal allowances and is not liable at all on foreign income.

(*a*) **Income from employments.** The rule here is that a non-resident's earnings are taxed in the UK as far as they are attributable to any duties of the employment which are performed in the UK. In cases where duties are partly carried on in the UK and partly overseas, separate contracts should be drawn up to deal with each, since under a separate contract the foreign income will escape UK tax, but without it the Inland Revenue may need convincing.

In this connection it is important to note that the *place at which the duties are performed* is crucial and not generally the time spent in the UK. If the duties are normally performed overseas, a visit to the UK of an overseas representative to receive instructions from his employer would normally be regarded by the Inland Revenue as *incidental* and not changing the status that the duties of the employment are performed overseas. On the other hand, it would not be regarded as incidental if a company director visits the UK to attend board meetings, since the duties of a company director attending a board meeting in London are carried out in London. Similarly, a courier visiting London with a party of American tourists who were going on to other countries would be regarded as performing his duties in London and not incidental to his foreign place of employment.

(*b*) **UK investment income.** Basically, a non-resident is taxable in the UK on all income from UK sources, except certain interest which is exempt (see 11.1). Dividends and non-exempt debenture interest is subject to Double Tax Relief under the Treaties and is given in the following way:

Example 12.5 A French shareholder receives a dividend from a UK company in 1985/86 of £70 and since it is subject to Tax Credit of £30, he will get Double Tax Relief as follows:

Dividend		£70
Plus Tax Credit	£30	
Less Double Tax Relief	15	15
French shareholder receives		85

Readers will notice that the French shareholder is treated exactly in the same way as the UK resident shareholder was treated on his foreign dividend (Example 12.4).

(*c*) Personal allowances (S.27, ICTA, 1970). Personal reliefs are given under S.5, ICTA, 1970, to individuals who claim them, but the annual tax return, which is the means of claiming these allowances, is not issued to non-residents. It follows therefore that these allowances are not available to non-residents, except under S.27. To qualify for relief under S.27 the non-resident must be:

(*i*) A British subject, including Commonwealth subjects or citizens of the Republic of Ireland, or

(*ii*) A person who is or has been in the service of the Crown, or

(*iii*) A person employed in the service of any missionary society.

(*iv*) A person employed in the service of any territory under Her Majesty's protection, or

(*v*) A resident of the Channel Islands or the Isle of Man, or

(*vi*) A former UK resident who is resident abroad for the sake of his health or the health of a member of his family resident with him, or

(*vii*) A widow whose late husband was in Crown service, or

(*viii*) A resident or national of a country with which the UK has a double taxation agreement providing for this relief. These countries are:

Austria	France	Japan	Singapore
Belgium	West Germany	Kenya	South Africa
Burma	Greece	Luxembourg	South West Africa (Namibia)
Denmark	Indonesia	Netherlands	Swaziland
Faroe Islands	Irish Republic	Netherland Antilles	Sweden
Finland	Israel	Norway	Switzerland
Fiji	Italy	Portugal	Zambia

A British woman married to a national of another country cannot claim to be a British subject for S.27 relief, because claims are dealt with in relation to the husband's status.

The S.27 relief amounts to personal allowances being given to the extent of the proportion the UK income bears to the total income:

Example 12.6 Todd is a British subject resident in France. He receives dividends from UK companies of £2,114 in 1984/85 and War Loan interest £70. His income in France, all earned, was £5,330. He subscribes £14 under covenant to a British charity and pays a premium of £25 p.a. on a policy on his life taken out in 1978, capital sum £1,000 to a British assurance company. Todd is married with two children under 11.

(*a*) *UK tax liability without claim under S.27*

Liable income: Dividend £2,114 + Tax credit £906 =		£3,020	
Less: Covenanted payment to charity		20	at 30% £6
Taxable income		3,000	
Tax due		906	
Tax paid		906	

(b) *S.27 Claim*

Liable income as under (*a*)		3,000	
Non-liable income:			
French salary	£5,330		
War Loan (Exempt S.99)	70	5,400	

World income		8,400
Less: Higher personal allowance	£3,155	
Life assurance	10	3,165
Taxable		5,235 at 30% = £1,570.50
Tax paid (tax credits)		906
Less proportion due on UK income	$\frac{3,000}{8,400}$ 1,570.50 =	560.89
Tax repayment (S.27 relief)		345.11

It will be noted that life assurance relief for non-residents is not given by deduction from the premium, but in the assessment.

12.12 Revision Test

Answers	*Questions*
1. Case IV deals with income from foreign securities, Case V with income from foreign possessions. The distinction is historical only, both incomes are treated in the same way.	**1.** Distinguish between Case IV and V and state the significance of the distinction?
2. It is the same as for Case III except that individuals not 'ordinarily resident' or 'domiciled' in the UK are assessed on the 'remittance' basis.	**2.** What is the basis of assessment for Case IV and V?
3. The 25% allowance has been reduced to 12½ per cent for 1984/85 and abolished from 5.4.1985.	**3.** What changes did the FA, 1984, make to the 'Special Allowances' for foreign trades, and traders going abroad?
4. Double Taxation Relief is given on foreign income, which is liable to UK tax if received by a resident, and is taxed in the country of origin as well. The relief is the lower of the two taxes.	**4.** Can you explain the term 'Double Taxation Relief'?
5. The dividend is normally paid through an agent of the foreign company in the UK. This agent (usually a bank) gives provisional DTR to the extent of the foreign	**5.** How is 'Double Taxation Relief' given on dividends from a foreign company received by a UK resident?

withholding tax, if less than UK tax.

---

6. This is 'Double Tax Relief' on income from a foreign country with whom the UK does not have a Double Tax Agreement. Normally, it is given in the same way as DTR.

6. What is meant by the term 'Unilateral Relief'?

---

7. An individual is treated as 'resident' in the UK unless he can satisfy all the following conditions:
(i) He visits the UK for a 'temporary' purpose only,
(ii) He visits without intending to maintain a place of abode,
(iii) He stays for less than 6 months in a year of assessment.

7. What do you understand by the term 'resident' in the UK in relation to income tax?

---

8. The Inland Revenue regard an individual, who visits the UK for annual periods of 3 months, but less than 6 months for 4 consecutive years as becoming resident in the 5th year.

8. When does a 'temporary visit' cease to be so regarded?

---

9. 'Ordinarily Resident' means habitually resident. An individual can be resident in more than one country, but not 'Ordinarily Resident'.

9. Explain the term 'Ordinarily Resident'

---

10. 'Domicile' is the country an individual regards as his natural home. It is the country one wishes to return to after long absence. Each individual has only one 'domicile'.

10. Explain the term 'Domicile'.

---

11. A 'non-resident' is taxable on his UK income only and is not entitled to tax-free personal allowances.

11. How are 'non-resident' individuals taxed?

---

12. S.27 relief is broadly given to non-resident British subjects, which

12. Can you explain S.27, ICTA, 1970 and who can claim it?

includes Commonwealth and Irish citizens. They are given part of the tax-free personal allowances in terms of tax, on the basis of the proportion the UK income bears to the 'World Income'.

13
The Treatment of Settlements and Trusts

The easiest way to reduce one's tax liability is to give away the source of the income, and parents have from time immemorial given away their assets to their children to make sure that their savings are not swallowed up by the Inland Revenue and also that the individuals for whom the money is intended in fact get it. Indeed, it is generally good advice for people to make a **Will** and lodge it with a bank to make sure that assets are disposed of in the manner intended. Settlement (trusts) can be created under a will or during one's life-time.

13.1 Tax Liability of the Deceased (SS.40 and 74, TMA, 1970)

When an individual dies income tax must be settled on all his income up to the date of death by his or her executors.

Example 13.1 Brown died on 5 January, 1985, at the age of 71 leaving his widow. His income for the period 6.4.1984 to 5.1.1985 was as follows:

Occupational pension		£5,600	taxed under PAYE £1,680
National retirement pension (including wife's)		1,760	
Dividends + tax credits (self)		3,400	
Dividends + tax credits (wife)		850	
Building society interest (wife)		350	
Bank deposit interest 1983/84 (self)		75	
Period 6.4.84 to 5.1.85 £45		45	
(*a*) 1984/85 assessment on Mr Brown's pensions		7,360	
Dividends (husband + wife)		4,250	
Building society interest (gross)		500	
Case III Schedule D (see Section 11.3)		45	
		£12,155	
Less: Personal allowance	£3,155		
Building society interest	500	3,655	
		8,500	× 30% = £2,550
Less: Tax paid PAYE	1,680		
Tax credits	1,275		2,995

Tax repayment		405

(*b*) Mrs Brown's position for 1984/85 is as follows:

Widow's pension		£445
Husband's occupational pension		800
Dividends (gross)		900
		2,145
Less: Personal allowance	£2,005	
Widow's bereavement allowance	1,150	3,155
Taxable		Nil
Tax paid on dividends		£270which is repayable.

13.2 Deceased Estates (SS.426–433, ICTA, 1970)

Under a Will beneficiaries are either **residuary legatees**—that is they have an absolute claim to the estate—or have a **life interest.** The most common form of arrangement is for the widow to receive a life interest in the estate—that is, receive the income—whilst the assets are held in trust until her passing, when the estate is divided among the children, who are the residuary legatees.

Income during the administration period. As soon as the person dies, bank accounts etc., are frozen and the executors have to deal with all financial matters. During the administration period sums paid to a beneficiary are treated as income of the beneficiary and, provided the whole of the estate is distributed, the income left over after fees, etc., have been paid is divided among the residuary legatees in accordance with the terms of the Will and will be treated as income of the beneficiaries in the period in which the income was received. The income is treated as having been received under deduction of tax and in the case of dividends, etc., the gross amount received has to be included in the annual return.

13.3 Treatment of Trustees

In all cases where under a Will the trustees have to administer the assets and the beneficiary receives a life interest, or where the settlor is still living, the trustees are charged with the tax and distribute the *net income* together with a Form 185E (Certificate of payment made and tax deducted before payment). Trustees are also liable to capital transfer tax, capital gains tax, capital gains tax and development land tax (all outside the scope of this book).

Example 13.2 Assume Anne, a widow, has a life interest in her late husband's estate and receives £1,750 from the trustees in 1984/85. The R185E gives the following particulars.

Income	*Basic rate of tax*	*Net amount of beneficiary's share of trust income*
£	£	£
2,000	600	1,400
	Building society interest	350
		1,750

Assuming that Anne's only other income is a widow's pension of £1,380, the computation will be as follows:

Pension		£1,380	
Trust income		2,000	
Building society interest (gross)		500	
		3,880	
Less: Personal allowance	£2,005		
Building society interest	500	2,505	
Taxable income		1,375×30%=£412.50	
Tax deducted R185E			600.00
Repayment			187.50

(*a*) **Assessment of untaxed income of a trust.** Untaxed income under Schedule A (rent) and Schedule D are normally assessed on the trustee, but if the income is paid direct to the beneficiary without deduction of tax the beneficiary pays the tax.

(*b*) **Expenses of administering the trust.** These expenses are not allowed in the assessments on the trustee, but deducted in arriving at the sums paid to the beneficiaries.

Example 13.3 John administers a trust set up by his deceased brother, the income to be shared among his brothers' three children. The income of the trust for 1984/85 was as follows:

Rent of £1,000 from letting an unfurnished house. During the year he paid £80 in repairs and £100 to the agent for collecting the rent, etc.; dividends from UK companies £1,050; and War Loan interest received £140. The 1984/85 trust statement is as follows:

Schedule A £1,000—expenses £180	=		£820
Dividends (gross) 10/7 × £1,050	=		1,500
Schedule D Case III (War Loan)	=		140
Income			2,460
Less: Trustee's expenses (gross)		£50	
Tax £2,460 × 30%		738	788
Distributable income one third each			1,672

13.4 Trusts where the Settlor is Still Living

Such settlements are quite common and are attractive from the point of view of capital transfer tax as well as income tax. In order to be effective these settlements must satisfy the following conditions:

(*a*) The settlement must be for a period of more than six years (S.434, ICTA, 1970), but see 3.9(f)—covenants in favour of charities.

(*b*) The settlement must be **irrevocable** (SS.445 and 446, ICTA, 1970). If the settlor or his wife has the right to revoke any part of the settlement, it is ignored. If this were not so, settlements would be a very easy form of tax avoidance.

(*c*) The settlor must not retain any interest in the settlement (S.447, ICTA, 1970). So long as the settlor retains an interest in the settlement, any income derived from it is regarded as his income. Once again a necessary provision to prevent tax avoidance.

13.5 Settlement by a Parent in Favour of Own Child (S.437, ICTA, 1970)

Income is treated as that of the parent while the child is unmarried and under eighteen. It should be noted that a settlement by a grandparent, or brother or sister qualifies. Moreover, if the income of a settlement does not exceed £5 and is an irrevocable settlement under which the income is accumulated and the parent is not resident in the UK for tax purposes, the settlement is not ignored.

13.6 Accumulation Settlements for Children (S.438, ICTA, 1970)

The most common form of creating a trust for the benefit of one's own minor children which enables one not to be assessed on the income tax is the **accumulation trust.** Under such a settlement the income is accumulated for each child until at least the age of 18. In this way a parent who is liable at a marginal rate of tax of 60 per cent on his investment income can settle sufficient capital in an **irrevocable** accumulation trust, which enables him to escape tax at 75 per cent but the trustees will be liable to tax at the basis rate of 30 per cent as shown in Example 13.2. On reaching the contingent age, say 18 or later, the trust is distributed among the beneficiaries and treated as a capital receipt in the hands of the beneficiaries.

Sometimes it is felt that the trustees should be able to use some of the money for the maintenance and education of the children and if this is provided for the trust becomes a discretionary trust. Tax is charged at 45 per cent.

13.7 Discretionary Trusts (SS.16–18, FA, 1973)

Discretionary trusts are subject to an additional tax of 15 per cent in addition to the basic rate, unless the trust is exempt as a charity or part of a superannuation fund. The income in the hands of the beneficiary is treated as having suffered tax at 45 per cent, except if it includes overseas tax the approriate double tax relief is available.

Example 13.4 Alfred created an accumulation trust for his son Paul in 1978 providing that the income be accumulated until he reached the age of 18 in December, 1993. The trustees have discretion to pay to Paul such sums as appropriate for his maintenance and education. During 1984/85 the trustees paid to Paul £400 out of trust funds. The income of the trust in 1984/85 was as follows:

Dividends from UK companies £1,105 + Tax credit 495	= £1,600	
Bank deposit interest	86	
Building society interest £35 $\times \frac{10}{7}$	50	
Taxable income	1,736 $\times$ 45%	
	= £781.20	
Less tax deducted at source: Dividends £495 + BSI 15	= 510	
Tax paid by Trustees		271.20

Payment to Paul is treated as the income of his father Alfred and has to be grossed at 45 per cent, that is £727.

If the trust is set up by the grandfather the £727 would be treated as income of the child Paul and would qualify for tax repayment of £327.15 on the basis of the Certificate R185E issued by the trustees.

13.8 Foreign Trusts

There are no special provisions for the income tax treatment of foreign trust income. Whether or not the income is liable to be taxed will depend on the tax law of the foreign country and the Double Tax Agreement. Usually the income has to be shown in the Annual Tax Return and will be assessable under Case IV or V subject to double tax relief. Where a foreign trust has advantages is in regard to capital gains tax, under which non-resident or not ordinarily resident persons are exempt but this is outside the scope of this book.

Before distributing the income to the beneficiaries the fees of the trustees have to be charged, after being grossed for tax, e.g. 30 per cent for ordinary trusts and 45 per cent for discretionary and accumulation trusts.

Example 13.5 Under a Will Mrs Williams, widowed in 1983/84, is entitled to the life interest in an estate of £100,000, the residuary legatees being her children. The solicitor administering the estate failed to set up a trust for a year, which resulted in the following tax loss for Mrs Williams.

(*a*) Position without a trust having been set up (Solicitor's charges £350):

1984/85	Pensions (including widow's pension)	£3,400
	Bank deposit interest (Case III)	400
	Building society interest received	700

Tax on building society interest		300	
Dividends including Tax Credits		12,000	
Income from estate (gross)		8,000	
Total income		24,800	
Less: Personal allowance	£2,005		
Widow's Bereavement allowance	1,150	£3,115	
Taxable		21,645	
		15,400 × 30% =	£4,620
		2,800 × 40% =	1,120
		3,445 × 45% =	1,550.25
Tax due			7,290.25

(*b*) The solicitor sets up the trust and charges his fee of £350 to the trust:

Pensions	3,400
Interest	400
Building society interest tax	1,000
Dividends + Tax Credits	12,000
Income from trust (gross)	7,500
	24,300
Less: Personal allowances	3,155
Taxable	21,145
Tax due	7,062.25

Tax assessment on Trust	Income	Tax	Net
Dividends	£8,000	£2,400	£5,600
Less: Expenses	500	150	350
Form R185	7,500	2,250	5,250

Tax saved by setting up the Trust:		
Tax paid under (*a*):		£7,290.25
Less Tax paid under (*b*):		7,062.25
Add tax paid by trust	£150	7,212.50
Tax saved		77.75

13.9 Revision Test

Answers	*Questions*
1. The 'residuary legatee' is the person who has an absolute title to either part or the whole of the estate.	**1.** Explain the term 'residuary legatee'.
2. The 'life interest' is the right a beneficiary has during his or her life time to income of the estate.	**2.** Explain the term 'life interest'.
3. The 'administration period' is the period from the date of death to the time of the distribution of the	**3.** Explain the term 'administration period' and its significance for income tax purposes.

estate, or setting up of the trust. The executors pay the tax on the income during the administration period.

---

4. Is it true that death, often results in an income tax repayment?

4. Yes, other things being equal the deceased's income ceases on death, but the tax-free personal allowances are not restricted, thus producing an overpayment for the year.

---

5. How are the trustees treated for income tax purposes?

5. The trustees have to administer the trust and are charged with the tax on income received by the trust. They pay all the taxes and distribute the 'net income' and issue forms R185E.

---

6. How are expenses of the trustees in the administration of the trust treated?

6. Expenses of the trustees are not deducted before the income is taxed, but are deducted before the 'net income' is distributed.

---

7. Making a settlement may have tax advantages, provided it is correctly made. Explain this statement.

7. Such a settlement must comply with the following conditions:
(a) It must be for more than 6 years, and
(b) It must be irrevocable, and
(c) The settlor must not retain an interest in the settlement.

---

8. Can a parent make a tax effective settlement in favour of his minor children?

8. No, S.437, ICTA 1970 prohibits this, except where the income is less than £5 per year.

---

9. What is the advantage of forming an 'Accumulation Settlement for Children'.

9. This is the most common form of settlement by parents. Under such a settlement the income is accumulated for each child until it reaches the age of 18. The settlement must be irrevocable.

---

10. What do you understand by the term 'Discretionay Trust' and how is such a trust treated for tax purposes?

10. A 'discretionary trust' gives the trustees discretion to apply and distribute the funds of the trust. It is subject to an additional tax of

15 per cent, which was not withdrawn by FA, 1984.

11. There are no special provisions for the income tax treatment of 'foreign trusts', although they may have capital gains tax advantages.	**11.** Are there any advantages in forming a 'foreign trust'?
12. The fees have to be grossed up at 30% in an ordinary trust and at 45% in a 'discretionary' or 'accumulation' trust, and are charged before the income is distributed.	**12.** How are the fees of trustees treated in the tax computation?

14
Tax Planning

Tax avoidance has already been referred to (see 2.6) and the simplest way to avoid paying tax is to have no income. The first rule therefore is not to allow tax planning to interfere with the enjoyment of the full fruits of one's income.

14.1 Common Sense and a Sense of Proportion

One must guard against the persuasive salesman of endowment and pension schemes, who quote assuming certain tax savings which are simply not in accordance with the facts. It is surprising how many people think that they pay tax at the higher or even highest rates, when in fact this is not the case. It is quite easy to over-insure oneself and to reduce one's standard of living on a long-term contract based on assumptions which turn out to be incorrect.

As a general statement, it is, of course, true that one can reduce income and tax on it by parting with the source of the income by giving capital away. Such schemes are worth consideration, but not to the extent of jeopardising one's future financial security. In this chapter an attempt is made to draw attention to tax planning opportunities as they arise from the time an individual starts work to the time he or she retires.

14.2 The Problem when Starting Employment

Young people when starting work seldom think how they can ensure that excessive tax is not paid.

Example 14.1 Leaving school in 1984, John starts work on 1.9.1984 with a monthly salary of £420. The employer uses the Emergency Code unless the Tax Office has notified him of a code number. Under this arrangement John will pay £81 each month until a code number has been obtained, arrived at as follows:

Salary for September	£420
Less: Tax-free pay Code 200 Month 1	167.42

Taxable pay 252.58 tax per Table B £75.60

If John had obtained the name and address and reference number of the Tax Office dealing with the employer from the employer and had written notifying the Inspector that he had started work and would he send him the 1984/85 Tax Return and complete it before starting work, there would be a good chance that the employer had been notified of the Code Number 200L, which would be reflected on P11 (Tax deduction working sheet) as follows:

Month	*Gross pay*	*Total gross pay*	*Tax-free pay*	*Taxable pay*	*Tax due*	*Tax Deducted*
	£	£	£	£	£	£
6	420	420	1,004.52			
7	420	840	1,171.94			
8	420	1,260	1,339.36			
9	420	1,680	1,506.78	173.22	51.90	51.90

It can be seen that John is not liable to pay tax under PAYE until November and the full monthly tax is not due until December; thus prudent tax planning will prevent the overpayment of tax of £299. Moreover, if John had not completed the Tax Return in time for the Code Number to be issued by March, 1985, he will overpay tax for 1984/85 and probably have to wait until August, 1985, or even later before getting his £299 for 1984/85 refunded and no **repayment supplement**—that is, interest on the tax overpaid is due.

14.3 Tax-efficient Savings

The young person starting work usually lives at home and is able to save part of his income. In fact, young unmarried people are probably the largest group of personal savers in the country.

(*i*) **Long-term savings.** The most efficient form is a pension scheme.

(*a*) **Superannuation schemes.** These schemes introduced by the employer, which staff can join. From a tax point of view, it is always a good idea to join, since both the employer's and employee's contributions can be paid from untaxed income. Moreover, since both contributions go into an exempt superannuation fund, any interest earned on money invested by the fund is also tax-free. The question often arises what to do when changing one's employment. The best way is to transfer one's pension rights to the new employment and if that is not possible, one can normally withdraw one's *own* contributions less 10 per cent tax, provided the membership of the fund is less than five years, otherwise the contributions are frozen and cannot normally be drawn before the age of 50 in the form of a pension. It is therefore quite possible to receive more than one small pension when retiring. Even if it is possible to withdraw one's contributions less tax at 10 per cent, it is usually wise to leave them in the scheme, since the employer's contributions and the interest earned are not recoverable. When taking up a new employment the questions arises, whether it is possible to purchase pension rights (see 10.21), known as Additional Voluntary Contributions (AVCs).

(*b*) **Providing oneself with a pension**, when the employer does not provide a scheme. This has already been referred to (see 3.10) and is a very popular way of providing for retirement in a tax-efficient way.

(*ii*) **Medium-term savings** for more than five years. This is often the period when a windfall of say £1,000 or less is used. Where to put this money may well depend on the average rate of tax payable.

Table 14.1. Net return of £1,000 invested for 5 years at 1984/85 tax-rate.

Tax rate %	*National Saving Certificates 26th Issue* £	*Clearing banks' Interest 6%* £	*Building Societies' Interest 9%* £	*Treasury Stock 10%* £
Nil	412	300	410	500
30	412	210	450	350
40	412	180	386	300
45	412	165	354	275
50	412	150	321	250
55	412	135	288	225
60	412	120	255	200
65	412	105	222	175
70	412	90	189	150
75	412	75	156	125

It can be seen that for higher rate tax payers, investing in National Savings Certificate and National Savings Banks, Ordinary Account up to interest of £70 (for both husband and wife) is a very tax efficient investment.

(*iii*) **Short-term savings** for less than four years. This is, of course, the most common of all.

Table 14.2 Net equivalent yield for liquid funds in 1984/85

Tax Rate %	*National Savings Bank Investment Account* %	*Clearing Banks* %	*Building Societies* %
Nil	11	6	7.25
30	7.7	4.2	7.25
40	6.6	3.6	6.21

45	6.05	3.3	5.7
50	5.50	3	5.17
55	4.95	2.7	4.66
60	4.40	2.4	4.14

It can be seen that National Savings Certificates is better than the paid-up share account of a building society, but since building societies offer term shares with higher rates and one month notice of withdrawal, this is not always the case. The bank deposit account comes a poor third but time investment get better returns.

14.4 The Age Allowance Trap

It was shown that building society interest with tax paid at source is often an attractive investment for basic rate (30 per cent) taxpayers, but in certain circumstances this is not so. It arises where age allowance has to be restricted (see 3.10).

Example 14.2 Assume that Mr Pensioner, aged 66 and married, has the following income in 1984/85:

National retirement and occupation pension £7,600		
Building society interest of £10,000		
Net interest 6.50% = £650, grossed × $\frac{100}{70}$		928
		8,528
Less: Age allowance	£3,966	
Less: 2/3 (£8,528–8,100) =	285	3,670
Taxable		4,858 × 30% = £1,457.40

This means that without the building society interest the tax would be £7,600—Age allowance £3,755 = £3,845 × 30% = £1,093.50
Therefore the tax on the building society interest £928 = 363.90
or 39 per cent.

It is clear therefore that Mr Pensioner should invest his £10,000 in National Savings rather than a building society.

14.5 Getting Married

Getting married is a suitable time for parents and grandparents to make gifts to the young couple and reduce their liability to capital transfer tax, but this is outside the scope of this book.

(*a*) **Wife's earnings election.** This has been dealt with in Section 4.3.

(*b*) **Purchasing the family home.** It has been accepted for a long time that unless frequent changes of address are contemplated it is financially advisable to purchase one's home rather than rent it. The reason is that mortgage interest can be deducted from taxable income (see 3.9(*a*)).

The most common form of mortgage used has been the **repayment mortgage**. The principle of this mortgage is that the borrower pays a fixed monthly sum in respect of both capital repayment and interest, but only the interest, of course, qualifies for tax relief. In other words, with a mortgage for twenty-five years this means that although the monthly payment is constant at the beginning it will be made up almost entirely of interest payments, but as the repayment proceeds the interest element will decline.

Example 14.3 Alfred took a mortgage on 1.4.83 for 25 years of £20,000 at 11.25% rate of interest. The position would be as follows:

1983/84	Year 1: Monthly repayment £201.60, yearly	£2,419
	Interest at 11.25%	2,250
	Repayment of principal	169
1984/85	Year 2: Repayments	2,419
	Interest at 11.25% on £19,831	2,231
	Repayment of principal	188
1985/86	Year 3: Repayments	2,419
	Interest at 11.25% on £19,643	2,210
	Repayment of principal	209

Another way to arrange the mortgage is the **endowment mortgage**. Under this arrangement the mortgage does not reduce, the borrower pays only the interest and takes an endowment policy to repay the capital. Although the initial cost under this system was higher since greater tax relief was received over the period, the average net cost was sometimes less.

The fine balance between the two systems was changed from 1983/84 onwards when MIRAS (Mortgage Interest Relief At Source) was introduced. Whilst the amount of tax relief remains unchanged, building societies, in an attempt to simplify administration, decided to average that relief which used to be great at the beginning and small at the end, over the whole term of the mortgage. Tax relief is now the same in year 1 as it is in year 25 and the initial advantage a purchaser with a repayment mortgage received in the early years of the mortgage has gone. The result of this change is to make the endowment mortgage more attractive. Since the 15 per cent tax relief on endowment policies written after 13.3.1984 has been withdrawn, the attraction has almost disappeared.

Example 14.4 Dennis, aged 39, takes out a 25-year mortgage of £25,000, in 1983/84 he is a basic rate taxpayer. His position is as follows:

1984/85	Monthly premium to insurance company (net) £31.45 yearly	£377.40
	Monthly mortgage interest (net) £171.35 yearly	2,056.20
		2,433.60
	Repayment mortgage (net)	2,424

However, endowment provides life cover and qualifies for bonuses estimating the maturity value of £30,600, giving a tax-free profit of £5,600 at the age of 65, when it is most welcome. It seems clear that the endowment mortgage is the better deal over the period.

A refinement of the endowment mortgage which is growing in popularity is the **pension mortgage**, where the mortgage is not linked to an endowment but to a pension policy, which qualifies for higher tax relief than an endowment policy (see 3.10(l)). The pension mortgage has risen in popularity since life assurance relief has been withdrawn.

Example 14.5 Assume that Dennis is self-employed or not working for a firm with a pension scheme. The position is as follows:

1984/85	Monthly premium to insurance company (net)	£41.71	yearly £500.52
	Monthly mortgage interest (net)	171.35	yearly £2,056.20
		213.08	2,556.72

Estimated maturity value £100,600 of which the maximum cash sum is £31,250 − mortgage £25,000 = tax free profit £6,250 and a pension for life of £8,129.

To conclude, it seems clear that the pension mortgage over the longer period is better than the endowment mortgage, which is better than the repayment mortgage, particularly for the higher-rate taxpayer provided taken out before 13.3.1984. Lastly, purchasing one's home is better than renting it because the mortgage interest is allowable for tax purposes, whilst rent is not. Moreover, not only will the value of the home increase with inflation, whilst the debt (mortgage) will not; in fact it reduces in relation to earnings and on the sale of the home it will be free of capital gains tax, whilst other investments are not. It is also a good idea to put the home in joint ownership with one's wife, because from a capital transfer tax point of view the wife can make arrangements to dispose of part of her belongings to the children and thus avoid capital transfer tax, which is outside the scope of this book.

14.6 Covenants

Chapter 13 and Section 4.7 briefly referred to **covenants** and their tax treatment. It is perhaps the simplest and most common form of tax-saving available. On the birth of a child, any relative (except the parents) can enter into a covenant for more than six years (see 13.5 and 13.6). All that is required is for the following document to be prepared and payments to be made accordingly:

'I Henry Taxpayer of 10 Chancellor's Lane, Tax Haven, covenant to pay my granddaughter Jane Mary Taxpayer of 15 Treasury Lane, Tax Haven, a gross amount of £500 on each of the following dates in each year, namely 1 October, 1 January and 1 April, for the period of 7 years, or for the period of our joint lives (whichever is the shortest period) the first payment to be made on 1 October, 1984.

Date:....................
Signed, sealed and delivered by Henry Taxpayer:

....

In the presence of:

....

(witness's signature and address)'

The most common form of covenant is for students and is entered into by the father of a student over 18 years of age. In this case one normally inserts: 'or until he (she) ceases to be receiving full-time education at any university, college, school or other educational establishment' after the 'period of 7 years'.

The procedure is simple. The **deed of covenant**, when completed, is sent to the tax-office dealing with the covenantor, who parts with the money. It has to be approved by the Inspector and well before the 1 October when the document is filed. On 1 October £500 − tax at 30% = £350 is paid over to the payee. At the end of the income tax year (5 April) the covenantor completes a Form R185 (AP), a certificate of deduction of income tax. The recipient then writes to his local HM Inspector of Taxes for a 'Repayment Claim Form' (R40), which is a special Tax Return for people with only taxed income to claim repayment. He completes that form, attaches the Form R185 (AP) and in due course will receive the tax repayment due.

Covenants in favour of charities need only be for *four* years and not seven. Moreover, the first £5,000 (£10,000 for 1985/86 onwards) gross each year covenanted to charities count as deductions from the higher rates of tax as well.

Lastly, deeds of covenant are a useful way to provide income for dependent relatives with low incomes whom one wants to support, provided the income of the elderly dependant cannot use up the whole of the age allowance. It must be remembered that to qualify for age relief the relative has to be 65 years old.

14.7 Gifts and Settlements

One way of reducing one's tax liability is, of course, the giving away of one's assets and the source of the taxable income. This has been referred to in Sections 13.4–13.6. Apart from the income tax considerations, the effect on capital transfer tax (outside the scope of this book) is the most important. The following exemptions should be kept in mind:

(*a*) Transfers each year up to £3,000 with a carry-forward of one year's unused allowance. In other words, a parent can give his children £6,000 in 1985/86 provided no gift was made in 1984/85.

(*b*) £5,000 on marriage, provided the donor is a parent of one of the marriage partners; £2,500 from a grandparent; and £1,000 gift from any other person to one of the partners in a marriage.

(*c*) Small gifts not exceeding £250 per person are also exempt.

The list of exemptions is not complete but the three above are probably the most important for 'tax planning'.

Gifts in excess of the exemption limit are accumulated and become liable to capital transfer tax when they exceed the threshold of £67,000 in 1985/86. Exceeding the threshold a life-time gift of up to £21,000 is subject to CTT at 15 per cent. On death the sum passing is added to the accumulated gifts and if the total exceeds £67,000 by up to £21,000 the rate is 30 per cent. So people are encouraged to transfer their wealth during their life-time.

The ten-year cumulation period. Lastly, S.93, FA, 1981, introduced a ten-year cumulation period, which means that any gift that was treated as a chargeable transfer and accumulated for capital transfer tax purposes will be excluded if ten years passed between the time of the gift and the chargeable date. In other words, a gift of £10,000 which was treated as chargeable transfer in May, 1974 (the tax applies after 26 March, 1974) is excluded from the accumulated sum after May, 1984, when calculating the threshold. This section is another reason for making life-time gifts and setting up trusts.

14.8 The Break-up of Marriage

During the traumatic experience of a break-up of a marriage and the sometimes long-drawn divorce proceedings, the tax aspects of any settlements are sometimes forgotten. These matters have been referred to in some detail in Section 4.8. The following matters should be kept in mind:

(*a*) All payments to the wife should be included in the Court Order or agreed alimony payment, since an agreement to pay for gas and electricity will not enable the payer to treat it as alimony payment and deduct tax at basic rate and get the gross sum deducted from the calculation of higher-rate liability.

(*b*) All payments in respect of children should be made in favour of the children. This will reduce the tax liability of the wife. It will not affect the husband's tax position.

(*c*) Mortgage interest can be claimed as a tax deduction even if the husband has left the matrimonial home, provided he still pays the interest and does not wish to purchase another house with a mortgage. If this circumstance does arise, however, the house should be transferred to the ex-wife together with the mortgage and the interest on the mortgage included in the alimony payment.

(*d*) The problem also arises with life assurance policies. One cannot claim in respect of premiums on the life of the wife, once the marriage has been dissolved. In these circumstances, as part of the settlement each individual should take over the life policies on their lives to continue to qualify for tax relief.

(*e*) The question of capital gains tax also arises, since one house (the owner's main residence) is exempt, but when a second home is purchased on the break-up of the marriage, the exemption on the former disappears. Once again, just as with mortgage interest the transfer of the former home to the ex-wife on suitable terms should be considered.

(*f*) Capital transfer tax has already been referred to with reference to gifts. It could apply to a settlement on the break-up of the marriage, although transfers between husband and wife are exempt.

14.9 Setting up in Business

This was referred to in Sections 9.1–9.2. The following points must be remembered:

(*a*) The first year's trading forms the basis of at least two year's assessment and for this reason the accounting date to which the accounts are made up should be chosen with care.

(*b*) Losses incurred in the first *four* years of trading can be allowed against the income of the last *three* years, the first year being 1978/79.

(*c*) Pre-trading expenses referred to in Section 6.8 qualify for deduction from the trading profit.

14.10 Forming a Partnership

This was referred to in Sections 9.5–9.10. The following points should be watched:

(*a*) A partnership has the advantage over a sole trader in that the capital and risks are shared. From the income tax point of view changes in the partnership are important and each partner's share has to be worked out.

(*b*) The question of an election under S.154, ICTA, 1970, when a partner leaves or joins the partnership should always be considered within the time limit provided, and in light of the provisions of F.A. 1985.

14.11 Forming a Company

Corporation tax, which applies to corporate bodies, is outside the scope of this book, but forming a company is often a good alternative to forming a partnership. The advantages are:

(*a*) **Limited liability**—unlimited liability being the main disadvantage of a partnership.

(*b*) **Private use of assets.** Particularly motor cars are treated more favourably in the case of a company director than in the case of a self-employed person, as is explained in Sections 10.10–10.12.

(*c*) **Business Expansion Scheme.** This scheme was introduced from 1981/82 and enables people to invest in certain trading companies and get this investment allowed against their taxable income. From 1983/84 onwards, individuals who have not had the relief before can claim up to £40,000.

To be eligible the investor must be a UK resident investing in a company with which he or his *associates* are not *closely connected.* Associates include a husband or wife, grandparents, parents, children and grandchildren amongst others, but aunts, uncles, brothers and sisters are all eligible under the scheme. 'Closely connected' covers three types of situation. Investors or their associates must not be employees or partners of companies they are planning to invest in nor paid directors, and must not own more than 30 per cent of ordinary shares in that company. One can be a director as long as all one reclaims is travelling and other expenses.

Certain other conditions must also be fulfilled:

(*i*) If the investor participates independently in the scheme he must invest at least £500 in each company, unless the investment is through a **business expansion fund** approved by the Inland Revenue, when the minimum investment can be as low as £30.

(*ii*) The investment must be in ordinary shares and not debentures or preference shares—in other words, in risk capital.

(*iii*) Shares must in general be held for five years.

(*iv*) The scheme is temporary and unless extended, ends on 5.4.1987.

Unfortunately, besides the venture risk, there is another risk inherent in approved funds. This concerns the timing of the tax relief. It is given within two years after either the end of the tax year in which the shares are issued, or the end of the company's first twelve months' trading, whichever is earlier. Consequently, one may qualify for tax relief at 75 per cent in 1983/84 when the investment in the approved fund is made, but if the funds are not actually invested by 5.4.1984 the taxpayer may have to wait until 1985/86 before relief is granted and the marginal rate of tax will be only 60 per cent.

Lastly, the question arises what happens after the five-year investment period is over, when the taxpayer may wish to realise his investment. This may be difficult unless the fund has definite arrangements for the realisation of capital after five years. The question of capital gains tax arises on any profit made on the sale. There are special rules, which allow one to deduct half the cost of the shares on which relief has been obtained to be deducted from the sale price for capital gains tax purposes in addition to the normal exemption of £5,900 available to everyone in 1985/86.

14.12 Working Overseas

There are three kinds of tax reliefs for working abroad (see 10.3) which enable employees who have work overseas and are absent for more than 30 days to receive a proportionate 25 per cent allowance of income up to 1983/84. Better still, if one goes to work abroad for a continuous period of 365 days or more, the allowance is 100 per cent, and if one is employed by a foreign employer abroad, although resident in this country, a 25 per cent reduction of the foreign income is due.

The same 25 per cent deductions are available for self-employed people as for employed people as regards the proportionate allowance and also the 100 per cent allowance for absence of 365 days. The 25 per cent allowances base has been reduced to 12½ per cent in 1984/85 and withdrawn after 5.4.1985.

14.13 Questions of Residence, Ordinarily Resident and Domicile

These questions fall into two parts:

(*a*) UK residents leaving this country and foreign residents coming to stay in this country. On the whole it is easier to be declared a non-resident and not liable to UK income tax on foreign income if one comes from abroad than when one leaves the UK. In this connection it is worth mentioning that an individual who is not resident or ordinarily resident in the UK is not liable to capital gains tax on properties, etc., sold in the UK.

(*b*) Residents leaving this country with a home in this country are treated as residents if they visit the UK any time during the year.

(*c*) The question of domicile is particularly important for individuals who were not born in the UK (see 12.9), since if they have foreign income it would pay them not to be too eager to acquire a domicile of choice in the UK.

A non-resident individual with British income can claim S.27, ICTA, 1970 relief (see 12.11).

14.14 Tax-Efficient Investment

The investment of a **windfall** has already been mentioned, but it is by no means unusual for people on retirement or redundancy to have a substantial sum to invest. Certain types of investment are particularly tax efficient:

(*a*) **Agricultural land.** Farmers are, of course, charged to income tax in the same way as other business people, but qualify for the averaging relief (see 6.12). For capital transfer tax purposes relief on agricultural land of 50 per cent if owned and 30 per cent if let is available if the farming business is carried on by a joint stock company and what is being sold are the shares.

(*b*) **Woodlands.** Successive governments have been persuaded that considerable financial support is needed to encourage investment in forests. Some 90 per cent of timber is imported into Britain and to reduce this dependence, grants are offered to potential owners of woodlands from the Forestry Commission and in the form of substantial tax reliefs. For income tax purposes when the woodlands are being established an election to be assessed under Schedule D will enable losses to be set against other income (see 8.1) and growing timber is excluded for capital gains tax and capital transfer tax, although the underlying land is brought into account for both these taxes. When the timber matures the woodlands can be sold or transferred and are then assessed under Schedule B (see 5.10) on the basis of the annual value for rating purposes, which should amount to a charge or no more than 50p per acre, irrespective of the income produced from the felling of timber. It has been reported that because of the very real tax advantages available commercial forestry companies can pay up 19 per cent dividends excluding tax credits (but see restriction for land so used after 13.3.1984).

(*c*) **Business assets.** The allowances available for income tax and corporation tax have been dealt with in Chapter 7. There are, however, substantial reliefs available from capital gains tax in the form of **roll-over relief**, when the gain on the sale of one business asset can be set against the purchase of another business asset, as long as the new asset does not cost less than the value of the asset sold. Moreover, after the age of 60 the self-employed person who has been in business for 10 years qualifies for retirement relief. The full relief is obtained if retirement takes place after reaching the age of 65 and is £100,000.

For purposes of capital transfer tax, a special **business property relief** is available; provided the business was owned for two years the relief is 50 per cent. Property transferred and used in the business is subject to a 30 per cent relief, and this relief also extends to the transfer of land and buildings owned by a trust, provided that immediately before the transfer the land and buildings were used in trade by the person beneficially entitled to an interest in possession in the trust.

(*d*) **Gilt-edged stocks.** Individuals subject to higher rates of income tax may benefit from purchasing stocks *ex-dividend* and selling them *cum-dividend*, thus turning the dividend liable to say 60 per cent into capital gain liable at 30 per cent or not at all, if the stock was held for over one year. New provisions affect bond-washing from 1985/86 for companies but most individuals are not affected.

14.15 Considerations on Retirement

It has already been explained that a growing number of people receive in addition to their National Retirement Pension an occupational pension through their employment or provide themselves with a pension by purchasing a **retirement annuity** (see 3.10(l)). What is not often realised is that the largest number of people below the poverty line—that is, in receipt of **supplementary benefit**—are retired people with only the National Retirement Pension to live on and less than £2,500 in savings.

Since 1981/82 it is possible to claim **retirement annuity relief** for the six years before the year of claim and this is particularly advantageous to recently retired people without occupational pensions.

Example 14.6 Assume a widower retired in 1982/83 and reached the age of 67 in 1984/85. He has only his National Retirement Pension and £6,000 invested in the National Savings Bank (Investment) Account. His position will be as follows:

1984/85 National Retirement Pension	£1,980
Interest (12% on £6,000)	720
Total income	2,700
Less: Age allowance	2,490
Taxable income	210 × 30% = £63.00

If he had purchased a retirement annuity for £5,000 in March 1984 the cost would be:

Retirement Annuity Policy		£5,000
Less: Cash repayment	£1,590	
Income tax relief (up to 1978/79) at 30%	1,500	3,090
Net cost		1,910

This investment will provide a retirement annuity for life of £470, guaranteed for five years, or a return on capital of 24.6 per cent compared to the National Savings Bank's 12 per cent.

Assuming the purchase of the retirement annuity was made in March, 1984, the position would be as follows:

1984/85 National Retirement Pension	£1,980
Interest (£2,910 × 12%)	349

Retirement annuity	470
Total income	2,799
Less: Age allowance	2,490
Taxable income	309 × 30% = £92.70

As a result of the exercise the widower increased his spendable income by £69, or 7.2 per cent, but the capital of £5,000 is lost.

(*i*) *The question whether to take a lump sum and a smaller pension.* This question arises quite frequently in cases where early retirement is taken. One cannot generalise since there are many alternatives and it is always worth-while obtaining as many quotations as possible. It is possible to invest the lump sum in order to accumulate without producing income for a given period and thus receive a larger income later.

One can turn the lump sum into a **purchased annuity**. An insurance company will quote on, say, the annuity a capital sum of £10,000 will purchase. This kind of annuity has to be distinguished from the **retirement annuity** referred to above, which is the pension provision of the self-employed and those in non-pensionable employment and qualifies for tax relief. The purchased annuity is the reverse of an endowment policy, turning capital into income. It does not qualify for tax relief, but the annuity itself is treated only in part as income, since part is in fact a return of the capital invested. Each quotation will show the non-taxable part of the annuity, which depends, of course, on the age and sex of the annuitant. The income element of the annuity is treated as investment income for tax purposes and not, as in the case of the retirement annuity or occupational pension, earned income.

(*ii*) *Possible switch from investment with building societies and bank deposits.* Building societies and banks, have a special arrangement under which they are charged the **composite rate** of tax, which is the average rate of tax chargeable to investors, based on a random sample. This rate may be 26 per cent instead of the basic rate of 30 per cent. In other words, since tax suffered by deduction from building society interest is not repayable, individual taxpayers, who are either not liable to income tax at all or are liable at a marginal rate of less than 30 per cent, subsidise the rest. Most of the individuals who do the subsidising are in fact retired people. So on retirement the question exists whether to switch from building society investment which may pay interest, after deduction of tax, of up to 9 per cent to say a National Savings Bank (Investment) account, which pays 12 per cent. The question of the age allowance trap should also be considered (see 14.4).

(*iii*) *Home income plans.* These plans arouse considerable interest, but the take-up rate is low. At the time of writing only two schemes are available: the Abbey National Building Society, in association with Royal Insurance, which has the larger share of the business, and

Hambro's Life Assurance plc. The general idea is for retired people to take a mortgage on their house, which is repaid on death out of the estate, and purchase an annuity with the proceeds. The maximum loan under both schemes is £30,000, but this depends on the valuation of the property. In order to qualify the applicant must be 75 years old if single, and the combined ages of married couples must be at least 150. The income of a mortgage of £30,000 producing an annuity, less mortgage interest, which qualifies for income tax relief, can produce an income up to £2,750 for a single man of 75 and up to £1,306 for a couple. The income of a single woman is much less, since women with their considerably longer life expectation get smaller annuities.

There are some snags in these schemes:

(*a*) The capital which parents wish to leave their children disappears, though this can be met with a **whole life policy** with an insurance company. The premiums will be high at the qualifying age and this will reduce the net income substantially.

(*b*) The income raised in this way may affect any supplementary benefit to which the claimant would be entitled.

(*c*) The amount of capital raised under this scheme has to be large and the cost in terms of interest, etc., is considerable.

14.16 Capital Conversion Schemes

There are numerous schemes available for reducing or eliminating potential liability to **capital transfer tax**, which although outside the scope of this book, has to be considered when tax planning is undertaken. The dilemma is usually to provide for the settlor's need of income to preserve his or her own living standards, while transferring and estate free from capital transfer tax. The question of **settlements** has been dealt with in Chapter 13 and **life-time gifts** are referred to in Section 14.7, but the more common arrangements are:

(*a*) **Deed of family arrangement.** Under S.47, FA, 1975, a deed of family arrangement signed by all the individuals affected by it can vary the terms of a Will within two years of death, thus altering the distribution of the estate and thus saving both capital transfer tax and income tax, since some of the income may escape tax at the higher rates.

Example 14.7 X died in May, 1980. Under the terms of his Will the income goes to his widow, but the capital is to be divided on her passing between his two children in equal parts. No capital transfer tax is payable in 1980/81, since transfers between husband and wife are exempt. The widow died in march, 1986 leaving £100,000 to be divided equally between her two children. Without a deed of family arrangement in 1980/81, capital transfer tax due in 1985/86 will be calculated as follows:

Value of estate (including husband's): £300,000

	Tax	Total
£	£	£
67,000	Nil	
22,000 × 30%	6,600	6,600
33,000 × 35%	11,550	18,150
33,000 × 40%	13,200	31,350
39,000 × 45%	17,550	48,900
49,000 × 50%	24,500	73,400
56,000 × 55%	30,800	104,200
11,500 × 60%	600	104,800
300,000		104,800

If a deed of family arrangement had been made giving £50,000 outright to the children in 1980/81, the capital transfer tax saved in 1985/86 would be:

1,000 × 60% =	£600
49,000 × 55% =	26,950
	27,550

A deed of family arrangement handing over £100,000 to the children in 1980/81 would have saved more tax in 1985/86. In this case CTT of £19,000 would have been payable in 1980/81 and the tax saved in 1984/85 would be calculated as follows:

1,000 × 60% =		600
56,000 × 55% =		30,800
43,000 × 50% =		21,500
		52,900
Less: CTT paid 1980/81	£19,000	
Less: Quick Succession Relief 19,000 × 60%	11,400	7,600
Net saving		45,300

(*b*) **Investment bonds.** Insurance-linked investment bonds are technically life assurance policies. Bonds are single premium insurance policies where the investor's money, after the deduction of a management charge, is invested in investment funds. Most insurance companies let the investor choose between equity funds, fixed interest funds, international property and managed funds etc., to allow for flexibility. The attraction of these bonds is that any income arising from this investment to the insurance company is taxed at the lower corporation tax rate of 37½ per cent compared to 50 per cent payable by investment holding companies on unfranked income.

The bonds do not provide income as such, since the income is re-invested by the insurance company. The investor get the benefit in the rise in the value of the bond. Moreover, the investor can live off his capital provided he withdraws no more than 5 per cent of the value of the bond, in which case no income tax liability arises. On the encashment of the bond, the proceeds are credited with having suffered tax at the basic rate. This is treated as a claw-back of life assurance relief (see 11.13). If the bondholder dies early, his family get the value of the bond at the time of death, or more if it has life cover written into it. This kind of investment is particularly for investors subject to tax at the higher rates who can postpone encashment until retirement, when tax liability will be at lower rates.

The disadvantage is that a considerable amount of capital has to be tied up for a long time—say, 10 years or more—to get the full advantage, depending on one's age, and the capital may be wanted earlier. The way to meet this contingency is to purchase the maximum number of bonds, the minimum sum to be invested in a single bond being £500. Thus an investment of £10,000 will be spread over 20 bonds and each one can be cashed separately without affecting the rest.

14.17 The Investment of Lump Sum (Redundancy) Payments

It is quite common for well-paid middle-aged executives to be made redundant or asked to retire early with a lump sum in excess of £20,000. Assuming the executive is in his early fifties, he or she will find a new position, but probably suffer a substantial reduction in pension rights, unless the pension rights from the employment given up can be transferred, which is still unusual. The tax treatment of the **golden handshake** has been explained (see 10.14), but the **maximum investment plan**, which combines the **capital conversion plan** (see 14.16) with an **endowment policy** (see 3.10(k)) deals with this situation.

Example 14.8 Z, an executive aged 54, is made redundant and finds a similar post with an income of £20,000 per year and rising. His redundancy payment, if invested, will attract tax at the higher rates, and apart from a loss in pension rights, since these could not be transferred to his new employment, he has not suffered from being made redundant. He invests £25,000 in an investment bond (see 14.16) and withdraws the 5 per cent which does not attract income tax and puts it into an endowment policy for 10 years. He intends to cash the bond on reaching 65 years, when he intends to retire and with the money realised from the bond and the with-profit endowment policy purchase an annuity to make up for the pension rights he lost when being made redundant. The calculations are as follows, based on a quotation from a leading insurance company:

(*a*) Immediate purchase of investment bond: £23,750 (95% of £25,000) On the basis of a 7.5% annual growth rate the value of the bond will be £46,968.
(*b*) Endowment policy: Gross premium per annum £1,470.59

On the basis of average bonus growth of 7.5%, after 10 years the maturity value will be £21,034.

As a result of this exercise the redundancy pay of £25,000 has grown to £46,968 + £21,034 = £68,002, and provided pension income after retirement is low the tax due on the encashment of the investment bond will be relatively small.

14.18 Revision Test

Answers	*Questions*
1. It is important to get a Code Number as soon as possible otherwise tax will be deducted at too high a rate.	**1.** What should one do when starting employment?
2. The most important long-term tax-efficient tax saving is to join a pension scheme or purchase pension rights, if the employment is not pensionable.	**2.** What are the most tax-efficient savings for a person starting work?
3. This arises when an individual aged over 65 receives interest subject to the composite rate, tax on which he cannot recover and which reduces the Age Allowance.	**3.** What is meant by the 'Age Allowance Trap'?
4. Since the 15 per cent life assurance has been withdrawn, the advantages of an endowment policy are less. They still exist when qualifying policies (taken out before 14.3.84) can be assigned and the balance be paid on a repayment mortgage.	**4.** Is it still advantageous to purchase one's home with an endowment policy?
5. It is quite true that a seven year covenant in favour of one's child aged over 18 for up to £2,200 will save up to £660, provided it is properly drawn up.	**5.** Covenants are the best way to help one's child through University. Comment on this statement.
6. The following matters should be borne in mind: (*i*) The date of break-up, particularly when the wife is working, (*ii*) All payments to the wife should be included in the Court Order, (*iii*) Alimony payments to the children should be payable to the children.	**6.** What matters should be considered when arrangements are made on the break-up of a marriage?

7. (*i*) If tax has been paid under PAYE some of it can be reclaimed. (*ii*) It is important to choose the right accounting date. (*iii*) Early business losses can be set against tax paid whilst employed.

7. What tax considerations should be borne in mind when setting up in business?

8. How is the profit to be divided. What interest on capital and what salaries should be paid to the partners. Should an election be made under S.154.

8. What tax considerations should be borne in mind when setting up a partnership?

9. The profit need not be distributed corporation tax is lower than the higher rates of income tax. There are favourable treatments for company cars, and members of the family can share the profits through dividends, thus reducing tax liability.

9. What tax advantages, if any, can be obtained by forming a company?

10. The cost of ordinary shares in a company qualifying can be deducted from untaxed income. The relief is extensive so are the conditions attached to the scheme.

10. Explain the term 'Business Expansion Scheme'. Has it any tax advantages?

11. The Finance Act, 1984 has reduced the benefits. After 5.4.1985, the Special Deduction has been withdrawn, but the 100% allowance for working abroad for more than 365 days still applies. Foreign income escapes tax if the recipient is non-resident.

11. What benefits can be obtained from working abroad?

12. If one retires without an occupational pension, one can purchase a Retirement Annuity and claim back Retirement Annuity Relief for six years.

12. Is it possible to benefit from the purchase of a Retirement Annuity on retirement and if so how?

Abbreviations

S	Section in statute
ICTA	Income and Corporation Taxes Act, 1970
FA	Finance Act
TMA	Taxes Management Act, 1970
CAA	Capital Allowances Act, 1968
CGTA	Capital Gains Tax Act, 1979
TC	Volume of Tax Cases, published by Inland Revenue
CAs	Capital allowances
STC	Simons Tax Cases
AC	Volume of annotated cases
KB	Kings Bench Division cases

Table of cases

Index

LANCASHIRE LIBRARY
ROSSENDALE